AF327147

KAWASAKI
JET SKI
1976-1983
SERVICE · REPAIR · MAINTENANCE

By
ANTON VESELY

SYDNIE A. WAUSON
Editor

JEFF ROBINSON
Publisher

CLYMER PUBLICATIONS

*World's largest publisher of books
devoted exclusively to automobiles and motorcycles*

12860 MUSCATINE STREET · P.O. BOX 20 · ARLETA, CALIFORNIA 91331

Copyright ©1982, 1984 Clymer Publications

All rights reserved. No part of this publication may be reproduced, stored in a retrieval system or transmitted, in any form or by any means, electronic, mechanical, photocopying, recording or otherwise, without the written permission of Clymer Publications.

FIRST EDITION
First Printing July, 1982

SECOND EDITION
Updated by Ron Wright to include 1982-1983 models
First Printing February, 1984

Printed in U.S.A.

ISBN: 0-89287-354-X

Production Coordinator, Marina Lerique

COVER: Photographed by Michael Brown Photographic Productions, Los Angeles, California. Assisted by Tim Lunde.

Jet Ski ridden by Greg Gracer.

CONTENTS

How to use this manual

Chapter organization

Notes, cautions and warnings

Photos, drawings and tables

Model identification

General maintenance hints

Special tips

Tools

Expendable supplies

Safety first

Clearing a submerged Jet Ski

Jump starting

Storage

Operating requirements

Starting difficulties

Poor idling

Misfiring

Flat spots

Power loss

Overheating

Backfiring

Engine noises

Piston seizure

Excessive vibration

Pre-ride checklist

End of day checklist

Maintenance schedule

Engine lubrication

Battery

Tune-up (every 25 hours)

On-shore cooling

Fuel filter and sediment bowl

Fuel vent check valve

Spark plugs

Spark plug heat range

Cylinder head nuts

Ignition timing

Carburetor

Cylinder compression

Tune-up (every 100 hours)

Cooling system cleaning

Bilge system cleaning

General lubrication

Steering

Impeller

Coupler rubber

Introduction

Tools

Break-in

Operating principles

Servicing engine in hull

Cooling system

Top end disassembly

Top end inspection

Top end assembly

Engine removal

Crankcase separation

Bottom end inspection

Bottom end assembly

Engine installation

QUICK REFERENCE DATA

40:1 GAS/OIL RATIO QUANTITIES

Oil	Gas
3.2 oz. (95 cc)	1 U.S. gal.
6.4 oz. (190 cc)	2 U.S. gal.
8.0 oz. (235 cc)	2.5 U.S. gal.
9.6 oz. (285 cc)	3 U.S. gal.
12.8 oz. (380 cc)	4 U.S. gal.
16.0 oz. (475 cc)	5 U.S. gal.

1982 AND LATER JS440 AND JS550 TUNE-UP SPECIFICATIONS

Spark plug gap	0.028-0.032 in. (0.7-0.8 mm)
Spark plug type	NGK B7ES; Champion N4G
Idle speed	
JS440	1,800 ±100 rpm
JS550	1,500 ±100 rpm
Needle adjustments	
Low-speed needle	
JS440	
1982	1 1/16 turns
1983	1 turn
JS550	1 turn
High-speed needle	
JS440	
1982	7/8 turn
1983	5/8 turn
JS550	5/8 turn

JS400/440 DRIVE TRAIN TORQUES

	Ft.-lb.	Mkg
Bearing box cover bolts	12	(1.6)
Bearing box mounting bolts	12	(1.6)
Coupler	20	(2.7)
Handle pole bracket bolts	16	(2.2)
Handle pole pivot bolt	10	(1.4)
Handle pole pivot nut	25	(3.5)
Impeller	45 in.-lb.	(0.5)
Intake grate bolts	7	(1.0)
Jet pump cover bolts	7	(1.0)
Jet pump mounting bolts	16	(2.2)
Jet pump outlet mounting bolts	12	(1.6)

JS550 DRIVE TRAIN TORQUES

Item	ft.-lb.	N•m
Bearing housing mounting bolt	12	16
Coupling torque	20	27
Pump mounting bolts	16	22
Pump cover bolts	7	10
Pump grate bolts	7	10
Impeller	14	20
Pump case bolts	48 in.-lb.	5.5

Spark plug gap	0.028-0.032 in. (0.7-0.8 mm)
Spark plug type	
U.S.	NGK B7ES; Champion N4G
Canada	NGK BR7ES

| Idle speed in water | 1,800 rpm |
| Idle speed out of water | 2,200 rpm |

Mixture screws	Low-speed (turns open)	High-speed (turns open)
1976	3/4	1 1/8
1977-1979	5/8	3/4
1980	5/8	1
1981	1	3/4

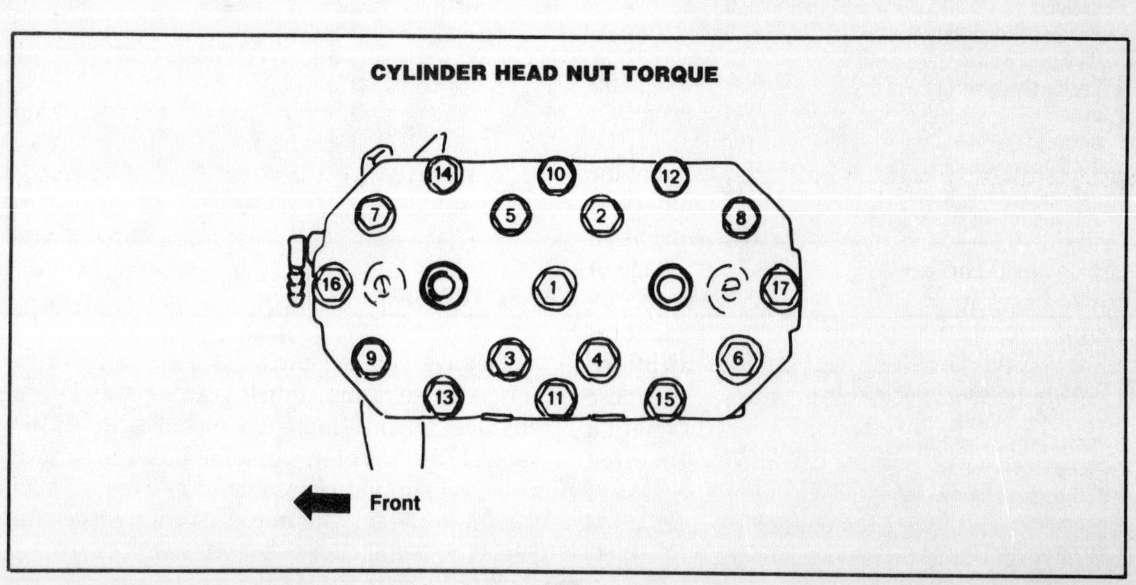

NOTE: If you own a 1982 or 1983 model, first check the Supplement at the back of the book for any new service information.

CHAPTER ONE

GENERAL INFORMATION

This book provides all maintenance and repair procedures for the Kawasaki JS series Jet Ski watercraft—from changing a spark plug to rebuilding an engine.

See **Figure 1** and **Figure 2** for identification of the Jet Ski part names used throughout this manual.

Table 1 is at the end of the chapter.

HOW TO USE THIS MANUAL

This manual has been specifically written and formatted for the amateur home mechanic. All procedures, tables, photos, etc., in this manual assume that the reader may be working on the Jet Ski or using this manual for the first time. This section is included to acquaint the home mechanic with what is in the manual and how to take best advantage of the information.

For the most frequently used general information and maintenance specifications refer to the *Quick Reference Data* pages. These first pages in the front of the book represent a compilation of the most commonly "referred to" facts. The *Quick Reference Data* pages save you from searching each chapter of the manual every time this information is needed.

To save time on all maintenance tasks, use the *Index*. The *Index* in the back of this manual has been carefully prepared and lists all major maintenance tasks by paragraph heading. Whether you want to remove a piston or simply clean the fuel filter, a quick look in the *Index* will tell you exactly what page to go to.

Throughout this book, keep in mind two conventions:

a. "Front" refers to the front of the Jet Ski. The front of any part describes the front of the part as it is normally mounted on the Jet Ski.

b. "Left" and "right" refer to the rider's left and right side when seated on the Jet Ski. For example, the throttle control is on the right handlebar. When the engine is removed from the Jet Ski, "right" and "left" refer to the engine as though it were mounted in the Jet Ski, not necessarily how it looks on a workbench.

To save yourself time, energy and possible future aggravation, finish reading this entire chapter. If you acquaint yourself with all the special features of this manual it can become a valuable and indispensable tool. This manual can help make your repairs more successful and your Jet Ski better maintained.

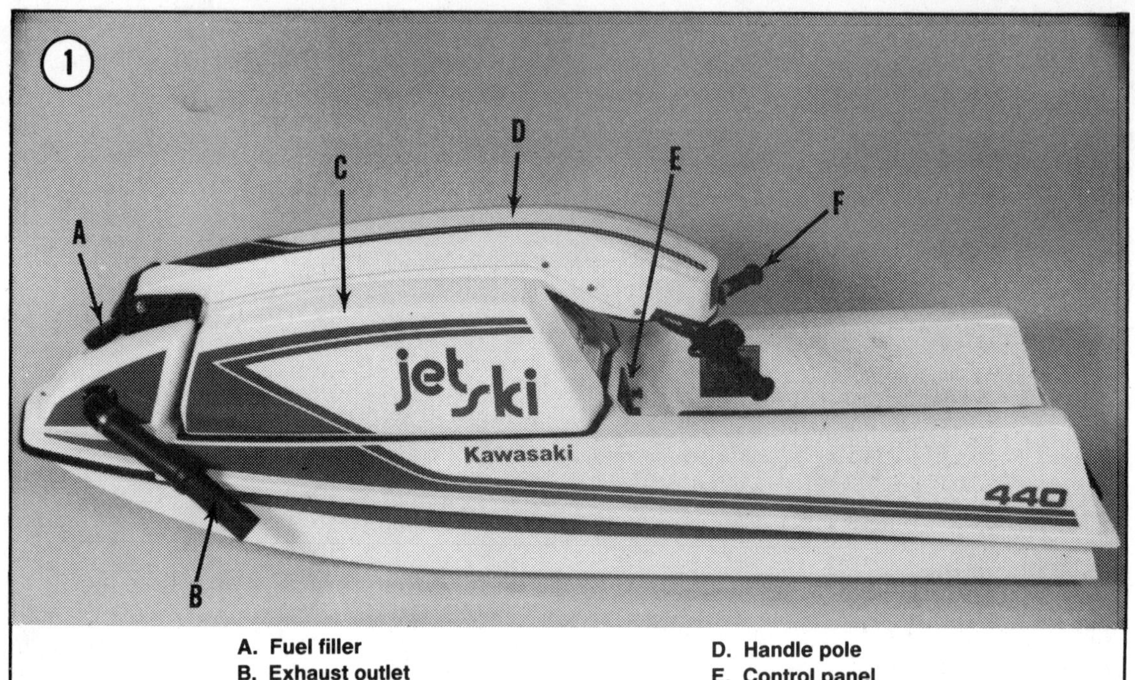

A. Fuel filler	D. Handle pole
B. Exhaust outlet	E. Control panel
C. Engine cover	F. Handlebar

1. Water muffler	5. Flame arrestor/carburetor	9. Expansion chamber
2. Fuel vent check valve	6. Spark plug	10. Exhaust pipe
3. Fuel tank outlet	7. Battery	11. Electric box
4. Fuel filter	8. Resonator	

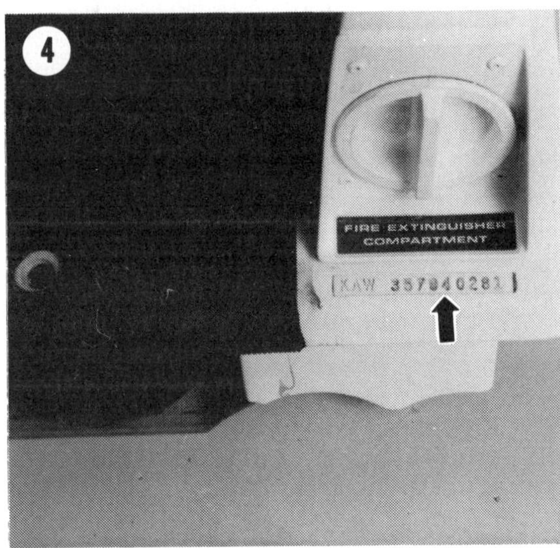

CHAPTER ORGANIZATION

This chapter provides general information on manual organization as well as special information and maintenance tips to aid all repair tasks. Read this entire chapter before performing any maintenance procedure.

Chapter Two, *Troubleshooting*, contains suggestions and tips for finding and fixing troubles fast. Troubleshooting procedures discuss symptoms and logical methods to pinpoint the trouble.

Chapter Three, *Lubrication, Maintenance and Tune-up*, includes all normal periodic and preventive maintenance tasks designed to keep your Jet Ski in peak operating condition.

Subsequent chapters describe specific systems such as engine, drive train, fuel and exhaust, and electrical systems. Each provides complete disassembly, repair, and assembly procedures in an easy to follow, step-by-step form. If a repair is impractical for a home mechanic or if it requires expensive, special factory tools to perform, you will be advised to see your Jet Ski dealer to save time and money, and to avoid damaging the Jet Ski.

NOTES, CAUTIONS AND WARNINGS

NOTES, CAUTIONS and WARNINGS appear throughout this manual and provide specific and important information to the reader. A NOTE provides extra or special information to make a step or procedure clearer or to provide a maintenance tip. Disregarding a NOTE could cause inconvenience but will not cause damage or personal injury.

A CAUTION is provided wherever mechanical damage of any type may occur. Failure to heed a CAUTION will probably cause some form of damage to the Jet Ski; however, personal injury is unlikely.

WARNINGS are the most serious and are included in a procedure where personal injury is likely to occur if the warning is not heeded. Mechanical damage may also occur. WARNINGS are definitely to be taken seriously.

PHOTOS, DRAWINGS AND TABLES

This manual contains literally hundreds of photos, drawings and tables that are used to support and clarify maintenance procedures. All tables are grouped at the end of each chapter. Each photo, drawing and table is referenced at least once within a specific procedure. When using a procedure, take full advantage of all the support data provided to make your job easier and help avoid costly errors.

MODEL IDENTIFICATION

When you order parts from your local dealer you will usually need the engine number (**Figure 3**) and hull number (**Figure 4**) of your

Jet Ski so the dealer can order the correct part. Record the numbers so you will have them when you need them. Compare new parts to old ones before you buy them. If the new part looks different from the old part, ask the dealer's parts or service manager to explain the difference to you.

In order to keep the Jet Ski as reliable as possible, the factory often makes improvements and refinements during a production run. Major design changes are often, though not exclusively, introduced with a new model. New models are not necessarily introduced by year but by model number suffix: for example, JS440-A1, A1A. See **Table 1** at the end of this chapter for model year and model suffix equivalents.

In order to take advantage of the constant improvements and changes, many of which can be incorporated on earlier models, try to make arrangements with your local Jet Ski dealer to examine and copy the factory Service Bulletins as they are released. These bulletins are very complete and announce all changes in parts, specifications, repair procedures and special tools as well as performance improvement tips.

GENERAL MAINTENANCE HINTS

Most of the service procedures described can be performed by anyone reasonably handy with tools. We suggest, however, that you carefully consider your own capabilities before attempting any operation which involves major disassembly of the engine and drive train.

Some crankshaft repair operations, for example, require the use of a press. It would be wiser to have them performed by a shop equipped for such work, rather than to try to do the job yourself with makeshift equipment. Other procedures require precision measurements and, unless you have the skills and equipment to make them, it would be better to have a well-equipped dealership do the work.

Repairs can be made faster and easier if the Jet Ski is clean before you begin work. Clean all oily or greasy parts with cleaning solvent as you remove them. *Never use gasoline as a cleaning agent.* It presents an extreme fire hazard. Always work in a well-ventilated area when using cleaning solvent. Keep a fire extinguisher, BC rated for gasoline fires, handy just in case.

Special tools are required for some service procedures. These may be purchased through dealers. If you are on good terms with the dealer's service department, you may be able to borrow what you need.

Much of the labor charge for repairs made by dealers is for removal and disassembly of other parts to reach the defective one. It is frequently possible to do all of this yourself, then take the affected part or assembly to the dealer for repair. Once you decide to tackle a job yourself, read the entire section pertaining to it. Study the illustrations and the text until you have a thorough idea of what's involved. If special tools are required, make arrangements to get them before you begin work. It's frustrating to get partway into a job and then discover that you are unable to complete it.

SPECIAL TIPS

The following items are specific suggestions that may improve the overall life of the Jet Ski and help avoid costly failures.

1. Use a non-permanent locking agent such as Loctite Lock N' Seal (blue Loctite) on all bolts and nuts, even if they are secured with lockwashers. This type of Loctite does not harden completely and allows easy removal of the bolt or nut. A screw lost from an engine cover or bearing retainer could easily cause serious and expensive damage before its loss is noticed.

When applying Loctite, use a small amount. If too much is used, it may not harden as intended. This type of locking agent hardens only when it is sealed away from air, so it won't lock a 10 mm nut onto an 8 mm bolt. Keep a tube of Loctite Lock N' Seal in your tool box. When used properly it is cheap insurance.

2. The Jet Ski operates in water and it is carefully assembled so that no water enters the fuel system, air intake and electrical system. Many repair procedures call for the use of a sealant such as General Electric RTV 108 silicone sealant. Use a sealant when called for,

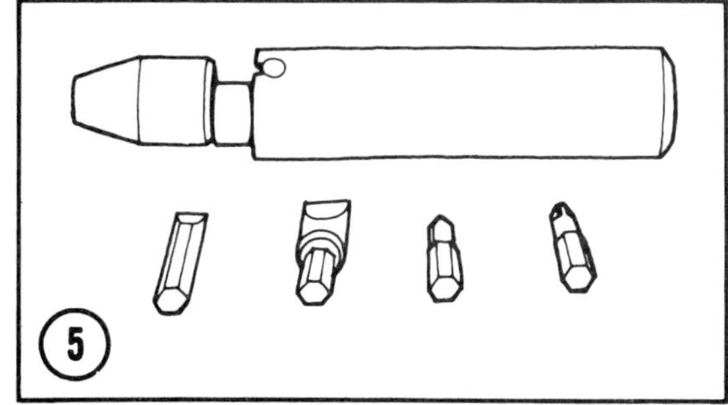

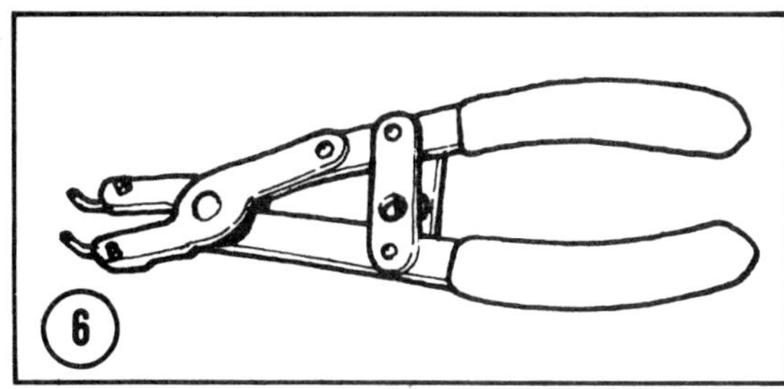

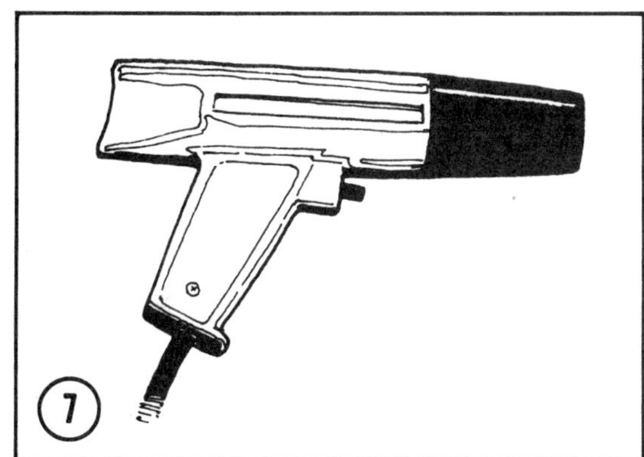

but don't apply so much that the excess leaks inside the parts being sealed. Too much sealant can cause as much damage as no sealant.

3. Many assembly procedures call for a penetrating rust inhibitor such as WD-40. This type of product not only lubricates but also actually penetrates the water on a wet part, in effect drying it out. WD-40 is a very handy lubricant to use on the many rubber tubes, hoses and grommets found on the Jet Ski.

4. When installing the "fold-over" type lockplates, always use a new one if possible. If a new lockplate is not available, always fold over a part of the plate that has not been previously folded. Re-using the same fold may cause the plate to break, resulting in a loose piece of metal adrift in the engine.

When folding the plate over, start the fold with a screwdriver and finish it with a pair of pliers. If a punch or chisel is used to make the fold, the fold may be too sharp, thereby increasing the chances of the plate breaking under stress. These lockplates are very inexpensive and we recommend you keep several in your tool box for field repairs.

5. When installing gaskets in the engine, always use gaskets *without* sealer, unless specifically designated.

TOOLS

To properly service your Jet Ski, you will need an assortment of ordinary hand tools. As a minimum, these include:

    a. Torque wrench
    b. Combination wrenches and socket wrenches (metric)
    c. Spark plug wrench
    d. Allen wrenches
    e. Screwdrivers (standard and Phillips)
    f. Impact driver
    g. Plastic mallet
    h. Small hammer
    i. Circlip pliers
    j. Pliers
    k. Feeler gauges (flat blade and round wire types)
    l. Vernier calipers

Some of the more specialized tools are described below, along with tools required for troubleshooting.

Impact Driver

See **Figure 5**. This tool makes removal of engine cover screws easy and eliminates damaged screw slots. Good ones are available at hardware or auto supply stores.

Circlip Pliers

See **Figure 6**. These pliers are used to remove circlips or snap rings that retain grease seals or bearings. They are available at hardware or auto supply stores.

Strobe Timing Light

See **Figure 7**. Although ignition timing adjustment should rarely be required on the Jet

Ski, you will probably want to check it anyway, especially if you modify the engine. The only way to check timing on CDI ignition is with a strobe light. The best kind to get is an inductive pickup xenon strobe light, where the sensor just clips over the spark plug lead.

Tachometer

If you want to set the idle speed exactly to specification, or to check ignition timing at exactly the specified rpm, you will need a tachometer suited for use on electronic ignition systems. Sun Instruments makes an Inductive Tach-Dwell Meter with a sensor lead that clips onto a spark plug lead. The meter is available at well-stocked auto parts stores.

Dial Indicator/Timing Gauge

See **Figure 8**. This measuring tool is required to precisely locate the position of the piston for accurate ignition timing.

Hydrometer

See **Figure 9**. This instrument tells the battery's state of charge and is available at auto supply stores.

Multimeter or VOM

See **Figure 10**. This instrument is invaluable for electrical system inspection and troubleshooting. You may be able to use a separate voltmeter and ohmmeter for some measurements, but for the serious hobbyist this tool is a must. It is available from electronics supply stores and mail order outlets.

Compression Gauge

See **Figure 11**. The compression gauge measures a cylinder's cranking compression. The measurement, when properly interpreted, indicates general cylinder, piston and ring condition. This instrument is available at auto supply stores.

EXPENDABLE SUPPLIES

Certain expendable supplies are required. These include water resistant grease such as Valvoline X-All, oil, liquid fastener-locking

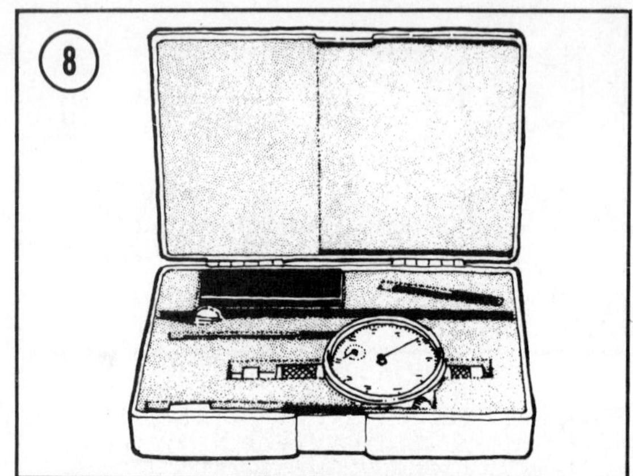

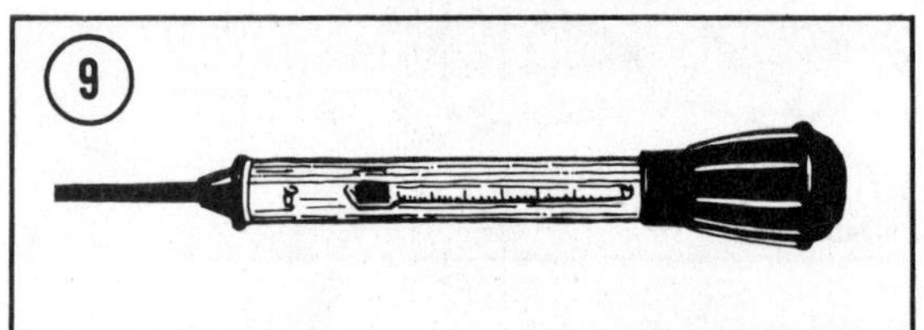

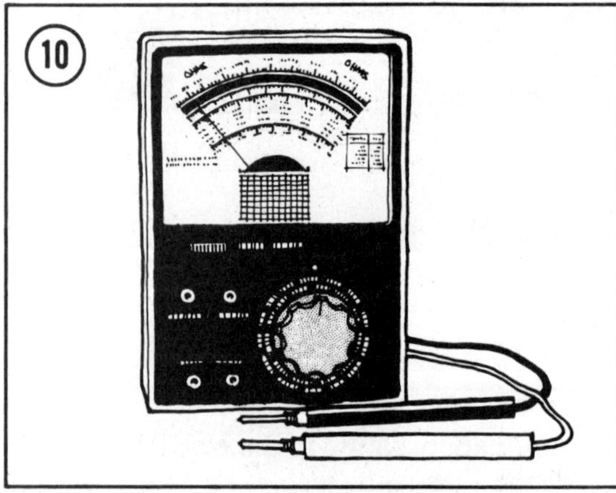

compound (Loctite Lock N' Seal and Stud N' Bearing Mount), silicone sealant such as General Electric RTV 108, rags and cleaning solvent. These items are available at most boating shops and auto supply stores.

SAFETY FIRST

A professional mechanic can work for years and never sustain a serious injury. If you observe a few rules of common sense and safety, you too can enjoy many hours safely servicing your own Jet Ski. You can also hurt yourself or damage your Jet Ski if you ignore these rules.

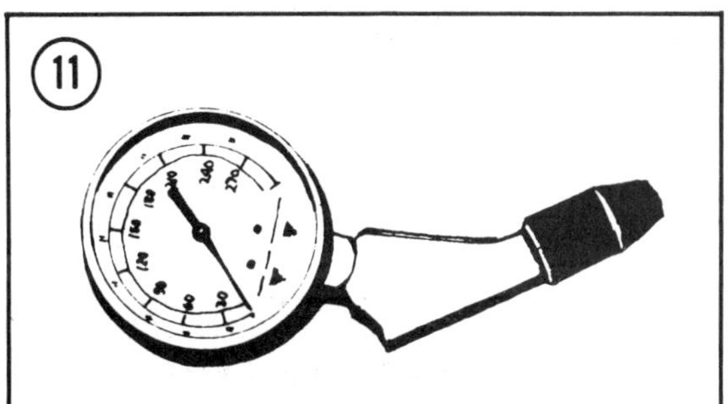

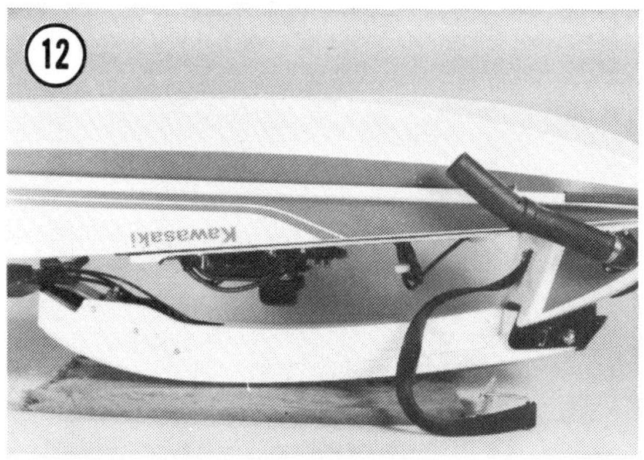

1. Never use gasoline as a cleaning solvent.
2. Never smoke or use a torch around flammable liquids.
3. If welding or brazing is required on the Jet Ski, remove the fuel tank and set it a safe distance away—at least 50 feet.
4. Always use the correct size wrench for turning nuts and bolts. If a nut is stuck, before you use a lot of force, think for a moment what would happen to your hand if the wrench were to slip.
5. Keep your work area clean and uncluttered.
6. Wear safety goggles in all operations involving drilling, grinding or the use of a chisel or air hose.
7. Don't use worn tools.
8. Keep a fire extinguisher handy. Be sure it is BC rated for gasoline and electrical fires.

CLEARING A SUBMERGED JET SKI

If the Jet Ski is submerged while the engine cover is off, water may get into the engine and the fuel tank. To prevent corrosion and serious damage to the engine, the following steps must be taken before trying to restart the engine.

CAUTION
To prevent corrosion damage inside the engine, accomplish this procedure as soon as possible after submerging the Jet Ski.

1. Remove the spark plugs and ground their leads to the engine to prevent damage to the CDI ignition system.
2. Using a protective pad, roll the Jet Ski over on its left side and then hold it upside down to allow the water to drain out of the engine (**Figure 12**).
3. Wait several minutes until no more water comes out, then open the throttle and crank the engine a few revolutions with the start button.

WARNING
Keep your hands away from the jet pump while cranking the engine.

4. Allow another minute for water to drain from the cylinders.
5. Repeat Steps 3 and 4 until all the water has drained from both cylinders, then turn the boat right side up.
6. Spray WD-40 or equivalent into both cylinders through the spark plug holes.
7. Install new dry spark plugs or spray the plugs with WD-40 to displace any water and reinstall them.
8. Start the engine and run it for *less than 15 seconds* to clear any remaining water out of the engine.

CAUTION
Do not run the engine for more than 15 seconds without a supply of cooling water or the rubber parts of the exhaust system will be damaged. Prolonged running without coolant will cause serious engine damage. Do not operate the engine at maximum speed out of the water.

9. If the engine doesn't start, take out the spark plugs and spray them again with WD-40. Reinstall them and try to start it again. If water fouling continues there may be water in the fuel.
10. Clean the fuel sediment bowl and filter; see *Fuel Filter* in Chapter Three. Water in the bowl may indicate that the fuel tank is contaminated.

11. If there is water in the fuel tank, use a pump or siphon to empty the contaminated fuel. Refill with fresh fuel.

> *NOTE*
> *It may be necessary to repeat this procedure several times before all water is removed from the engine. Continued trouble may require disassembly of the fuel pump to drain water; see **Carburetor Disassembly** in Chapter Six.*

12. To dry out the electrical components and keep them from rusting, remove the magneto cover plug and spray WD-40 or equivalent into the cover (**Figure 13**). Do not put oil in the magneto cover.

13. Install the engine cover.

14. To completely clean all water out of the crankcase and cylinders, run the boat *in water* for at least 5 minutes.

JUMP STARTING

Ideally, your Jet Ski's battery should be removed and charged if it runs down. However, the Jet Ski can be started with a booster battery and jumper cables if necessary. Be sure that the booster battery and the Jet Ski battery are both 12 volts.

> *WARNING*
> *When the machine is being jump started, highly explosive hydrogen gas forms in the cells of the battery. Some of this gas escapes through the filler openings and may form an explosive atmosphere around the battery. Sparks, flames or a lighted cigarette can ignite the gas, causing a battery explosion and possible serious personal injury.*

> *WARNING*
> *Electrolyte splashed into the eyes is extremely dangerous. Wear safety glasses while working with batteries. If electrolyte is splashed into the eye, call a doctor immediately, force the eye open and flood it with cool water for at least 5 minutes.*

1. Remove all the filler caps from both batteries.

2. Cover the open vents of each battery with a cloth.

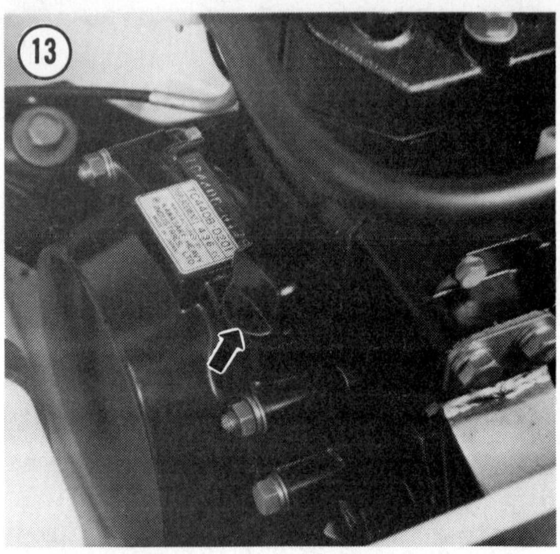

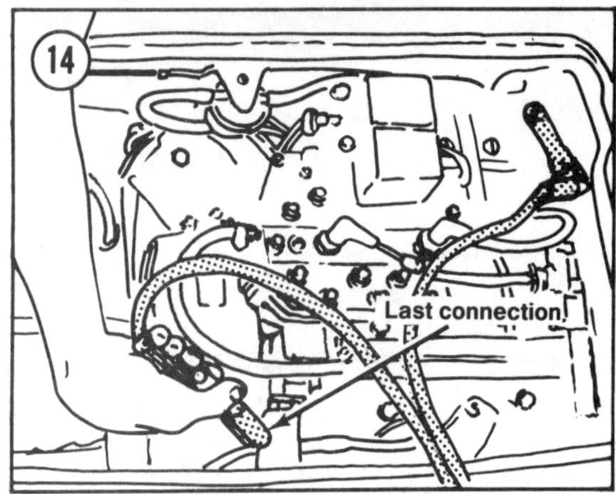

3. Connect a jumper cable between the positive (+) terminals of the 2 batteries.

4. Connect one end of the remaining jumper cable to the negative (-) terminal of the booster battery.

> *CAUTION*
> *If the two batteries are connected in reverse polarity (+ to -) the electrical system will be seriously damaged.*

5. Connect the other end of the remaining jumper cable to the expansion chamber brace (**Figure 14**).

> *WARNING*
> *Do not make this last connection at the carburetor or battery. Take care that you*

do not short the cables together and do not lean over the battery when making this last connection. Do not jump start a frozen battery. It could explode.

6. After starting the Jet Ski, disconnect the jumper cable at the expansion chamber brace first, then the other connections.
7. Install the battery filler caps.

STORAGE

Several months of inactivity can cause problems and a general deterioration of the Jet Ski's condition if proper care is neglected. This is especially true in areas of weather extremes. You should prepare your Jet Ski carefully for "hibernation."

Preparation for Storage

Most people store their Jet Skis in their home garages. If you do not have a garage, the Jet Ski can be covered with a tarp and stored outside in a secure area where you can keep an eye on it.

Careful preparation will minimize deterioration and make it easier to restore the Jet Ski to service later. Use the following procedure.
1. Wash the Jet Ski completely, dry it and thoroughly drain the water from the engine compartment. Wax all painted and polished surfaces.
2. Lubricate all controls. See *General Lubrication* in Chapter Three.

WARNING
Some fuel may spill during these procedures. Work in a well-ventilated area at least 50 feet from any sparks or flames, including gas appliance pilot lights. Do not smoke in the area. Keep a BC rated fire extinguisher handy.

3. Drain all gasoline from the fuel tank, interconnecting hoses, filter and carburetor. Remove the fuel pump end cover and the rubber gasket from the side of the carburetor (**Figure 15**). There is a filter screen under the gasket on 1976-1980 models. Clean the filter screen and reinstall the screen, gasket and cover on the carburetor. Run the engine in 15 second periods to use up all the fuel in the carburetor.

WARNING
The exhaust gases are poisonous. Do not run the engine in a closed area. Make sure there is plenty of ventilation.

CAUTION
Do not run the engine for more than 15 seconds without a supply of cooling water or the rubber parts of the exhaust system will be damaged. Prolonged running without coolant will cause serious engine damage. Do not operate the engine at maximum speed out of the water.

As an alternative, the tank should be filled to minimize water condensation and a fuel preservative may be added to the fuel. These preservatives are available from many motorcycle shops and marine equipment suppliers.
4. Remove the carburetor's cover and clean the flame arrestor element. See *Carburetor Disassembly* in Chapter Six. Open the throttle and spray a penetrating rust inhibitor such as WD-40 down into the carburetor bore. Install the flame arrestor and cover.
5. Remove spark plugs and add a small quantity of motor oil to each cylinder. Crank the engine a few revolutions to distribute the oil and install the spark plugs.

CAUTION
Do not add more than a small amount of oil to the cylinder or the crankshaft oil

seals may be blown out when the engine is cranked.

6. To keep the water in the water muffler from freezing and cracking the muffler, remove the exhaust pipe/expansion chamber in one piece and pour about 3 ounces of automotive antifreeze through the resonator and into the water muffler. See *Exhaust Removal* in Chapter Six.

7. Remove the battery and coat the cable terminals with petroleum jelly; see *Battery Removal* in Chapter Seven. Check the electrolyte level and refill with distilled water if it is low. Store the battery in an area where it will not freeze and recharge it once a month.

8. Clean the cooling system; see *Cooling System Cleaning* in Chapter Three.

9. After cleaning, all water should be cleared from the cooling system. Disconnect the hose at the front of the exhaust pipe (**Figure 16**) and blow air back through the engine until all water is cleared from the system. Reconnect the hose.

10. Clean the bilge system; see *Bilge System Cleaning* in Chapter Three. Before reconnecting the bilge hoses at the breather fitting, blow air through each of them until all water is cleared from the bilge system.

11. Spray the whole engine with a penetrating rust inhibitor such as WD-40. Wipe off the excess.

12. Remove the magneto cover plug to allow moisture to evaporate.

13. Place the engine cover on the Jet Ski, but prop it up off the gasket so that air can circulate freely throughout the engine compartment.

14. Cover the Jet Ski with material that will allow air circulation. Don't use plastic.

Removal From Storage

1. Lubricate all controls. See *General Lubrication* in Chapter Three.

2. Install the battery; see *Battery Installation* in Chapter Seven.

3. Fill the tank with fresh fuel and check for leaks.

4. Inspect or replace the fuel filter element; see *Fuel Filter* in Chapter Three.

5. Inspect the fuel vent check valve; see *Fuel Vent Check Valve* in Chapter Three.

6. Perform a tune-up as described in Chapter Three.

7. Check all rubber bilge and cooling hoses for cracking and weathering. Replace any faulty parts. Check the hose connections under the jet pump cover.

8. Make sure your fire extinguisher has a full charge.

9. Inspect your life jacket and make sure your boat registration is up to date.

Table 1   MODEL YEAR/SUFFIX DESIGNATION

Year	Model Suffix	Hull Number Begins
1976	JS400-A3	017250675
1977	JS440-A1	070700976
1978 early	JS440-A1A	150001277
1978 late	JS440-A2	162000178
1979	JS440-A3	245001178
1980 early	JS440-A4	316070480
1980 late	JS440-A4A	326350580
1981	JS440-A5	352000181

Table 2   GENERAL SPECIFICATIONS
(JS400/440 1976-1981)

General	
Engine type	2-stroke twin cylinder, piston port, 180° firing, water-cooled
Lubrication system	Premixed gas/oil — 40:1
Starting system	Electric starter
Ignition system	CDI (capacitive discharge ignition)
Charging system	Alternator, rectifier/regulator
Carburetion	Mikuni BN38
Fuel tank capacity	3.5 U.S. gal. (13 liters, 2.9 Imp. gal.)
Engine (JS400)	
Displacement	24.3 cu. in. (398 cc)
Max. horsepower	24.5 @ 6,000 rpm
Max. torque	24 ft.-lb. (3.3 mkg) @ 4,500 rpm
Compression ratio	5.8:1
Port timing	
Intake	Open 74.3° BTDC; Close 74.3° ATDC
Transfer	Open 58.6° BBDC; Close 58.6° ABDC
Exhaust	Open 82.3° BBDC; Close 82.3° ABDC
Engine (JS440)	
Displacement	26.6 cu. in. (436 cc)
Max. horsepower	27 @ 6,000 rpm
Max. torque	27 ft.-lb. (3.7 mkg) @ 4,500 rpm
Compression ratio	6.1:1
Port timing	
Intake	Open 74.3° BTDC; Close 74.3° ATDC
Transfer	Open 58.0° BBDC; Close 58.0° ABDC
Exhaust	Open 82.3° BBDC; Close 82.3° ABDC
Drive Train	
Jet pump type	Axial flow, single stage
Jet pump diameter	4.8 in. (121 mm)
Jet pump thrust	
400	220 lb. (100 kg)
440	243 lb. (110 kg)
Steering	Pivoting outlet nozzle
Braking	Water drag
Electrical	
Ignition system	CDI (capacitive discharge ignition)
Advanced timing	25° BTDC @ 6,000 rpm, 0.139 in. (3.53 mm)
Charging system	Alternator, rectifier/regulator
Alternator output	45W @ 6,000 rpm
Battery	12V, 16AH
Dimensions and Performance	
Length	82 in. (214 cm)
Width	24 in. (61 cm)
Height	25 in. (64 cm)
Draft	4 in. (100 mm)
Dry weight	243 lb. (110 kg)
Max. speed	
400	31 mph (50 kph)
440	33 mph (53 kph)
Fuel consumption	
(full throttle)	
400	2.9 U.S. gal./hr. (11 liter/hr. 2.4 Imp. gal./hr.)
440	3.2 U.S. gal./hr. (12 liter/hr. 2.7 Imp. gal./hr.)
Cruising range	
(full throttle)	
400	29 mi. (47 km), 55 minutes to Reserve
440	28 mi. (45 km), 50 minutes to Reserve
Noise level	
400	79 dbA @ 50 ft. @ full throttle
440	81 dbA @ 50 ft. @ full throttle

CHAPTER TWO

TROUBLESHOOTING

There's one kind of "trouble" you can expect to run into occasionally if you like to push the Jet Ski to its performance and handling limits—that is submerging. If the engine cover has come loose and the engine compartment is full of water, refer to *Cleaning a Submerged Jet Ski* in Chapter One. That kind of problem is as regular as a tune-up for some riders. This chapter deals with other causes of trouble.

Diagnosing mechanical ills is relatively simple if you use orderly procedures and keep a few basic principles in mind. Never assume anything. Don't overlook the obvious. If the Jet Ski won't start, is the stop button OFF? Is there fuel in the tank? Is the engine cranking slow because the battery is discharged? Is the engine flooded with fuel from using the choke too much?

If you are riding along and the engine suddenly quits, check the easiest, most accessible problem spots first. Is there sufficient fuel in the tank? Has a spark plug wire fallen off? Is there water in the fuel filter sediment bowl? Is the fuel vent check valve allowing air to enter the tank as it should?

If nothing obvious turns up in the first check, look a little further. Learning to recognize and describe symptoms will make repairs easier for you or a mechanic at a shop. Describe the problems accurately and fully. Saying that "it won't run" isn't the same as saying "it quit at high speed and wouldn't start" or that "it sat in my garage for 3 months and then wouldn't start."

Gather as many symptoms together as possible to aid in diagnosis. Note whether the engine lost power gradually or all at once, what color smoke (if any) came from the exhaust and so on.

You don't need fancy equipment or complicated test gear to determine whether repairs can be attempted at home. A few simple checks could save a large repair bill and time lost while the Jet Ski sits in a dealer's service department. On the other hand, be realistic and don't attempt repairs beyond your abilities. Service departments tend to charge heavily for putting together a disassembled engine that may have been abused. Some won't even take on such a job—so use some common sense and don't get in over your head.

OPERATING REQUIREMENTS

An engine needs 3 basics to run properly: correct fuel/air mixture, compression and a spark at the right time. If one or more are missing, the engine won't run. The spark is the weakest link of the 3 basics. More problems result from fouled plugs than from any other source. Keep that in mind before you begin tampering with carburetor adjustments and the like.

If a Jet Ski has been sitting for any length of time and refuses to start, check the fuel delivery system. This includes the tank, fuel valve, lines, filter and carburetor. Water may have collected in the tank. Fuel deposits may have gummed up the carburetor fuel or air passages. Fuel tends to lose its potency after standing for long periods. Condensation may contaminate it with water. Drain old fuel and try starting with a fresh tankful.

Compression, or the lack of it, usually enters the picture only in the case of older machines. Worn or broken pistons, rings and cylinder bores could prevent starting. Generally, a gradual power loss and harder and harder starting will be readily apparent in this case.

STARTING DIFFICULTIES

Fuel Flow

Check fuel flow first. If fuel is in the tank, check for water in the fuel filter sediment bowl. The 1976 400 cc filter elements can swell and block fuel flow when contaminated with water. The fuel valve may be clogged, the fuel lines may be stopped up or kinked, the fuel filter may be clogged or leaking air at the ring nut or the fuel vent check valve or vent line may be plugged. If the carburetor is getting enough fuel, turn to the electrical system next.

Electrical System

The CDI system won't produce a spark if the battery turns the engine over too slowly. If the battery has run down, refer to *Battery* in Chapter Seven.

If the battery is okay, remove the spark plugs and check them for water or fuel fouling. Reconnect the plug caps and lay the plugs against the cylinder head so the base makes a good connection and turn the engine over with the starter. A fat, blue spark should jump across the electrodes. If there is no spark or a weak one, you have electrical system trouble. Check for a defective plug by replacing it with a known good one. Don't assume a plug is good just because it's new.

If the plug has been cleared of guilt, but there's still no spark, start backtracking through the system. If the contact at the end of the spark plug wire can be exposed, it can be held about 1/8 inch from the head while the engine is turned over to check for a spark. Remember to hold the wire only by its insulation to avoid a nasty shock. If the plug wires are dirty, greasy or wet, wrap a rag around them so you don't get shocked. If you do feel a shock or see sparks along the wire, clean or replace the wire and/or its connections. If there's no spark at the plug wire, look for loose connections to the ignition coil or igniter. Improper installation of the stator exciter coil will keep the engine from starting; see *Stator Coil Installation* in Chapter Seven.

If you have just submerged the Jet Ski and it won't start, dry off the plug and plug wire. Spray WD-40 into the magneto cover opening.

Note that spark plugs of an incorrect heat range (too cold) may cause hard starting. Set the gap to specifications. Refer to Chapter Seven for checkout procedures for the entire electrical system and individual components.

If a healthy spark occurs at the right time and there is adequate fuel flow to the carburetor, check the carburetor itself. Make sure all fuel and air passages are clean. Check that the carburetor is mounted snugly and no air is leaking past the mounting flange.

Compression

An accurate compression check gives a good idea of the condition of the engine's basic working parts. Refer to *Compression Test* in Chapter Three for regular compression inspection.

Hard starting and low power may also be caused by faulty *primary* compression in the crankcase. This can be caused by a leaking crankshaft seal, base gasket, or any source of crankcase leakage. If you suspect faulty crankcase compression, take the Jet Ski to your dealer for crankcase pressure testing.

POOR IDLING

Poor idling may be caused by incorrect carburetor adjustment, incorrect timing or ignition system defects. Check the fuel vent check valve for an obstruction. Also check for loose carburetor mounting bolts or a faulty carburetor flange gasket.

MISFIRING

Misfiring under heavy load, as when accelerating, is usually caused by bad spark plugs, but it can be caused by too lean or too rich a fuel mixture— see *Carburetor Adjustment* in Chapter Three. Misfiring can be caused by a weak spark or dirty plugs. Check for fuel contamination. If misfiring occurs only at certain throttle settings, refer to Chapter Six for the specific carburetor circuits involved.

FLAT SPOTS

If the engine seems to die momentarily when the throttle is opened and then recovers, check for dirty fuel passages in the carburetor, water in the fuel or an excessively lean or rich low speed mixture.

POWER LOSS

Exhaust fumes leaking within the engine compartment can slow and even stop the engine. Water in the fuel, weeds in the jet pump, improper fuel and oil and carburetor maladjustment can cause low power. Poor condition of rings, pistons or cylinder will cause a lack of power and speed. Check the ignition timing. Improper stator trigger coil installation will retard the ignition timing; see *Stator Coil Installation* in Chapter Seven.

OVERHEATING

If the engine seems to run too hot all the time, be sure you are not idling it for long periods. The Jet Ski cooling system does not circulate water at idle speed. Make sure the cooling system isn't clogged with sand; see *Cooling System Cleaning* in Chapter Three.

Spark plugs of the wrong heat range can burn pistons. An excessively lean fuel mixture may cause overheating. Check ignition timing. Broken or worn rings may permit compression gases to leak past them, heating heads and cylinders excessively. Use the proper grade and mixture of gas and oil. Check for air leaks at cylinder base gasket or intake manifold.

BACKFIRING

Check that the timing is not advanced too far. Check the fuel for contamination. Make sure the fuel mixture is not too lean.

ENGINE NOISES

Experience is needed to diagnose accurately in this area. Noises are hard to differentiate and harder yet to describe. Deep knocking noises usually mean main bearing failure. A slapping noise generally comes from a loose piston. A light knocking noise during acceleration may be a bad connecting rod bearing. Pinging, which sounds like marbles being shaken in a tin can, is caused by too much ignition advance, fuel with too low an octane rating or too lean a fuel mixture. Pinging should be corrected immediately or piston damage will result. Compression leaks at the head/cylinder joint will sound like a rapid on-and-off squeal.

PISTON SEIZURE

Piston seizure is caused by incorrect piston clearances when fitted, fitting rings with improper end gap, too thin an oil being used, incorrect spark plug heat range or incorrect ignition timing. Overheating from any cause may result in seizure.

EXCESSIVE VIBRATION

Excessive vibration may be caused by loose engine mounts, worn engine or drive shaft bearings, loose jet pump bolts, a bent drive shaft or a damaged jet pump or impeller.

NOTE: If you own a 1982 or 1983 model, first check the Supplement at the back of the book for any new service information.

CHAPTER THREE

LUBRICATION, MAINTENANCE AND TUNE-UP

This chapter covers all the regular maintenance you have to perform to keep your machine in top shape. Regular maintenance is the best guarantee of a trouble-free, long lasting Jet Ski. In addition, while performing the routine jobs, you will probably notice any developing problems at an early stage when they are simple and inexpensive to correct.

Tables 1-3 are at the end of the chapter.

PRE-RIDE CHECKLIST

Before a day of riding, always prepare your Jet Ski as follows:

1. Release built-up vapor pressure from the fuel tank by loosening the fuel filler cap. When the pressure has been released, tighten the cap securely.
2. Check the throttle cable clamp pivot at the carburetor (**Figure 1**). If it is dry, lubricate with waterproof grease; see *General Lubrication* in this chapter.
3. Lubricate the choke and steering controls with WD-40, LPS or equivalent penetrating rust inhibitor; see *General Lubrication* in this chapter.

The throttle cable housing must *not* be lubricated or it will collect sand and dirt.

4. Check steering and throttle cable operation. Make sure that the throttle lever returns to the fully closed position when it is released (**Figure 2**). Make sure the pivot retainer clip is secure. If binding, rough spots or excessive play are noticed, make the necessary adjustments; see *Steering* and *Carburetor* in this chapter.
5. Remove the engine cover and check for fuel leakage. Do not operate the Jet Ski until leaks are stopped and spilled fuel is washed out.
6. Roll the Jet Ski onto its left side to allow any water in the engine compartment to run out. You can protect the Jet Ski's finish by laying a towel under its left side before rolling it over.

> *CAUTION*
> *Do not turn the Jet Ski on its right side or water in the exhaust system may drain into the engine's exhaust ports and cause serious engine damage.*

7. Remove any weeds or foreign objects from the water inlet, jet pump and drive shaft. Check the jet pump cover and intake grate. If they are loose, tighten the mounting screws.
8. Inspect the hull for damage.
9. Turn the Jet Ski upright and check the amount of fuel in the tank. Add more if needed and turn the fuel valve to ON.
10. Check the electrolyte level in the battery; see *Battery* in this chapter.

11. Tighten any loose bolts, nuts or hose clamps. Pay special attention to the following:
   a. Fuel hoses and tank outlet retainer nut
   b. Cooling water and bilge hoses
   c. Exhaust system clamps
12. Inspect your fire extinguisher. Make sure it is fully charged.
13. Run the engine for about 5 seconds and stop the engine with the kill switch.

> *WARNING*
> *The exhaust gases are poisonous. Do not run the engine in a closed area. Make sure there is plenty of ventilation.*

> *CAUTION*
> *Do not run the engine for more than 15 seconds without a supply of cooling water or the rubber parts of the exhaust system will be damaged. Prolonged running without coolant will cause serious engine damage. Do not operate the engine at maximum speed out of the water.*

END OF DAY CHECKLIST

Before putting your Jet Ski away for the day, complete the following procedures:
1. After taking the Jet Ski out of the water, lift the rear end 10 in. or more to allow water in the expansion chamber to drain away from the engine.
2. Clear the excess water out of the exhaust system by starting the engine and running it for *no more than 5 seconds.*
3. Stop the engine and remove the engine cover. If there is water in the engine compartment, roll the Jet Ski onto its left side to drain the water out. A towel or other pad placed under the Jet Ski will protect its finish.
4. Dry the engine compartment and reinstall the engine cover.
5. Before storing the Jet Ski, loosen the engine cover strap so its elasticity will be retained and move the engine cover so that air can circulate freely.

MAINTENANCE SCHEDULE

Table 1 is a recommended maintenance schedule.

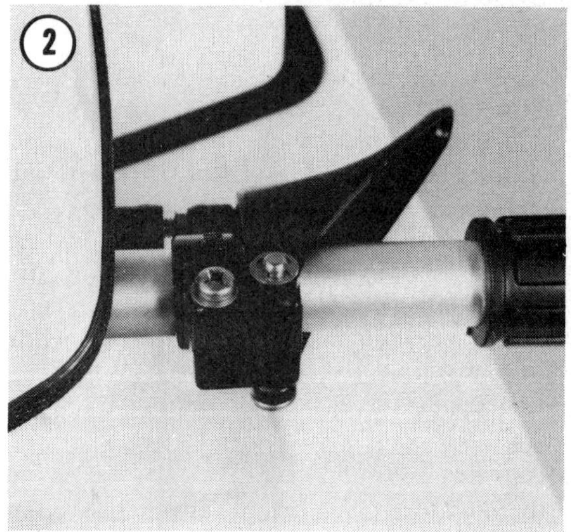

> *CAUTION*
> *If it is necessary to run the engine during maintenance, the Jet Ski should be in water. A temporary cooling system must be used if this is not possible; see* **On-shore Cooling** *in this chapter.*

ENGINE LUBRICATION

> *WARNING*
> *Some fuel may spill during these procedures. Work in a well-ventilated area at least 50 feet from any sparks or flames, including gas appliance pilot lights. Do not smoke in the area. Keep a BC rated fire extinguisher handy.*

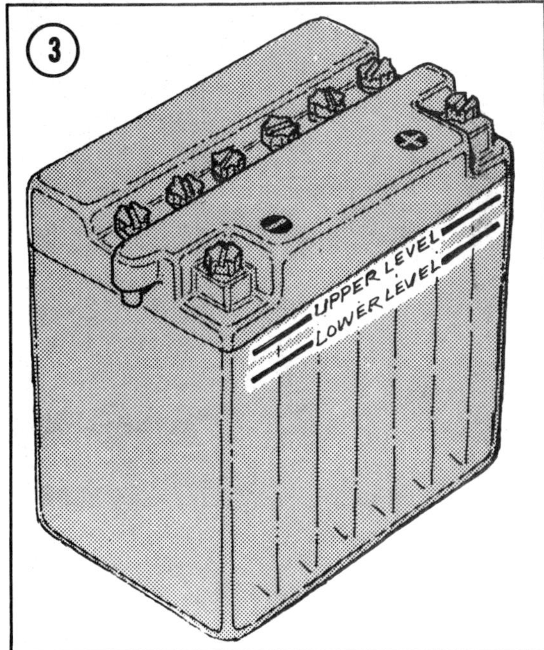

The engine is lubricated by oil mixed with gasoline in a 40:1 gas/oil ratio. Regular, unleaded, or leaded premium gasoline can be used. Use only oil rated by the Boating Industry Association (BIA) for "Service TC-W" (two-cycle water cooled). Mix the oil and gasoline thoroughly in a clean container larger than the quantity being mixed, to allow room for agitation. Always measure the quantities exactly. See **Table 2** for specific gas/oil qualities.

Use a baby bottle or graduate to measure oil. Pour the required amount of oil into the mixing container and add about 1/2 the required amount of gasoline. Agitate the mixture thoroughly, then add the remaining fuel.

CAUTION
Do not mix castor bean oils with petroleum oils. A gum will form which may cause serious engine damage.

BATTERY

The battery electrolyte level should be checked regularly, particularly during hot weather. The battery is marked with electrolyte level limit lines (**Figure 3**). Always maintain the fluid level between the lines, adding distilled water as required. Distilled water is available at most supermarkets and its use will prolong the life of the battery, especially in areas where tap water is hard (has a high mineral content).

To inspect the fluid level in all the cells, it may be necessary to unhook the retaining straps and lift the battery out of the engine compartment.

WARNING
Battery electrolyte contains sulfuric acid, which can destroy clothing and cause serious chemical burns. Electrolyte splashed into the eyes is extremely dangerous. Wear safety glasses. In case of contact, flood with water for at least 5 minutes and call a doctor immediately if the eyes were exposed.

Don't overfill the battery or you'll lose some electrolyte, weakening the battery and causing corrosion. Never allow the electrolyte level to drop below the top of the plates or the plates may be permanently damaged.

CAUTION
If electrolyte is spilled on the Jet Ski, wash it off immediately with plenty of water.

TUNE-UP
(EVERY 25 HOURS)

Tune the engine every 25 hours of operation. Refer to **Table 3** at the end of the chapter for tune-up specifications. The following list summarizes routine engine tune-up procedures. Detailed instructions follow the list.

Consult Chapter Two for troubleshooting procedures when you suspect more serious trouble.

1. Clean the fuel filter and fuel tap sediment bowl. Inspect fuel lines for cracks or leakage.
2. Inspect the fuel vent check valve.
3. Inspect the spark plugs, clean them, adjust the gap, or replace them if necessary.
4. Torque the cylinder head nuts.
5. Inspect and adjust the carburetor (if required).
6. Check and record cylinder compression.

ON-SHORE COOLING

If it is necessary to run the engine during maintenance, the Jet Ski should be in water. A temporary cooling system must be used if this is not possible.

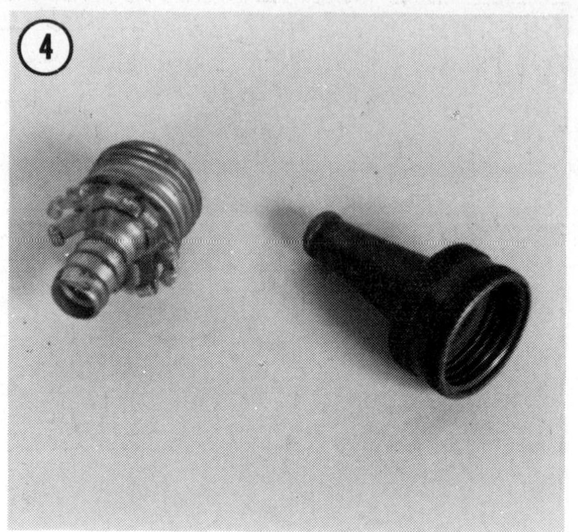

CAUTION
Do not run the engine for more than 15 seconds out of the water or the rubber parts of the exhaust system will be damaged. Prolonged running without coolant will cause serious engine damage. Never operate the engine at maximum speed out of the water.

All that is needed for an on-shore cooling system is an ordinary 3/8 in. garden hose adapter, such as those shown in **Figure 4**, and a hose. Most hardware stores can furnish the adapter.

1. Screw the adapter onto the garden hose.
2. Disconnect the rear end of the coolant hose that runs to the exhaust manifold and attach the garden hose adapter to the hose (**Figure 5**). Attach the garden hose to a faucet, but do not turn the water on yet.
3. Start the engine and turn the water on as soon as the engine is running. Turn the water off as soon as the engine stops. The engine requires 2.5 qt./minute (2.4 liters/minute) of coolant when idling, and 9 qt./minute (8.5 liters/minute) at high speed.

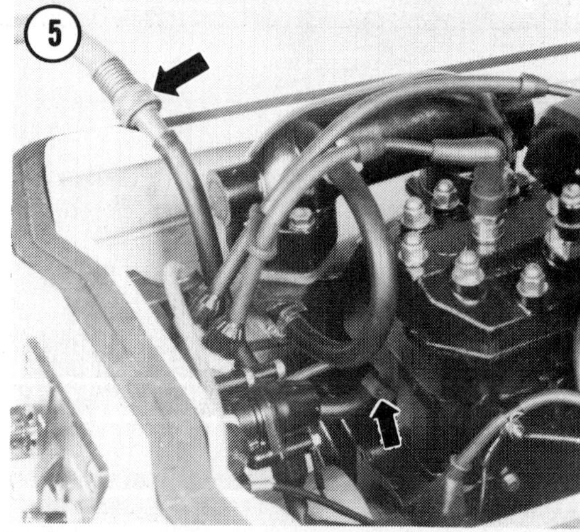

CAUTION
Too slow a coolant flow will cause exhaust system and engine damage. Too fast a coolant flow may kill the engine and flood the cylinders; this may cause hydraulic locking of the engine and severe damage. If the engine dies while using an on-shore cooling supply, shut the water off immediately.

4. After the job is finished, disconnect the garden hose and adapter, reconnect the engine cooling hose and tighten its clamp.

FUEL FILTER & SEDIMENT BOWL

A fuel filter and sediment bowl, mounted on the right side of the engine compartment (**Figure 6**), keep dirt and water from entering

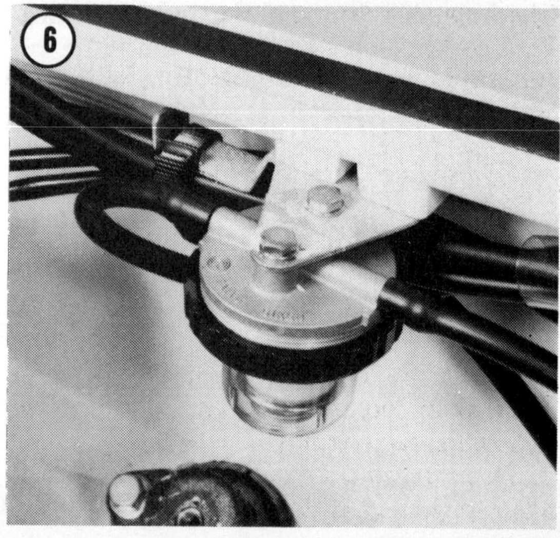

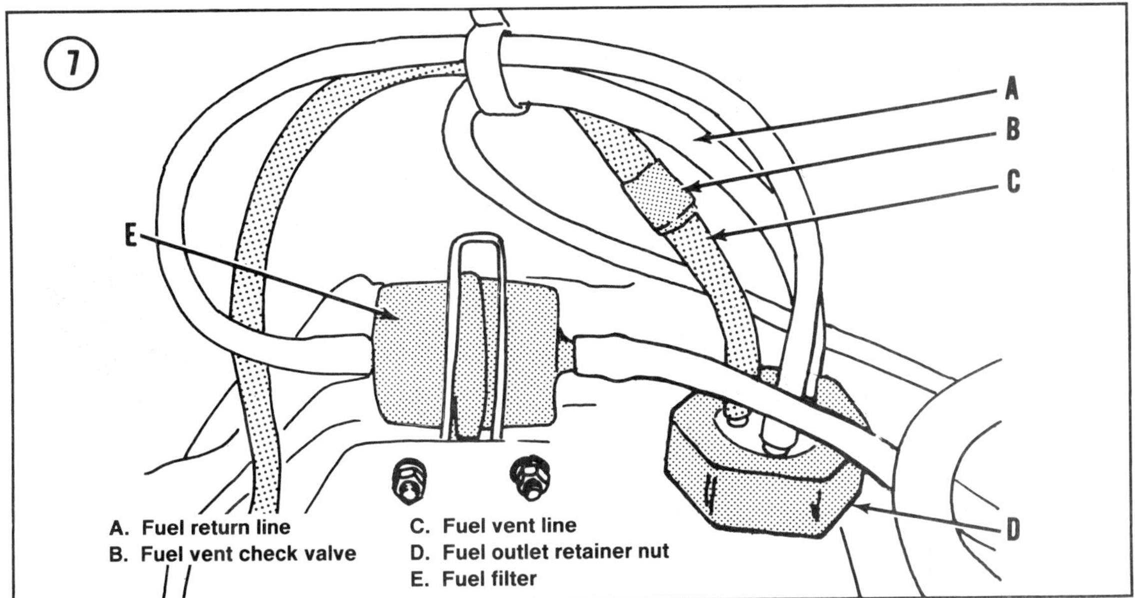

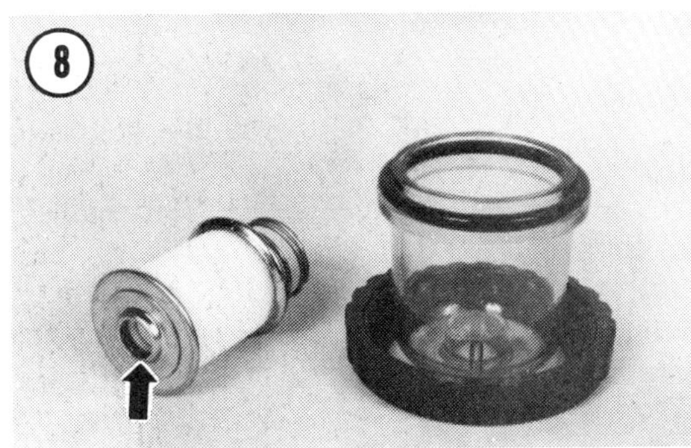

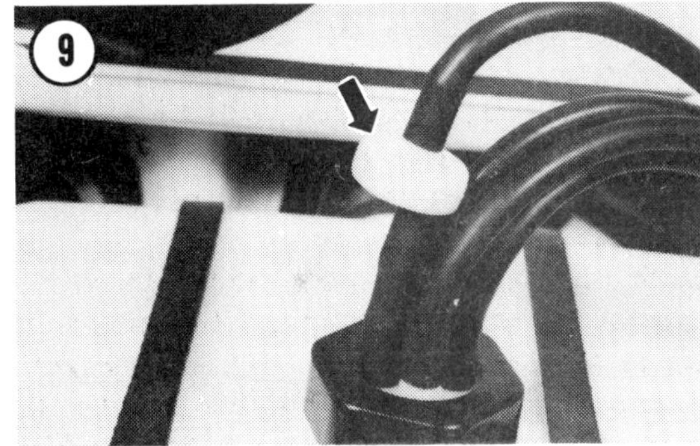

the carburetor. Clean the filter at each tune-up or whenever there is water in the bowl.

The 400 cc Jet Skis have a disposable fuel filter mounted on top of the fuel tank (**Figure 7**). Change this filter at each tune-up or whenever it becomes contaminated with water.

> *WARNING*
> *Some fuel may spill during these procedures. Work in a well-ventilated area at least 50 feet away from any sparks or flames, including gas appliance pilot lights. Do not smoke in the area.*

1. Release built-up vapor pressure from the fuel tank by loosening the fuel filler cap, then tighten the cap securely.
2. Place a rag under the sediment bowl to catch any spilled gasoline, then unscrew the sediment bowl ring and remove the bowl, spring and filter.
3. Clean the filter and bowl in solvent.
4. Check that the small rubber O-ring is in place inside the filter neck (**Figure 8**), then push the filter up onto the outlet tube.
5. Install the bowl with its large O-ring and tighten the mounting ring securely. Be sure that the O-ring seals properly or air may be drawn into the bowl.

FUEL VENT CHECK VALVE

The fuel vent check valve (**Figure 9**) allows air to enter the fuel tank as fuel is used up and prevents fuel from leaking out when the Jet Ski is tipped over. To inspect the valve, disconnect the hose from the tank to the check valve. If the check valve is operating correctly, you should be able to draw air through the valve, but you should not be able to blow through the valve. See *Fuel Vent Check Valve* in Chapter Six for more information on the check valve.

SPARK PLUGS

Spark Plug Inspection

1. Grasp the spark plug leads as near to the plug as possible and pull them off the plugs. Clear away any dirt near the spark plugs.

CAUTION
Dirt could fall into the cylinders when the plug is removed, causing serious engine damage.

2. Remove the spark plugs with a 13/16 inch spark plug wrench.
3. Inspect the spark plugs carefully. The most common spark plug problem on a Jet Ski is water fouling. Water or a water/oil emulsion on the plug electrodes indicates water in the fuel or inside the engine. A plug with this condition should be replaced with a clean, dry plug. If this is not possible, the water fouled plugs may be dried with electrical contact cleaner or with a penetrating rust inhibitor (WD-40 or equivalent).

Look for a broken center porcelain or severely eroded electrodes. If deposits are light the plug may be cleaned with a wire brush or in a spark plug sandblast cleaner, but the price of a new plug is cheap insurance for reliability. Check the spark plug gasket. If it's completely flattened, install a new one.

CAUTION
Never sandblast an oily or wet plug. The grit will stick to the plug and later drop into the engine. After sandblasting a plug, clean it thoroughly.

4. If the plug is reusable, file the center and side electrodes so their corners are sharp. Less voltage is required to jump the gap when the electrode corners are sharp.
5. Measure the gap with a round wire spark plug gauge (**Figure 10**). Adjust the gap by bending the side electrode only. The gap should be 0.028-0.032 in. (0.7-0.8 mm).
6. Apply a small amount of aluminum anti-seize compound (available at auto parts

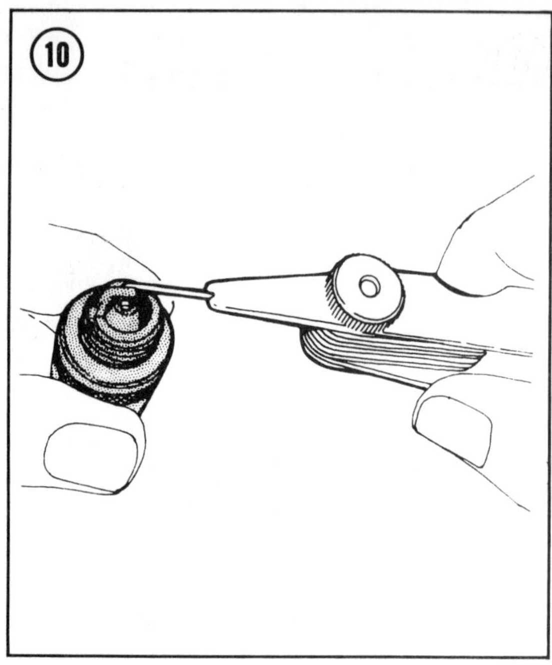

stores) to the plug threads. Don't use oil or grease—they'll turn to pure carbon and make the plug harder to get out the next time.
7. Clean the seating area on the cylinder head and thread the plug in by hand until it seats. Then tighten the plug 1/8 to 1/2 turn with a spark plug wrench. If you use a torque wrench, the proper torque is 20 ft.-lb. (2.8 mkg).

Figure 11 illustrates various spark plug conditions that can tell you something about the engine's condition.

Normal Condition

If the plug has a light tan-or gray-colored deposit and no abnormal gap wear or erosion, good engine, carburetion, and ignition condition are indicated. The plug in use is of the proper heat range and may be serviced and returned to use.

Carbon Fouled

Soft, dry, sooty deposits are evidence of incomplete combustion and can usually be attributed to rich carburetion. This condition is also sometimes caused by weak ignition, retarded timing or low compression. Such a plug may usually be cleaned and returned to service, but the condition which causes fouling should be corrected.

NORMAL USE

OIL FOULED

CARBON FOULED

OVERHEATED

GAP BRIDGED

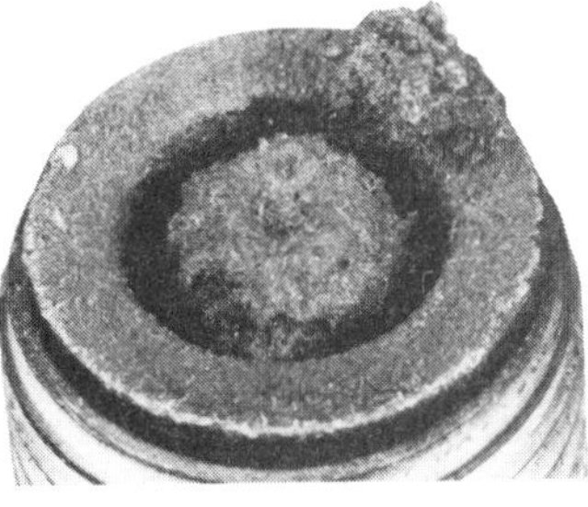

SUSTAINED PREIGNITION

WORN OUT

Photos courtesy of Champion Spark Plug Company.

Oil Fouled

This plug has a black insulator tip, a damp, oily film over the firing end and a carbon layer over the entire nose. The electrodes will not be worn. Common causes for this condition are:
   a. Too much oil in the fuel
   b. Poorly mixed fuel
   c. Wrong type of oil
   d. Low idle speed or prolonged idling
   e. Weak ignition
   f. Spark plug heat range too cold
Oil fouled spark plugs may be cleaned in an emergency, but it is better to replace them. It is important to correct the cause of fouling before the engine is returned to service.

Gap Bridging

Plugs with this condition exhibit gaps shorted out by combustion deposits between the electrodes. If this situation is encountered, check for an improper oil type or a clogged exhaust. Be sure to locate and correct the cause of this spark plug condition. Such plugs must be replaced with new ones.

Overheated

Overheated spark plugs exhibit burned electrodes. The insulator tip will be light gray or even chalk white. The most common cause for this condition is using a spark plug of the wrong heat range (too hot). If it is known that the correct plug is being used, other causes are:
   a. Lean fuel mixture
   b. Engine overloading or lugging
   c. Loose carburetor mounting
   d. Timing advanced too far
Always correct the fault before putting the bike back into service. Such plugs cannot be salvaged; install new plugs.

Worn Out

Corrosive gases formed by combustion and high voltage sparks have eroded the electrodes. Spark plugs in this condition require more voltage to fire under hard acceleration, often more than the ignition system can supply. Replace them with new spark plugs of the same heat range.

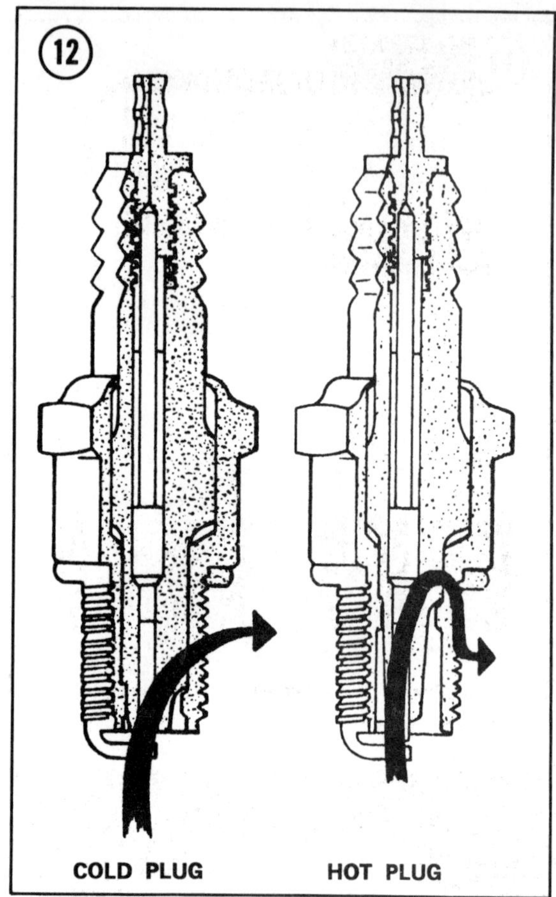

Preignition

If electrodes are melted, preignition is almost certainly the cause. Check for carburetor mounting or intake manifold leaks, also overadvanced ignition timing. It is also possible that a plug of the wrong heat range (too hot) is being used. Find the cause of preignition before placing the engine back into service.

SPARK PLUG HEAT RANGE

The proper spark plug is very important for maximum performance and reliability. The proper heat range requires that a plug operate hot enough to burn off unwanted deposits, but not hot enough to burn up or cause preignition. **Figure 12** shows "hot" and "cold" spark plugs. A cold plug dissipates heat faster than a hot plug because the heat has a shorter path to travel from the hot tip of the plug to the cylinder head. A spark plug of the correct heat

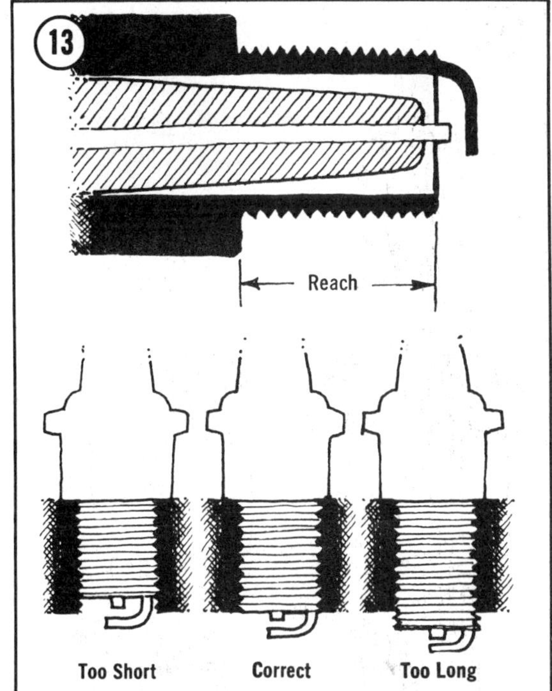

range will show a light tan color on the portion of the insulator within the cylinder after the plug has been in service.

The spark plug recommended by the factory is usually the most suitable for your machine, since spark plugs of the wrong heat range can cause extensive engine damage. Because the Jet Ski engine is water-cooled and is generally operated at a constant throttle opening, cylinder head temperature is relatively stable. This means that an engine that is in good condition, tuned properly, with the proper fuel/oil mix being used should not need a spark plug of a different heat range. Refer to **Table 3** at the end of the chapter for the recommended spark plugs.

> *CAUTION*
> *Ensure that the spark plug used has the correct thread reach (**Figure 13**). A thread reach too short will cause the exposed threads in the cylinder head to accumulate carbon, resulting in stripped cylinder head threads when the proper plug is installed. Too long a reach may cause plug/piston contact and serious damage.*

CYLINDER HEAD NUTS

Re-torque the cylinder head nuts at each tune-up as described in *Cylinder Head Installation* in Chapter Four.

IGNITION TIMING

The Jet Ski uses a CDI (capacitive discharge ignition) system. The solid state CDI has no wearing parts and, once set properly, should not require adjustment unless you want to alter the engine's performance characteristics.

To inspect or adjust the timing, refer to Chapter Seven, *Ignition Timing*.

CARBURETOR

The carburetor should be adjusted only when the engine is fully warmed up. Don't "fiddle" with the carburetor if any problem may be caused by a faulty spark plug or water in the fuel system.

> *CAUTION*
> *If it is necessary to run the engine during maintenance, the Jet Ski should be in water. A temporary cooling system must be used if this is not possible; see **On-shore Cooling** in this chapter.*

Choke Cable

1. The choke butterfly valve in the carburetor should be all the way open when the choke knob is pushed in (**Figure 14**).
2. The choke butterfly valve should be completely closed when the choke knob is pulled all the way out.

3. Use the adjuster nuts at the cable bracket (**Figure 15**) to move the cable up or down to take up any excess slack in the choke cable. Tighten the nuts when finished and push the rubber cable boot down over the end of the adjuster to keep water and sand out of the cable.

Throttle Cable

1. When the throttle lever is released, the idle adjust screw should rest against the throttle stop.

2. Squeeze the throttle lever to open the throttle fully and check that the throttle bellcrank is all the way down against its stop (A, **Figure 16**).

3. To adjust, loosen the set screw in the bellcrank connector (B, **Figure 16**), then squeeze the throttle lever all the way against the handle grip, push the bellcrank down against its stop and tighten the connector set screw.

4. You can make minor adjustments at the throttle control lever by loosening the cable locknut (**Figure 17**), turning the adjuster (B) and then retightening the locknut.

5. Swing the handlebar as far as it will go in each direction and make sure that the throttle cable does not catch or bend sharply at the steering pivot nut.

> *CAUTION*
> *Do not try to lubricate the throttle cable. Lubricants can attract and hold sand and dirt in the cable. The throttle lever must return to the fully closed position when released.*

Idle Speed

The proper idle setting for the Jet Ski is the lowest at which it will run reliably and have just enough thrust to circle back to the rider after a spill. See **Table 3** for the standard speed specifications. Experimentation with different idle speed settings is the usual way to set the best idle speed. Turn the idle adjust screw as required (**Figure 18**).

> *WARNING*
> *The exhaust gases are poisonous. Do not run the engine in a closed area. Make sure there is plenty of ventilation.*

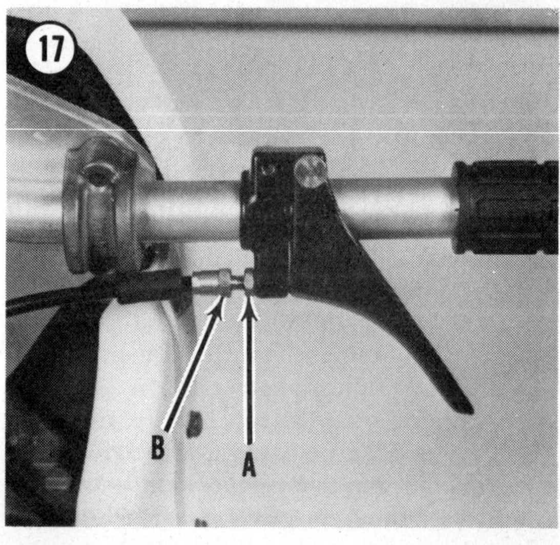

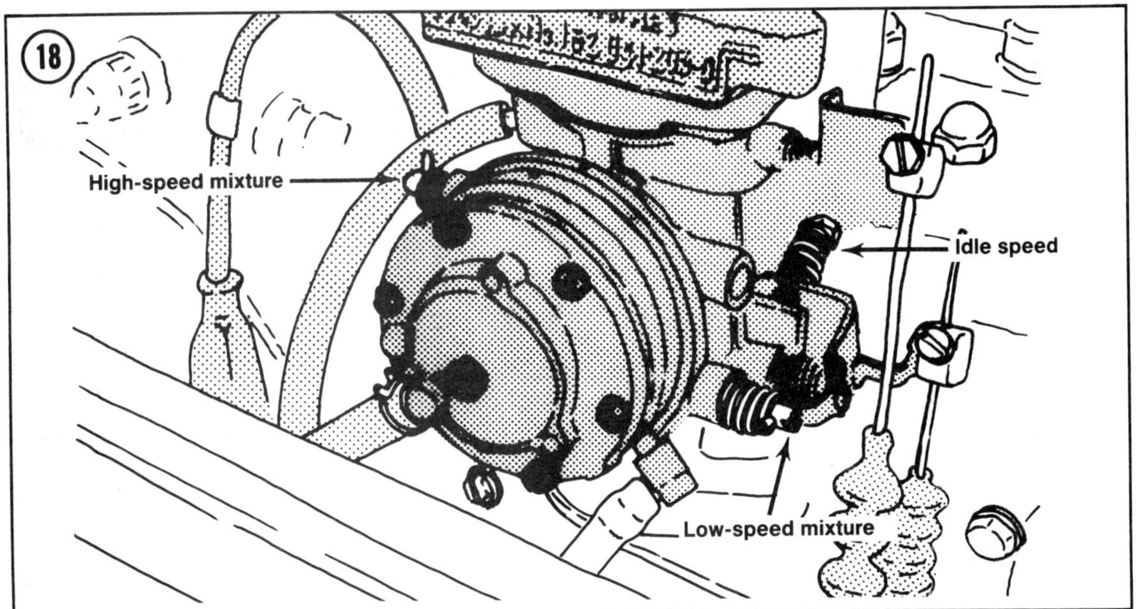

If you want to set the idle speed exactly to specification, Sun Instruments makes an Inductive Tach-Dwell Meter with a sensor lead that clips onto a spark plug lead. The meter is available at well stocked auto parts stores.

Mixture Screws (Initial Adjustment)

To set the mixture screws (**Figure 18**), turn each one in until it seats lightly and then back it out the number of turns specified in **Table 3**.

> *CAUTION*
> *Never force the mixture screws into their seats. You'll damage the screw or its seat in the carburetor.*

> *CAUTION*
> *Do not ride the Jet Ski with the high-speed screw turned in (clockwise) more than specified or the engine may be damaged by too lean a fuel mixture.*

Mixture Screws (Adjustment Under Load)

The following mixture screw adjustments must be made with the Jet Ski in water.

> *WARNING*
> *The Jet Ski produces a large thrust at high engine speeds. Keep a 100 ft. (30 m) area clear in front of the Jet Ski in case the anchor rope fails. Keep your clothing, hands and feet away from the jet pump intake and outlet.*

Low-speed adjustment

1. Put the Jet Ski in at least 2 ft. (0.6 m) of water.
2. Secure the Jet Ski with a strong rope (minimum 500 lb. test) connected at one end to the rear of the Jet Ski and the other end to a stationary object (**Figure 19**). Be sure to choose an object that is strong enough to withstand the full thrust of the Jet Ski.
3. Remove the engine cover and set both mixture screws at their normal initial settings. See **Table 3**.
4. Start the engine and warm it up. Check that the idle speed is normal.
5. Turn the low speed mixture screw in clockwise until the idle speed starts to drop, then back it out 1/4 turn. If the idle speed has changed, reset it to normal.

6. Check that the anchor rope has no slack and is secure at both ends, then give the throttle 2 or 3 quick applications to see that the engine revs without stalling or hesitation and returns to a smooth idle. If it hesitates, readjust the low speed mixture screw until the engine will rev from idle smoothly.

High-speed adjustment

CAUTION
The Jet Ski pumps a large volume of water at high engine speeds. Provide a 50 ft. clear area behind the Jet Ski.

1. Make sure that the pump intake stays submerged at full throttle by putting a 50 lb. (25 kg) weight on the riding platform.
2. Check that the anchor rope has no slack and is secure at both ends, then gradually give the engine full throttle.
3. Turn the high-speed screw in (clockwise) until the engine begins to misfire and lose speed.
4. Slowly turn the high-speed screw back out until the highest smooth rpm is reached.

CAUTION
Do not ride the Jet Ski with the high-speed screw turned in (clockwise) more than specified or the engine may be damaged by too lean a fuel mixture.

5. After adjusting the high-speed mixture under load, install new spark plugs and check the mixture to make sure you haven't set it so lean that engine damage will result. Ride the Jet Ski a short distance at full throttle then, without releasing the throttle, use the kill switch to stop the engine. Remove the spark plugs and examine them.
   a. If the insulator is white or burned, the fuel mixture is too lean.
   b. Black, sooty deposits show the mixture is too rich.
   c. If the insulator is light tan or gray colored, the mixture is correct.

NOTE
These plug readings are correct only for the standard heat range spark plug.

CYLINDER COMPRESSION

A cylinder cranking compression check is not *required maintenance*, but it is the quickest way to check the internal condition of the engine: rings, head gasket, etc. It's a good idea to check compression at each tune-up, write it down and compare it with the reading you get at the next tune-up. This will help you spot any developing problems before they cost too much repair money.

1. Make sure the cylinder head nuts are all torqued properly.

2. Warm the engine to normal operating temperature. Make sure the choke is OFF. Check around the spark plugs and the cylinder head gasket to make sure there is no gas leakage.

3. Stop the engine and remove both spark plugs.

4. Insert the plugs in the caps and ground both plugs to the expansion chamber.

CAUTION
If the plugs are not grounded during the compression test, the CDI ignition could be damaged.

5. Screw the compression gauge into one spark plug hole or, if you have a press-in type gauge, hold it firmly in position.
6. Check that the kill switch is OFF, hold the throttle wide open and crank the engine several revolutions until the gauge gives its highest reading. Record the reading.
7. Repeat the test for the other cylinder. There should be no more than a 10% difference in compression between cylinders.

When interpreting the results, the actual reading is not as important as the difference from the last check. Individual gauge calibrations vary widely. A significant drop (more than 15 psi) since the last check (made with the same gauge) may indicate engine top end problems.

If the compression is 100 psi or more, compression is normal. If either cylinder reads

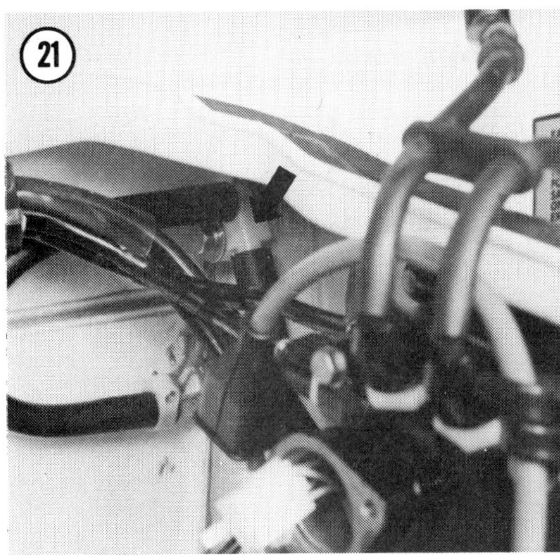

less than about 90 psi, check your readings with a recently calibrated gauge. It may be time to rebuild the top end.

TUNE-UP
(EVERY 100 HOURS)

Every 100 hours of operation, perform the following additional services.

Flame Arrestor

Inspect and clean the flame arrestor element; see *Flame Arrestor* in Chapter Six.

Throttle Valve

Inspect the throttle valve nylon bushing for excessive wear and make sure the throttle return spring is closing the throttle firmly. See *Carburetor Cleaning and Inspection* in Chapter Six.

Magneto Rotor Nut

Torque the magneto rotor nut as described in *Rotor Installation* in Chapter Seven.

COOLING SYSTEM CLEANING

The cooling system can become blocked by sand and salt deposits if it is not flushed occasionally. Clean the cooling system every 25 hours of operation or whenever you suspect that a blockage may have occurred. You will need a garden hose and adapter, as described under *On-shore Cooling* in this chapter.

1. Obtain a garden hose and a 3/8 in. (10 mm) adapter (**Figure 4**). Screw the adapter onto the garden hose.
2. Find the cooling outlet hose that connects the exhaust manifold log to the expansion chamber. Disconnect the hose from the expansion chamber (lower end).
3. Attach the garden hose adapter to the cooling hose from the exhaust pipe (**Figure 20**).
4. Attach the garden hose to a faucet, turn the water on full and allow it to run for 5 minutes.
5. Turn off the water, remove the garden hose and connect the cooling hose to the expansion chamber. Tighten the clamp.

BILGE SYSTEM CLEANING

The bilge system can become clogged and should be flushed out every 25 hours of operation or whenever a blockage is suspected. You will need a garden hose and adapter, as described under *On-shore Cooling* earlier in this chapter.

1. Find the plastic breather fitting and disconnect the 2 bilge hoses from it. On 1979 and later Jet Skis the breather fitting is above and behind the battery on the bulkhead (**Figure 21**). On the 1976-1978 models the breather

fitting is on the right side of the engine compartment (**Figure 22**).

2. Connect the garden hose and adapter to the hose from the bilge filter, roll the Jet Ski onto a protective pad under its left side to allow the engine compartment to drain, turn the water on and let it run for about a minute. Turn the water off and clean the engine compartment.

3. Connect the garden hose adapter to the other hose (from the hull bulkhead) and run water through it for several minutes.

4. Make sure the small breather hole on top of the fitting is clear. See **Figure 22** for 1976-1978 models; see **Figure 23** for 1979-on models. Reconnect the bilge hoses.

GENERAL LUBRICATION

Lubricate the jet pump bushing (Step 5, following) after every weekend's use. Lubricate the other items every 25 hours of operation. Use WD-40 or an equivalent penetrating rust inhibitor, unless another lubricant is specified.

1. At the handlebar, lubricate the throttle lever pivot and the steering cable end pivot and sliding shaft (**Figure 24**).

2. Pull out the choke knob and lubricate its shaft.

3. Lubricate the choke fitting pivot at the carburetor (A, **Figure 25**) and the carburetor throttle cable fitting pivot (B) with Valvoline X-All or another high-quality waterproof grease.

4. Remove the breather plug from the magneto cover, spray the inside of the magneto cavity with WD-40 and reinstall the plug (**Figure 26**).

5. Fit a hand grease gun filled with Valvoline X-All or equivalent onto the grease fittings of the bearing box (**Figure 27**) and the jet pump

bushing (**Figure 28**). Pack them with grease until resistance is felt.

> *CAUTION*
> *Do not force grease in after the housings are full or you may damage the grease seals.*

6. Remove the jet pump cover and lubricate the steering cable end pivot, the sliding shaft and the upper and lower steering nozzle pivots (**Figure 29**). Reinstall the jet pump cover and tighten the mounting screws securely.

7. Disassemble and grease the handlebar pivot.

Steering Pivot Lubrication

The steering must be disassembled to grease the steering pivot.

1. Pull the steering cable connector fitting free from its ball (**Figure 30**).

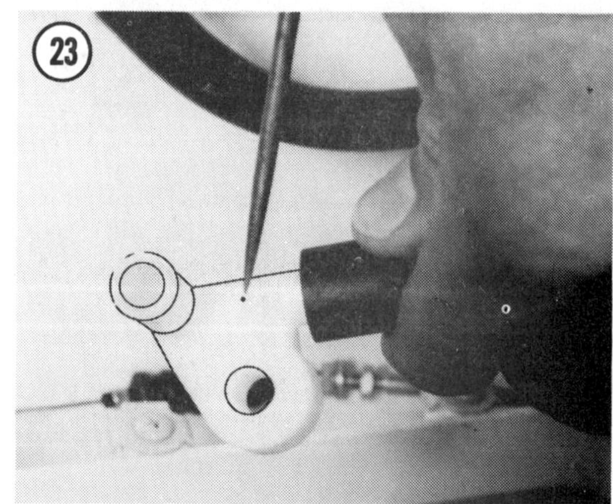

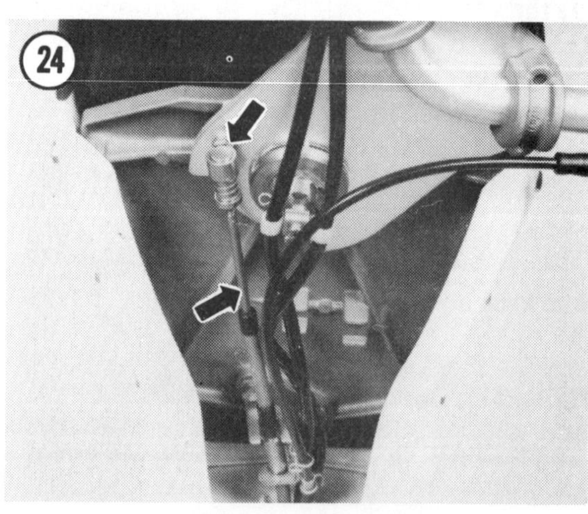

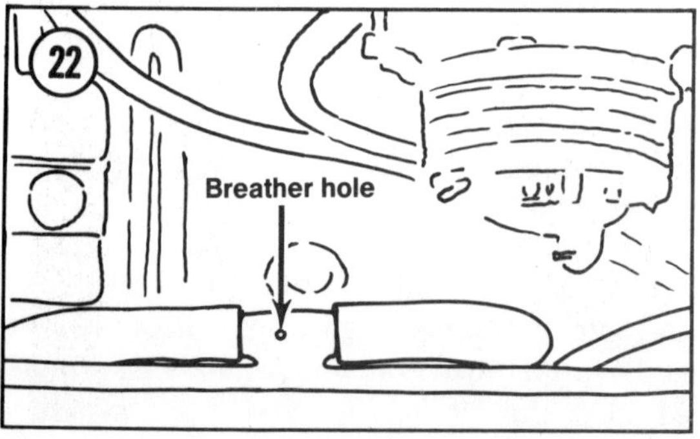

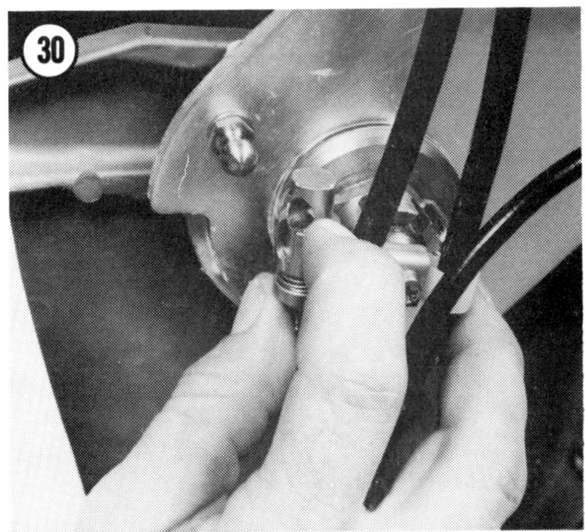

2. *On 1979 and later Jet Skis*: Remove the wiring clamp screw and clamps from the pivot (**Figure 31**).

3. *On 1979 and later Jet Skis*: Remove the cotter pin from the pivot nut and remove the nut, washer and bushing (**Figure 32**).

4. *On 1976-1978 Jet Skis*: Unscrew the 2 locknuts from the steering plate pivot and remove the washer and bushing (**Figure 33**).

5. Remove the steering plate from the support and take out the nylon bushing disc (**Figure 34**).

6. Apply a water-resistant grease such as Valvoline X-All to lubricate the nylon pivot bushings. Assemble the steering support, plate, bushings and washer.

7. *On 1979 and later Jet Skis*: Install the castellated lock nut and tighten it just enough so that the handlebar rotates smoothly without too much drag and with a minimum of vertical free play. Install a new cotter pin and spread the ends (**Figure 35**).

8. *On 1979 and later Jet Skis*: Install the wiring clamps and clamp screw.

9. *On 1976-1978 Jet Skis*: Install the adjuster nut and tighten it just enough so that the handlebar rotates smoothly without too much drag and with a minimum of vertical free play. Install the second nut and tighten it while holding the adjuster nut to keep it from turning.

10. Connect the steering cable fitting to its ball.

STEERING

Steering Cable Adjustment

1. Center the handlebar (**Figure 36**).

2. With the handlebar centered, the steering nozzle should be the same distance from each side of the hull cavity (**Figure 37**).

3. If the steering nozzle is not centered correctly, raise the handle pole, loosen the locknut just below the steering cable connector on the handlebar and pull the connector free of the ball (**Figure 30**).

4. Turn the connector to adjust the linkage, then reconnect it and check the alignment again. When the alignment is correct, tighten the locknut. If additional adjustment is required, adjust the connector at the jet pump steering nozzle in the same manner.

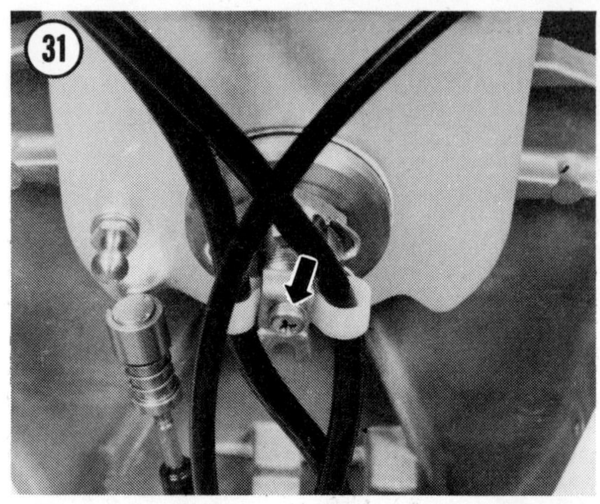

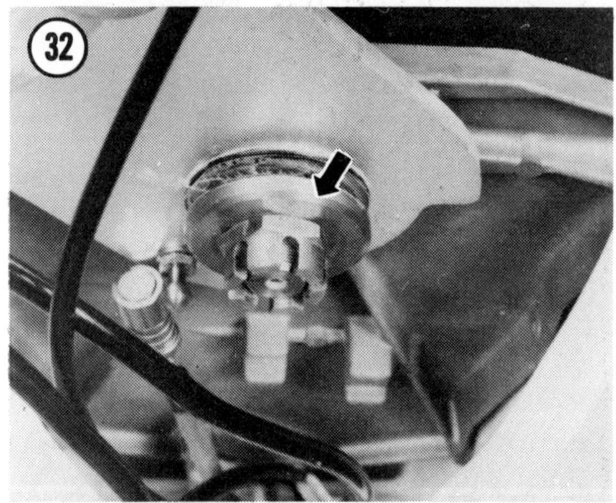

5. To be sure the alignment is correct, measure the distance between the nozzle and the edge of the pump cavity with the handlebar turned all the way to each side. The distance should be the same at both extremes.

IMPELLER

Inspect the impeller blade for nicks, deep scratches or gouges every 25 hours of operation or whenever the Jet Ski's performance deteriorates while the engine seems to be running well. See *Jet Pump Removal* and *Impeller Inspection* in Chapter Five.

COUPLER RUBBER

Inspect the coupler rubber for wear every 100 hours of operation; see *Coupler Rubber Inspection* in Chapter Five.

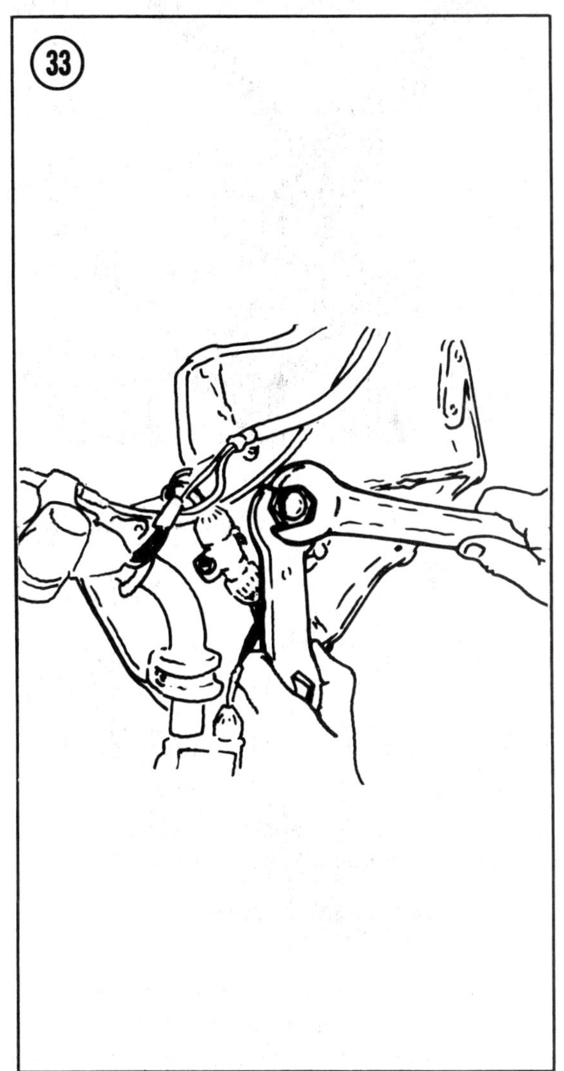

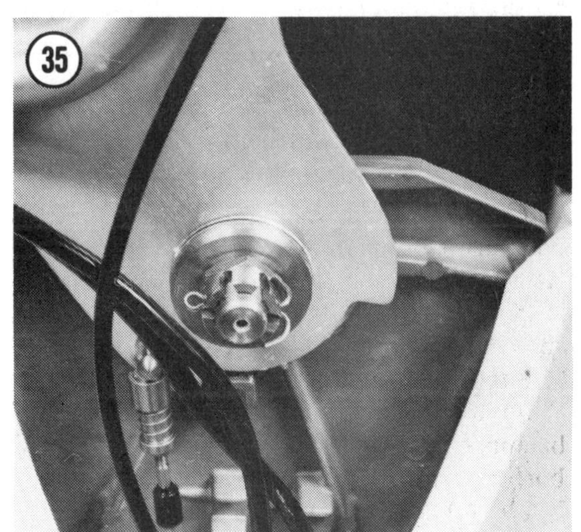

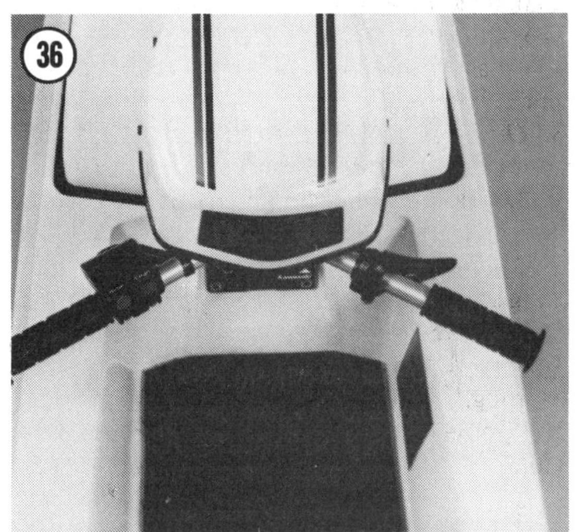

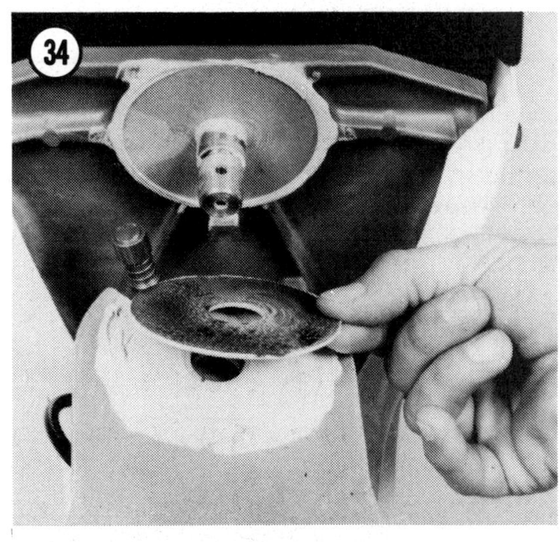

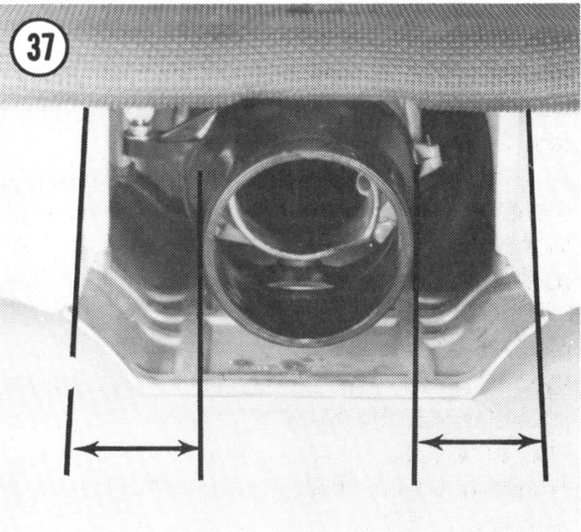

Table 1   JS400/440 MAINTENANCE SCHEDULE

Weekly Maintenance	
Battery electrolyte level	Check/add water if necessary; check more frequently in hot weather
Throttle lever	Check for smooth opening and return Grease the fitting at carburetor
Steering	Smooth but not loose; adjust if necessary
Nuts, bolts, fasteners	Check jet pump cover and grate, fuel hoses, fuel tank outlet nut, cooling water and bilge lines and exhaust system clamps for looseness; tighten if necessary
Jet pump	Inspect intake, pump and drive shaft Remove any foreign objects
Fuel leaks	Inspect engine compartment
Engine noise or vibration	Check
Stop switch	Check operation
Fire extinguisher	Check for a full charge
Every 25 Hours of Operation	
All items above, plus:	
Fuel system	
400cc	Inspect filter, replace if necessary
440cc	Clean sediment bowl and filter
Spark plugs	Clean, set gap, replace if necessary
Carburetor	Check/adjust cable play, idle speed and mixture if necessary
Cylinder head nuts	Check torque
Impeller	Remove, inspect for damage and wear
Throttle lever pivot, choke and steering cable ends, steering nozzle pivots, inside magneto housing	Lubricate with WD-40
Drive shaft bearing box, jet pump bushing, handlebar pivot	Lubricate with grease
Steering	Check, adjust if necessary
Cooling system	Clean
Bilge system	Clean
Every 100 Hours of Operation	
All items above, plus:	
Flame arrestor	Inspect and clean
Ignition timing	Inspect, adjust if necessary
Rotor nut	Check torque
Exhaust system	Decarbonize pistons, cylinder head, exhaust manifold
Coupler rubber	Inspect, replace if worn
Throttle shaft	Inspect spring and nylon bushing at carburetor

Table 2   40:1 GAS/OIL RATIO QUANTITIES

Oil	Gas
3.2 oz. (95 cc)	1 U.S. gal.
6.4 oz. (190 cc)	2 U.S. gal.
8.0 oz. (235 cc)	2.5 U.S. gal.
9.6 oz. (285 cc)	3 U.S. gal.
12.8 oz. (380 cc)	4 U.S. gal.
16.0 oz. (475 cc)	5 U.S. gal.

Table 3   JS400/440 TUNE-UP SPECIFICATIONS

Spark plug gap		0.028-0.032 in. (0.7-0.8 mm)	
Spark plug type			
U.S.		NGK B7ES; Champion N4G	
Canada		NGK BR7ES	
Idle speed in water		1,800 rpm	
Idle speed out of water		2,200 rpm	
Mixture screws	Low-speed (turns open)		High-speed (turns open)
1976	3/4		1 1/8
1977-1979	5/8		3/4
1980	5/8		1
1981	1		3/4

3

NOTE: If you own a 1982 or 1983 model, first check the Supplement at the back of the book for any new service information.

CHAPTER FOUR

ENGINE

INTRODUCTION

This chapter provides complete service and overhaul procedures for the Kawasaki Jet Ski 440 and 400 cc engines. **Table 1** provides wear limit specifications for the engine. **Table 2** provides tightening torques. All tables are at the end of the chapter. Routine inspections and adjustments, including a cranking compression test, are given in Chapter Three.

This chapter is written in a general teardown sequence. If you only need to remove one particular part, follow the *Disassembly* procedures until you have the part you want. Then refer to the *Inspection* procedure for that part and finally go on to the *Installation* procedure for that part.

Service procedures for all models are virtually the same. Where differences occur, they are identified. Right now, before you start any work, go back and read the *Service Hints* in Chapter One. You will save yourself a lot of mistakes with those hints fresh in your mind.

TOOLS

Several specialized tools will be helpful in the disassembly and inspection procedures in this chapter.

Removal of the magneto rotor requires a means of locking the engine when loosening and tightening the rotor nut. A very handy tool for this purpose is a universal rotor holder (**Figure 1**). To remove the rotor from the crankshaft, a special Kawasaki 4-bolt rotor puller (**Figure 2**) will be required. Your Jet Ski dealer, or any Kawasaki motorcycle dealer, should be able to provide you with these tools.

Inspection measurements require a precision inside and outside micrometer, dial

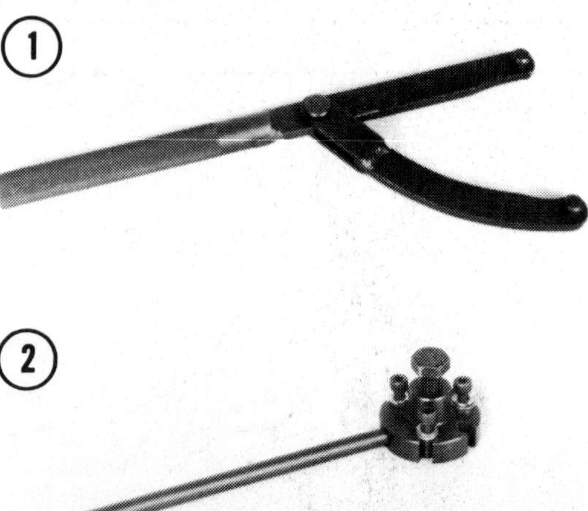

gauge or the equivalent (**Figure 3** and **Figure 4**). If you don't have the right tools, remove the parts and have your dealer or machine shop take the required measurements.

BREAK-IN

Following cylinder repair (boring, honing, new rings, etc.) and major lower end work, the engine should be broken in just as though it were new. The performance and service life of the engine depend greatly on a careful and sensible break-in.

OPERATING PRINCIPLES

During this discussion on 2-stroke operating principles, assume that the crankshaft is rotating counterclockwise in **Figure 5**. As the piston travels downward, a transfer port (A) between the crankcase and the cylinder is uncovered. The exhaust gases leave the cylinder through the exhaust port (B), which is also opened by the downward movement of the piston. A fresh fuel-air charge, which has previously been compressed slightly, travels from the crankcase (C) to the cylinder through the transfer port (A) as the port opens. Since the incoming charge is under pressure, it rushes into the cylinder quickly and helps to expel the exhaust gases from the previous cycle.

Figure 6 illustrates the next phase of the cycle. As the crankshaft continues to rotate, the piston moves upward, closing the exhaust and transfer ports. As the piston continues upward, the air/fuel mixture in the cylinder is compressed. Notice also that a vacuum is created in the crankcase at the same time. Further upward movement of the piston uncovers the intake port (D). A fresh fuel-air charge is then drawn into the crankcase through the intake port because of the vacuum created by the upward piston movement.

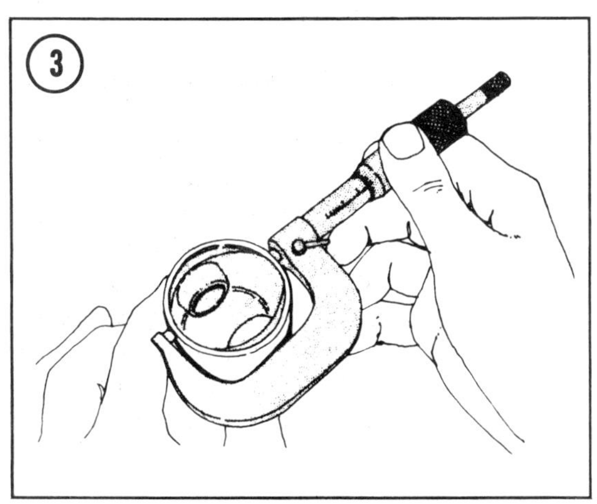

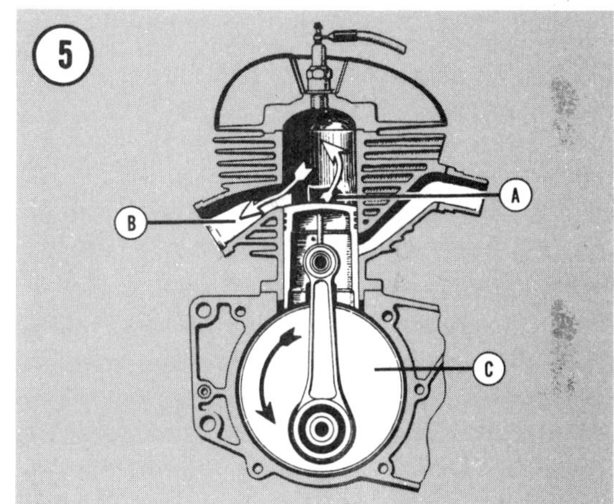

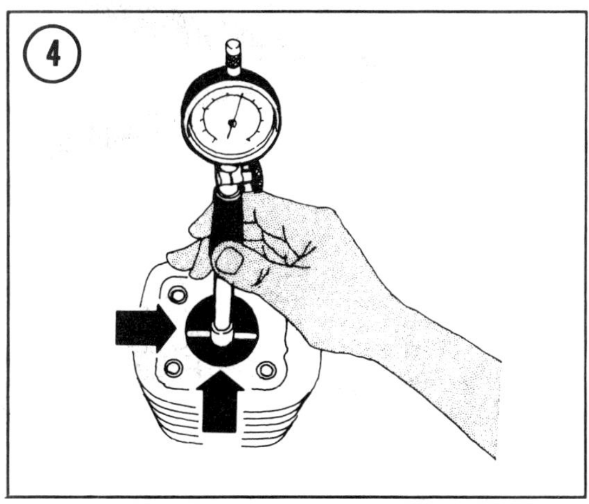

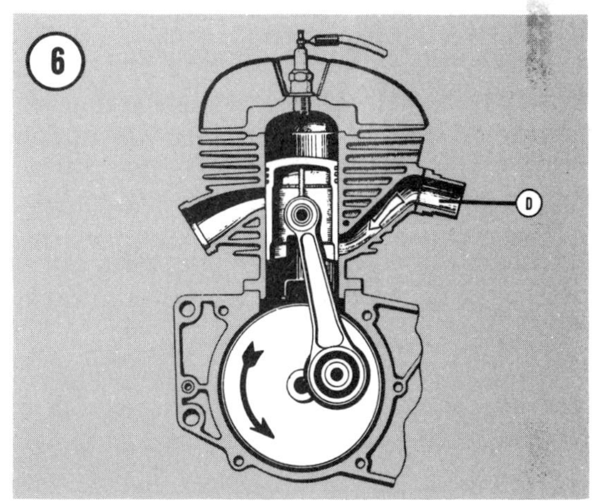

The third phase is shown in **Figure 7**. As the piston approaches top dead center, the spark plug fires, igniting the compressed mixture. The piston is then driven downward by the expanding gases.

When the top of the piston uncovers the exhaust port, the fourth phase begins, as shown in **Figure 8**. The exhaust gases leave the cylinder through the exhaust port. As the piston continues downward, the intake port is closed and the mixture in the crankcase is compressed in preparation for the next cycle.

It can be seen from this discussion that every downward stroke of the piston is a power stroke.

SERVICING ENGINE IN HULL

The engine has been laid out so that most "top end" repairs (cylinder head, cylinder block and piston) can be done with the engine still in the hull. However, for repairs to the "bottom end" (crankshaft, connecting rods and bearings), the engine must be removed from the hull for separation of the crankcases. Although the engine "top end" can be left attached during engine removal, we recommend that you remove it first. It makes the engine much lighter and easier to handle.

COOLING SYSTEM

The Jet Ski uses the same water you ride on to cool the engine. The water is supplied by a fitting on the jet pump just downstream from the impeller. The amount of cooling water flow depends on the speed of the engine. At idle, practically no water flows through the cooling system. As speed increases, more water flows through the cooling system.

In addition to cooling the engine's internal parts, the water cools the exhaust system and keeps the engine compartment temperature from becoming dangerously high. If the engine were run without cooling water, the engine's internal parts would be damaged within a matter of minutes; but even sooner (within 30 seconds or so), the rubber exhaust resonator would overheat and melt or burn.

The cooling system should be cleaned periodically and whenever the engine shows signs of overheating; see *Cooling System Cleaning* in Chapter Three.

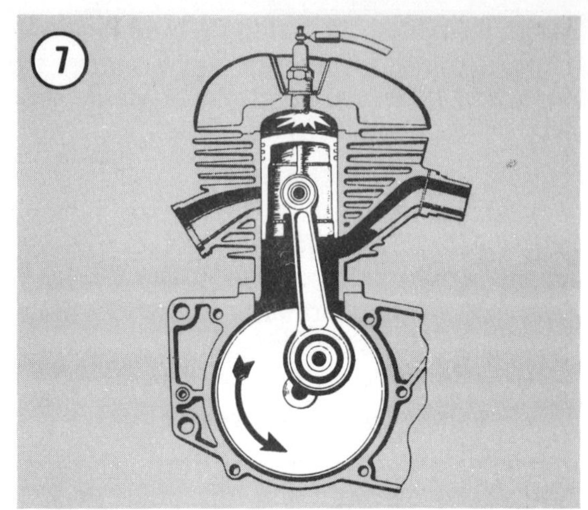

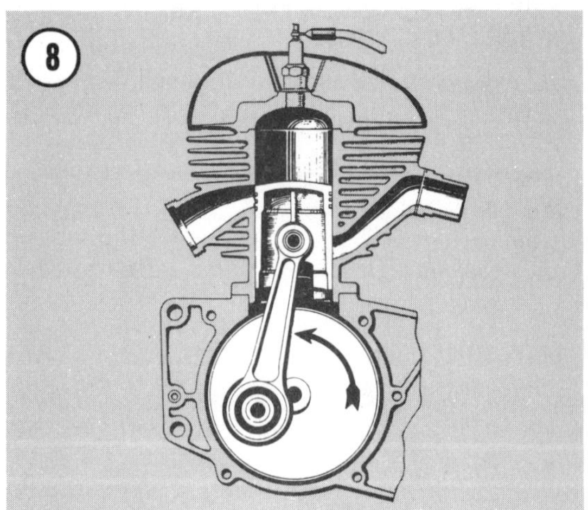

Coolant Flow

See **Figure 9**. From the fitting at the front of the jet pump, water flows through a rubber hose to a metal tube that goes through the hull and into the engine compartment. On 1979 and later models, the tube enters the engine compartment at the left side of the bulkhead. On 1976-1978 Jet Skis, the tube enters the engine compartment at the right side of the bulkhead.

The water is then conducted by a rubber hose to a fitting on the lower rear end of the exhaust manifold. The water flows through and cools the exhaust manifold, then enters the cylinder block. The water flows around the iron cylinder liners and up into the cylinder head.

A rubber hose conducts the water from a fitting at the front of the cylinder head to a

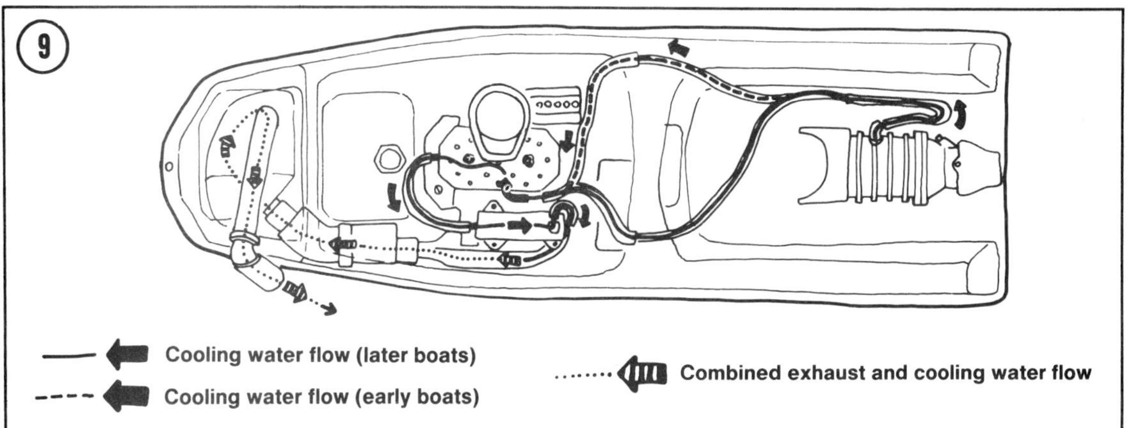

fitting at the front of the exhaust pipe. The water circulates around the exhaust pipe water jacket, then enters the expansion chamber through a hose from the rear of the exhaust pipe to the chamber. In the expansion chamber the water mixes with exhaust gases, then runs down through the rubber resonator and into the water muffler. When the water reaches a given level in the water muffler it is expelled from the Jet Ski through the exhaust hose.

NOTE
Some water usually remains in the expansion chamber after the engine is shut off. The water could enter the engine's exhaust ports if the Jet Ski is turned over on its right side. For this reason the Jet Ski should not be turned over on its right side unless all water has been cleared from the expansion chamber.

TOP END DISASSEMBLY

Refer to **Figure 10**. The engine "top end" consists of the cylinder head, cylinder block, pistons and rings, piston pins and connecting rod small-end bearings.

Before working on the top end, clean all dirt and grease from the outside of the engine.

Cylinder Head Removal

To avoid possible warping of the cylinder head, wait until the engine has cooled down before removing the head.

1. *On 1979 and later Jet Skis:* Disconnect the battery negative (-) ground cable at the engine (**Figure 11**).

2. *On 1976-1977 Jet Skis:* Disconnect the battery negative (-) ground cable at the battery.
3. Pull the spark plug caps off the plugs, then remove the spark plugs.
4. Disconnect the water hose from the fitting at the front of the cylinder head (A, **Figure 12**).
5. Remove the intake cover bolts and the cover (B, **Figure 12**).
6. *On 1978 and later Jet Skis:* Remove the nuts holding the carburetor brace to the cylinder head (**Figure 13**).
7. *On 1981 and later Jet Skis:* Remove the flame arrestor element. Close the choke to keep parts from dropping down the carburetor, then remove the 3 flame arrestor holder bolts and the holder (**Figure 14**).
8. Remove the cylinder head nuts and washers (**Figure 15**).

CAUTION
Make sure that you have removed all the fasteners. If the parts are hard to separate, check for any fasteners you may have missed.

NOTE
On 1981 and later engines, nuts No. 10 and 11 have been eliminated.

9. Lift off the cylinder head and head gasket, taking care not to drop any parts into the cylinder (**Figure 16**). You may need to tap the head lightly with a soft mallet to loosen it, but don't try to pry it off or you may damage the gasket surfaces.

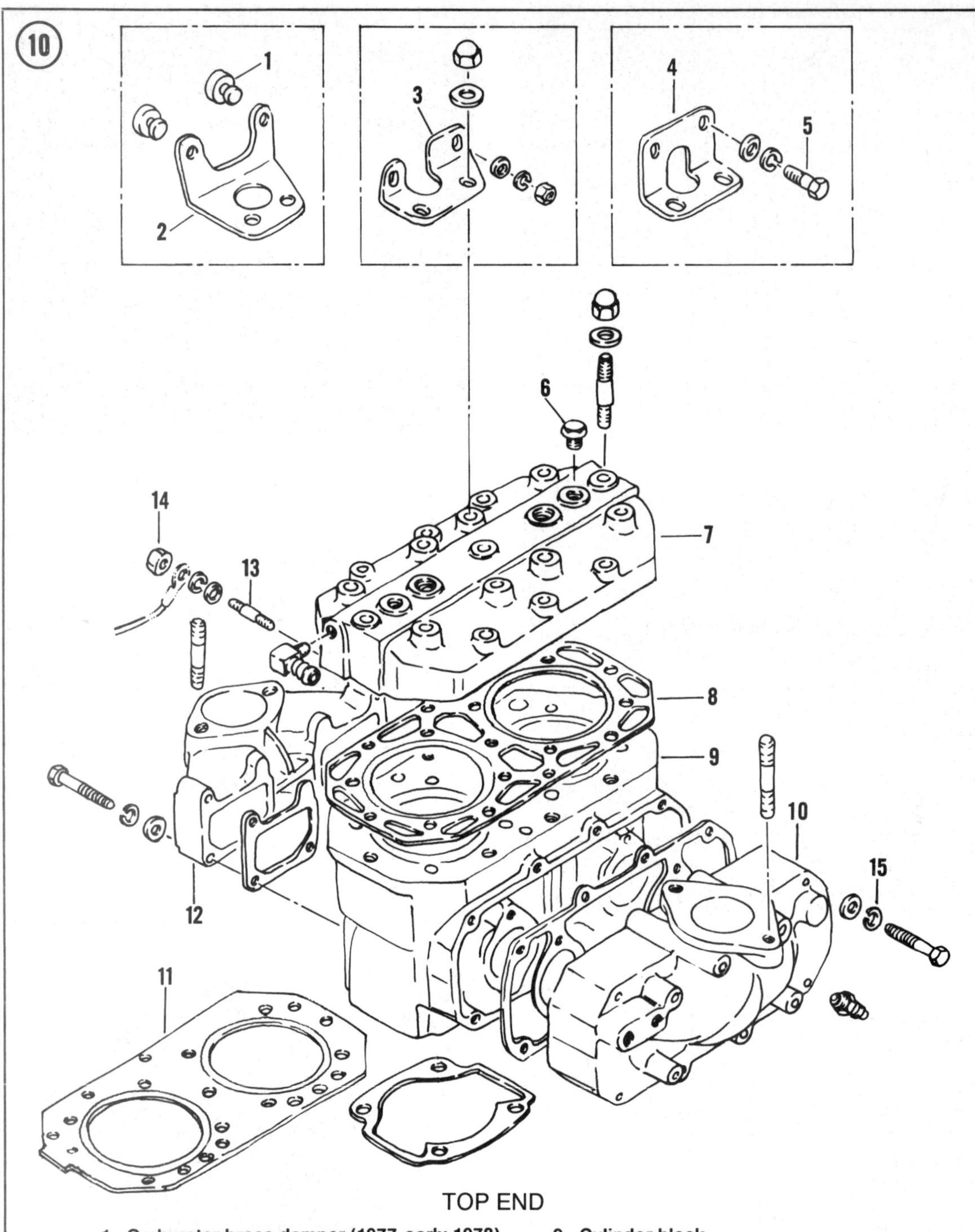

TOP END

1. Carburetor brace damper (1977-early 1978)
2. Carburetor brace (1977-early 1978)
3. Carburetor brace (late 1978-1980)
4. Carburetor brace (1981 and later)
5. Bolt (1981 and later)
6. Plug (1976-early 1980)
7. Cylinder head
8. Head gasket (1976-1980)
9. Cylinder block
10. Exhaust manifold
11. Head gasket (1981 and later)
12. Intake manifold
13. Stud (1979 and later)
14. Nut (1979 and later)
15. Lockwasher (1976-1980)

A
B
B
B
B

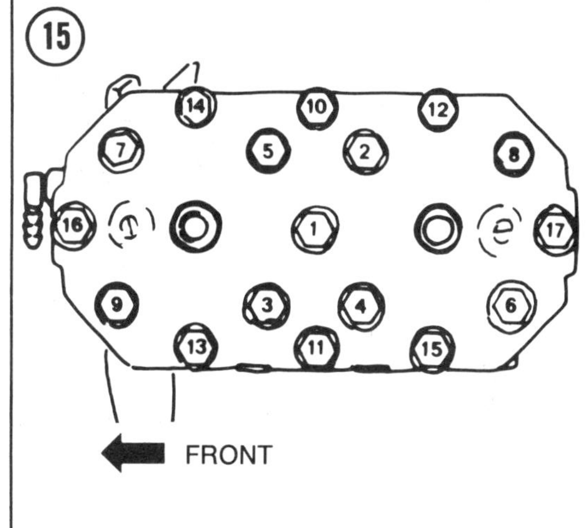
14
7
16
9
13
10
5
1
3
11
12
2
4
15
8
17
6
FRONT

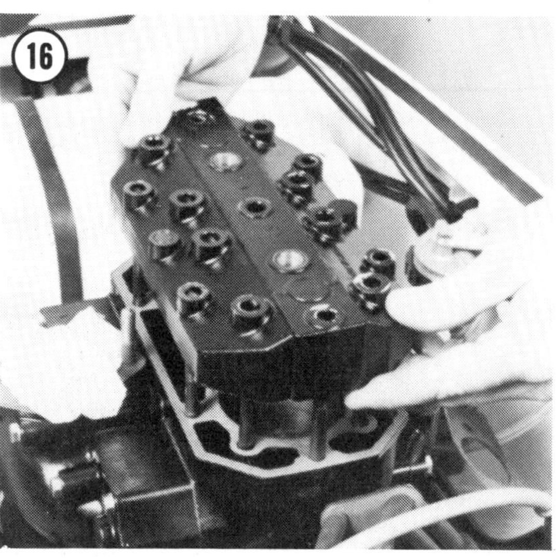

Cylinder Block Removal

The cylinder block can be removed after removing the cylinder head. Removal of the intake and exhaust manifolds is easiest after the cylinder block is removed from the engine.

The 1981 and later Jet Skis have cast iron cylinder blocks. Earlier Jet Skis have aluminum blocks with cast iron liners.

1. Remove the carburetor and the exhaust pipe/expansion chamber assembly; see *Carburetor Removal* and *Exhaust Removal* in Chapter Six.

2. Disconnect the cooling water supply hose at the bottom rear of the exhaust manifold (**Figure 17**).

3. Disconnect the electric box ground wire at the upper rear intake manifold bolt (**Figure 11**).

4. Lift off the cylinder block (**Figure 18**). You may need to tap the cylinder lightly with a soft mallet to loosen it. Be careful not to damage the cylinder.

5. Stuff clean rags around the connecting rods to keep dirt and loose parts from entering the crankcase.

Manifold Removal

Do not remove the manifolds from the cylinder block unless the gaskets are leaking or you want to inspect the manifold.

1. Remove the intake (**Figure 19**) or exhaust (**Figure 20**) manifold bolts and washers.

2. Remove the manifold and gaskets from the cylinder block. You may need to tap the manifold lightly with a soft mallet to loosen it.

> *CAUTION*
> *Make sure that you have removed all the fasteners. If the parts are hard to separate, check for any fasteners you may have missed.*

Piston Removal

Before removing a piston, hold the connecting rod tightly and rock the piston as shown in **Figure 21**. Any rocking motion (do not confuse with normal side-to-side sliding motion) indicates wear of the piston pin, connecting rod bore, needle bearing or a combination of all. Pay particular attention to inspection of these items.

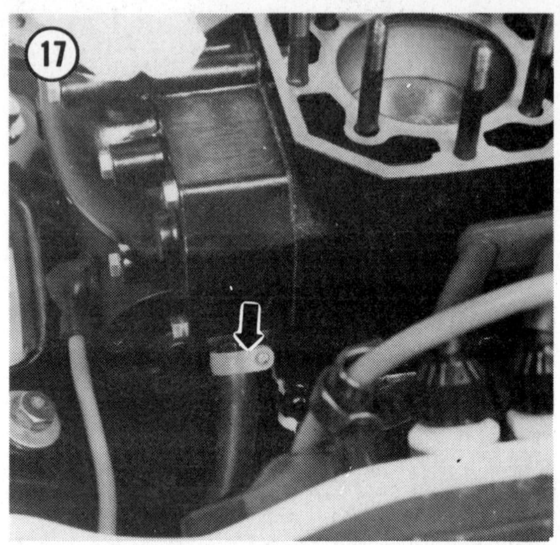

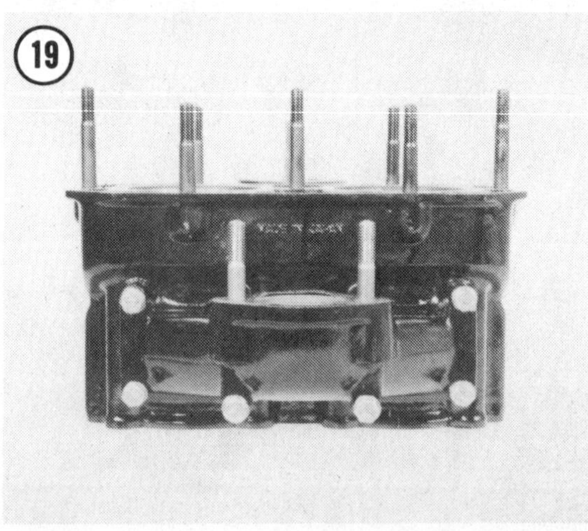

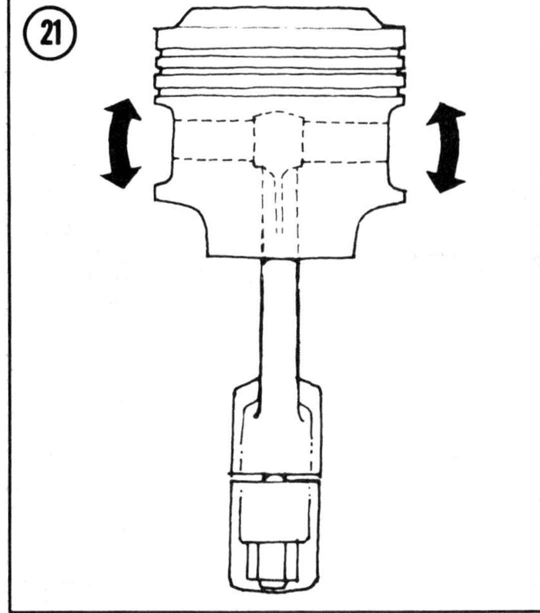

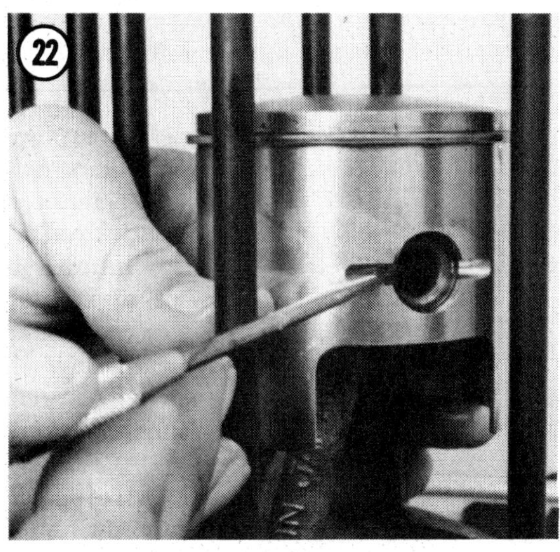

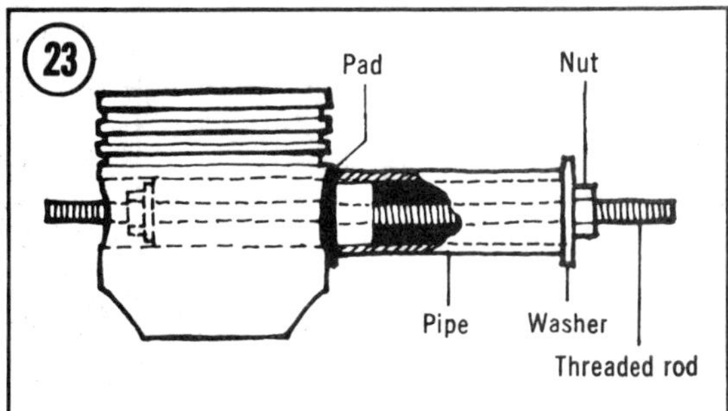

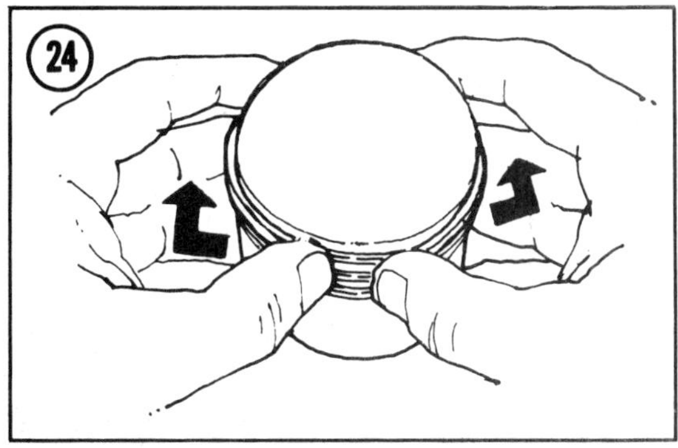

1. Raise the piston and pry out the piston pin circlip with needle nose pliers or an awl (**Figure 22**). The circlip can spring out forcefully, so protect your face, and don't drop the clip into the engine.

2. Push the piston pin out the side of the piston from which you removed the circlip.

> *CAUTION*
> *Do not try to hammer the pin out. You could bend the connecting rod or damage the rod bearing.*

> *NOTE*
> *It may be necessary to heat the piston slightly with a rag soaked in hot water or use a homemade tool to push the pin out, as shown in **Figure 23**.*

3. Lift off the piston and mark it to identify it as the front or rear piston. Remove the needle bearing from the connecting rod. Keep each piston together with its own pin, bearing and piston rings to avoid confusion during reassembly.

4. Remove the piston rings by spreading the ring ends with your thumbs (**Figure 24**), then pushing the other side of the ring up off the piston.

TOP END INSPECTION

Decarbonizing

Wipe away any soft deposits on the cylinder head, piston crowns and exhaust ports. Hard deposits can be removed with a wire brush or *soft* metal scraper. Be careful not to gouge the aluminum surfaces. Burrs will create hot spots which can cause preignition and heat erosion.

Clean the spark plug hole threads with a fine wire brush, then clean the head and cylinder thoroughly with solvent.

Cylinder Head Warp

Place a straightedge across the gasket surface at several points. Measure warp by inserting a feeler gauge between the straightedge and cylinder head at each location (**Figure 25**). Any warp should be less than the service limit in **Table 1**. If a small amount is present, the head can be resurfaced by rubbing it in a figure-8 pattern on a piece of plate glass covered with 320 grit emery cloth.

Cylinder Inspection

1. Do not remove the carbon ridge at the top of the cylinder bore unless you are going to bore or hone the cylinder. The ridge helps the top ring's compression seal.
2. Check the cylinder wall for scratches; if evident, the cylinder should be rebored.
3. Measure the cylinder bore with a cylinder gauge or inside micrometer near the top, middle, and bottom of the cylinder (**Figure 26**). Measure 2 ways—in line with the piston pin and at a right angle to the pin. If any measurement exceeds the wear limit in **Table 1**, or if the taper or out-of-round is greater than 0.002 in. (0.05 mm), the cylinder must be rebored oversize and a new oversize piston and rings installed. The cylinder can be bored once to 0.020 in. (0.50 mm) oversize.

> *NOTE*
> *Get the new piston before you have the cylinder bored. You'll need it to get the proper piston/cylinder clearance.*

Piston Inspection

1. Carefully clean the carbon from the piston crown with a chemical remover or with a *soft* scraper.
2. Check the top of the piston for erosion of the metal and replace it if any is found. Erosion of the piston crown is often caused by an very lean fuel/air mixture. This condition should be corrected immediately after a new piston has been installed and the engine reassembled.
3. Check the skirt of the piston for brown varnish deposits. More than a slight amount is evidence of worn or sticking rings which should be replaced. Also check the skirt for galling and abrasion—a symptom of piston seizure. If light galling is present, smooth the affected area with No. 400 emery paper. However, if galling is severe or if the piston is scored deeply enough to feel the scratches easily with your fingernail, replace the piston.
4. Clean the carbon and gum from the ring grooves with a broken ring or a groove cleaner (**Figure 27**). Any deposits left in the grooves will contribute to ring sticking and may result in piston seizure. Examine each ring groove for burrs, dented edges and wear. Examine the piston carefully for hairline cracks at the top

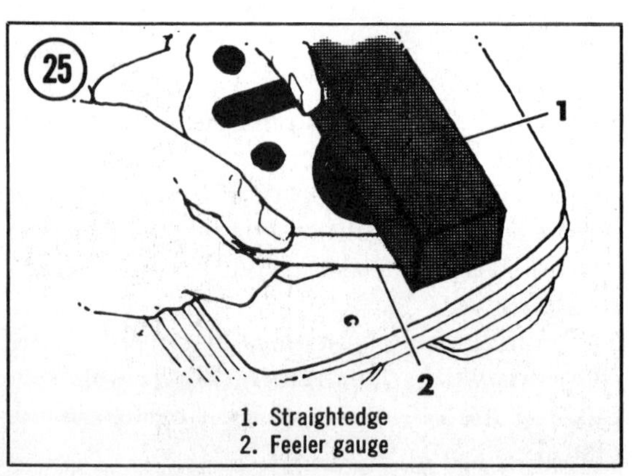

1. Straightedge
2. Feeler gauge

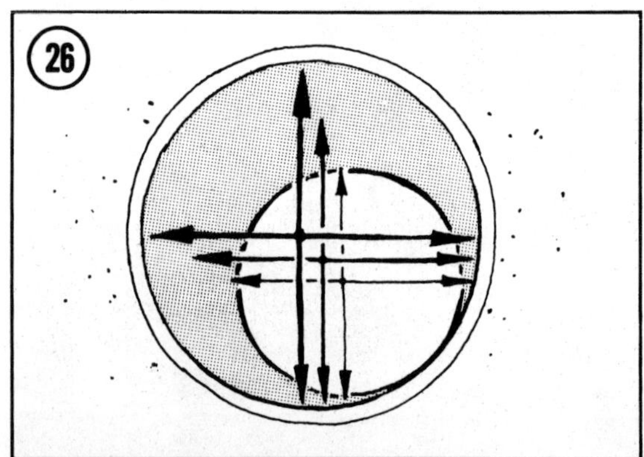

edges of the transfer cutaways (**Figure 28**). If any cracks are found, replace the piston.

5. Check piston wear by measuring the outside diameter with a micrometer. Take the measurement 3/16 in. (5 mm) above the bottom of the piston skirt, at a right angle to the piston pin bore (**Figure 29**). If the diameter of the piston measures less than the wear limit in **Table 1**, install a new piston.

Piston/Cylinder Clearance

The most accurate way to check piston/cylinder clearance is to measure the inside diameter of the cylinder just above its bottom edge (where it will have undergone the least amount of wear), then subtract the piston diameter as measured in *Piston Inspection*. The clearance should be within the range specified in **Table 1**.

You can also measure installed piston/cylinder clearance with a feeler gauge near the bottom of the cylinder (**Figure 30**). The piston should be just free enough to slide with a light push (with no rings on the piston). This method is *not* as accurate as micrometer measurement calculation.

If a cylinder has not worn past the acceptable inside diameter limit, and installing a new piston will bring the clearance within tolerance, the cylinder block need not be bored. However, in no case should the piston/cylinder clearance be less than the minimum.

Piston Ring Inspection

On 1981 and later engines, one tapered profile piston ring is used on each piston. On 1976-1980 engines, 2 flat rings are used on each piston.

Measure the top ring for wear by inserting it into the bottom of the cylinder where the cylinder is least worn. Seat the ring squarely in the cylinder by pushing it in slightly with the top of a piston. Measure the installed end gap

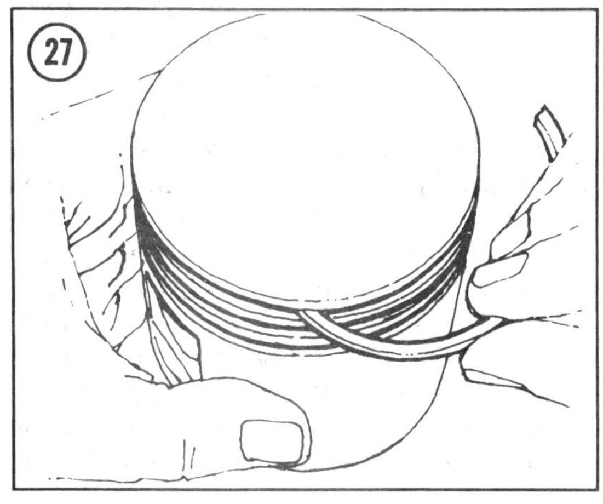

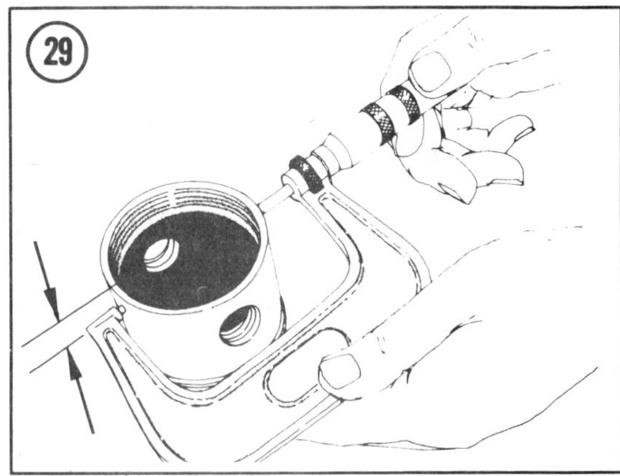

with a feeler gauge (**Figure 31**). A new ring's gap should be no smaller than the limit in **Table 1**.

If the gap is smaller than specified, hold a small file in a vise, grip the ends of the ring with your fingers and enlarge the gap to the required minimum (**Figure 32**). As old rings wear, the gap will increase. Discard any rings whose installed gap exceeds the limit in **Table 1**.

Always install new rings when installing a new piston or when you have any doubt about the condition of the rings.

On 1976-1980 engines: Check the side clearance of each ring with a feeler gauge (**Figure 33**). Refer to **Table 1**. If the clearance is excessive, replace the rings, piston or both.

Piston Pin and Needle Bearing Inspection

Measure the inside diameter of the piston pin holes and the outside diameter of the piston pins with a micrometer. A piston pin must be replaced if its diameter in any place is under the service limit in **Table 1**; the piston must be replaced if its pin hole diameter exceeds the service limit.

Clean the needle bearing assembly in solvent and dry it thoroughly. With a magnifying glass, examine the bearing assembly for cracks at the corners of the bearing slots and also on the needles themselves (**Figure 34**). If any are found, replace the bearing. This bearing should be replaced routinely when the piston is replaced.

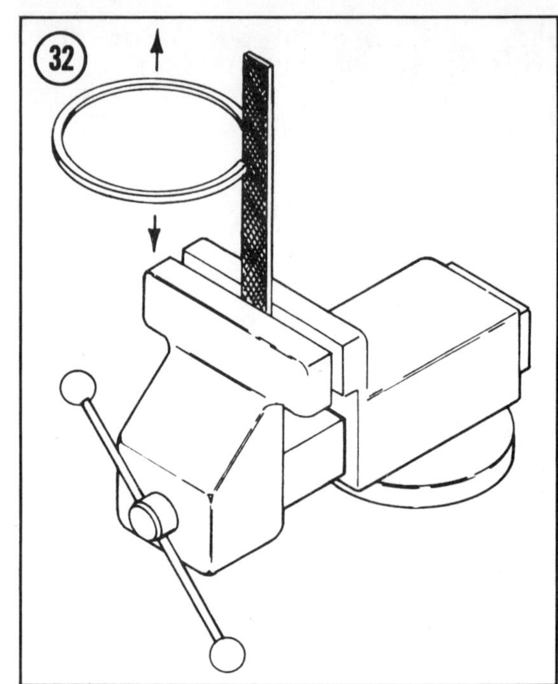

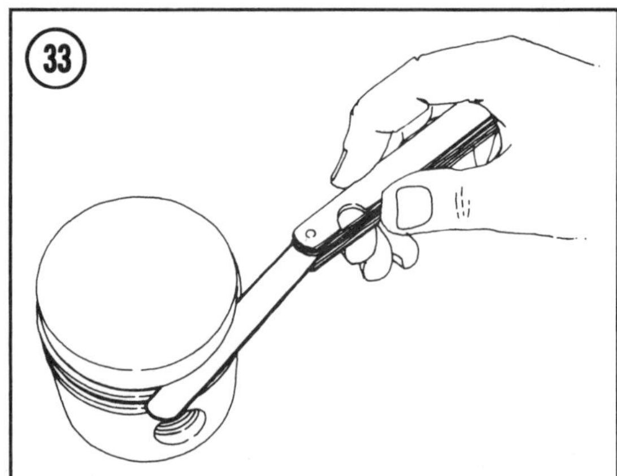

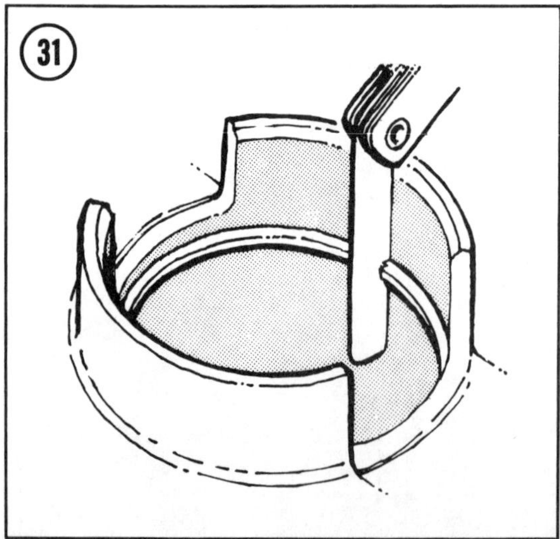

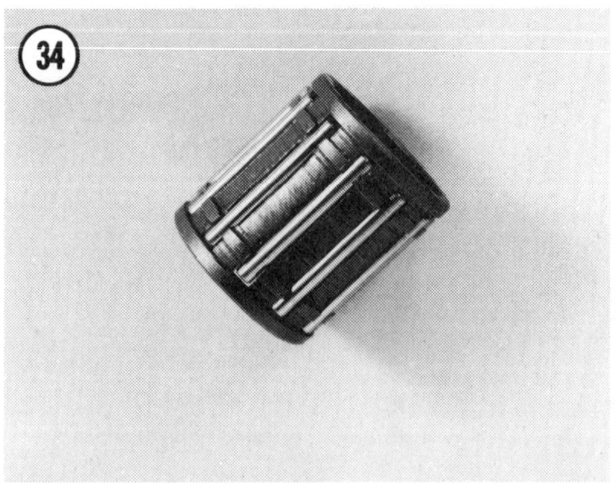

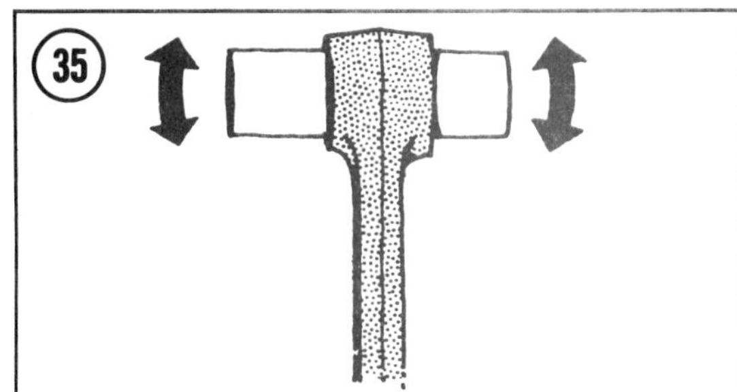

Oil the bearing and pin and install them in the connecting rod. Slowly rock the pin and check for radial play (**Figure 35**). If any play exists, the pin and bearing should be replaced, provided the rod bore is in good condition.

Connecting Rod Inspection

The connecting rods can be inspected after the engine's top end has been removed. If the connecting rods fail to pass any of these inspections, a new crankshaft assembly should be installed. See *Crankshaft Removal* in this chapter.

1. Check the rod for obvious damage such as cracks and burns.

2. Measure the inside diameter (ID) of the small end of the connecting rod with a snap gauge and micrometer (**Figure 36**). The inside diameter should be smaller than the limit given in **Table 1**.

3. Check the big-end bearing side play with a feeler gauge (**Figure 37**). The play should be less than the limit in **Table 1**. If it is greater, the crankshaft assembly should be rebuilt or replaced.

4. Check the connecting rod big-end bearing radial (up-and-down) play; you can make a quick check by simply rocking the connecting rods back and forth (**Figure 38**). If there is more than a very slight rocking motion (some side-to-side sliding is normal), you can measure the connecting rod big-end bearing radial play without splitting the crankcases. Refer to *Crankshaft Inspection* in this chapter for the procedure.

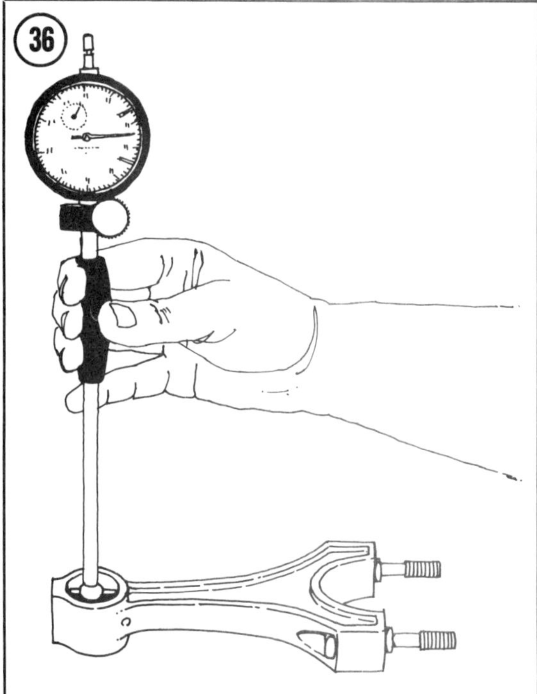

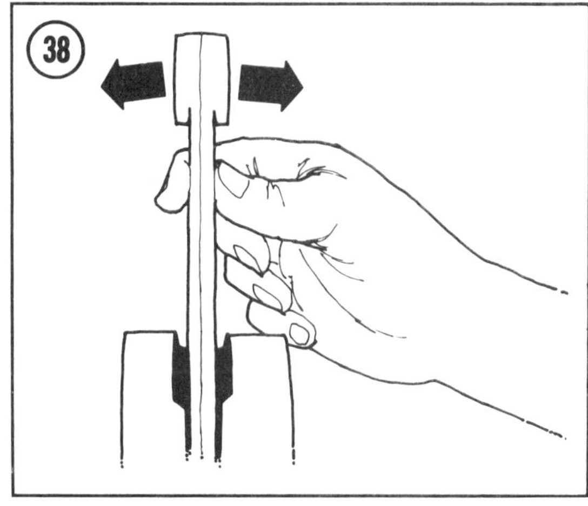

TOP END ASSEMBLY

Refer to **Figure 10**.

Piston Installation

1. Install the rings on the pistons. Spread the ends of the piston ring with your thumbs and install it in the proper piston groove. The side of the ring with letter or number marks always faces *up* (**Figure 39**).

2. Lightly oil the needle bearing assembly and install it in the connecting rod (**Figure 40**).

3. Oil the piston pin and push it into the piston until the end extends slightly beyond the inside of the boss (**Figure 41**).

4. Place the piston over the connecting rod with the arrow on the piston pointing to the left (exhaust) side of the engine (**Figure 42**). Line up the pin with the bearing and push the pin into the piston until it is even with the circlip grooves.

> *CAUTION*
> *Do not try to hammer the pin in. You could bend the connecting rod or damage the rod bearing. Do not damage the needle bearing when installing the piston pin.*

> *NOTE*
> *It may be necessary to heat the piston slightly with a rag soaked in hot water or use a homemade tool to pull the pin in, as shown in Figure 23.*

5. Install new circlips where removed. Make sure the clip is fully seated in the groove and

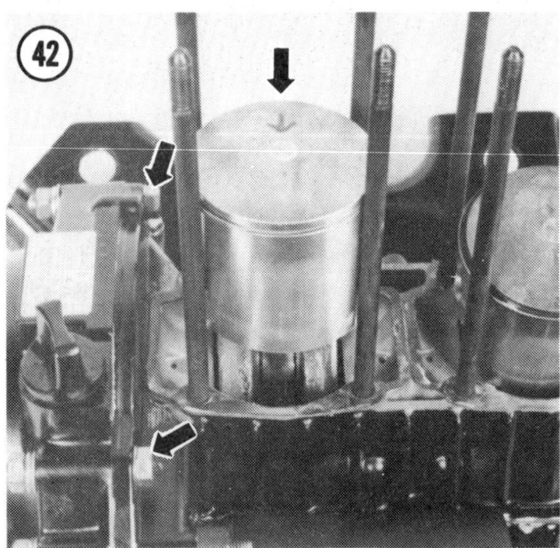

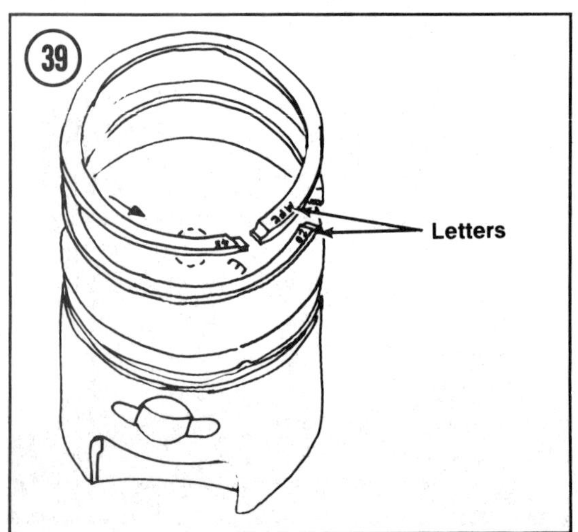

that the circlip gap lies at the top or bottom of the groove (**Figure 43**).

> *CAUTION*
> *Do not reuse an old circlip. The old clip was probably weakened during removal and its use could lead to serious engine damage.*

Manifold Installation

Install new manifold gaskets. On 1981 and later models, use flat washers only on the exhaust manifold bolts. On earlier models, use washers and lockwashers. Leave the upper left intake manifold nut loose until the electric box ground wire is attached. Torque the bolts in a crisscross pattern to 50 in.-lb. (0.6 mkg).

> *NOTE*
> *When installing manifold bolts, check that each one sticks up the same amount before you screw them all in. If not, you've got a long bolt in a short hole and vice versa.*

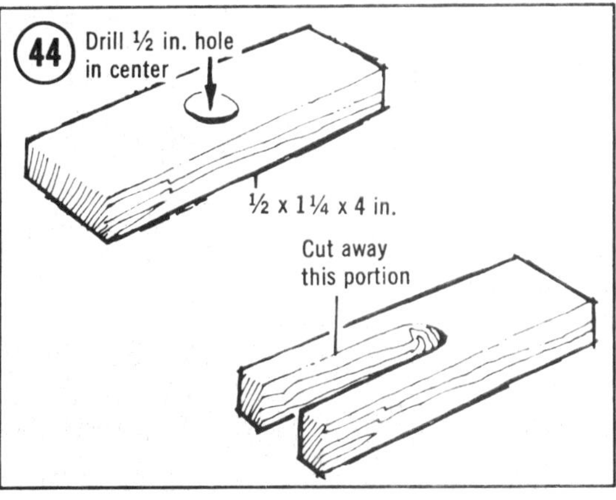

Cylinder Block Installation

1. Take the rags out of the crankcase openings. Check that the top surface of the crankcase and the bottom surface of the cylinder are clean.

2. Install new cylinder base gaskets on the crankcase. Make sure they are properly aligned with the crankcase openings.

3. Place a piston holding tool under one piston and turn the crankshaft until the piston is down firmly against the tool. This will make cylinder installation much easier. You can make such a tool out of wood as shown in **Figure 44**.

4. Oil the piston rings and cylinder walls. Check that the piston rings are seated in the ring grooves and the ring end gaps are correctly lined up with the locating pins (**Figure 45**).

5. *If the magneto cover was removed*: Slip the 2 upper magneto cover bolts into their holes from the rear (cylinder) side of the crankcase flange (**Figure 42**).

6. Install the cylinder block on the crankcase studs, compressing each piston ring with your fingers as the cylinder starts to slide over it (**Figure 46**). If the rings are hard to compress,

you can use a large hose clamp as a cheap, but effective compressor (**Figure 47**). Make sure the cylinder block is fully seated on the crankcase.

7. Connect the cooling water supply hose at the rear of the exhaust manifold. Tighten its clamp.

8. Connect the electric box ground wire to the upper rear intake manifold bolt (**Figure 11**).
9. Install the cylinder head as described in this chapter.

10. Install the carburetor and the exhaust pipe/expansion chamber assembly; see *Carburetor Installation* and *Exhaust Installation* in Chapter Six.

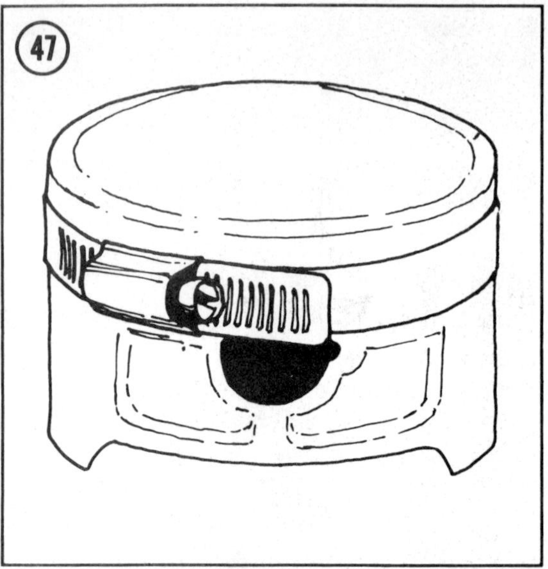

Cylinder Head Installation

1. If the water cooling hose fitting was removed from the cylinder head, apply sealant to its threads and install it.

2. *On 1976-early 1980 engines:* If the cylinder head plugs were removed (**Figure 10**), coat the threads with sealant and tighten them securely.
3. Lightly coat a new head gasket with non-hardening sealer, being careful not to block any of the gasket holes. Install the gasket with the wider part of the cylinder sealing rings on top. On 1981 and later models, the tab at the front of the gasket should align with the boss cast in the cylinder head (**Figure 48**).
4. Install the cylinder head, making sure that the water hose fitting is pointing forward. Install the cylinder head nuts and washers finger-tight.
5. If you removed the carburetor, install it now. See *Carburetor Installation* in Chapter Six.
6. *On 1981 and later Jet Skis:* Close the choke to keep parts from dropping down the carburetor, then install the flame arrestor holder with bolts, washers and lockwashers. Install the flame arrestor element.
7. *On 1978 and later Jet Skis:* Install the carburetor brace nuts and the bracket (**Figure 10**).
8. Tighten the cylinder head nuts gradually in the sequence shown in **Figure 49**. Torque them to 16 ft.-lb. (2.2 mkg).

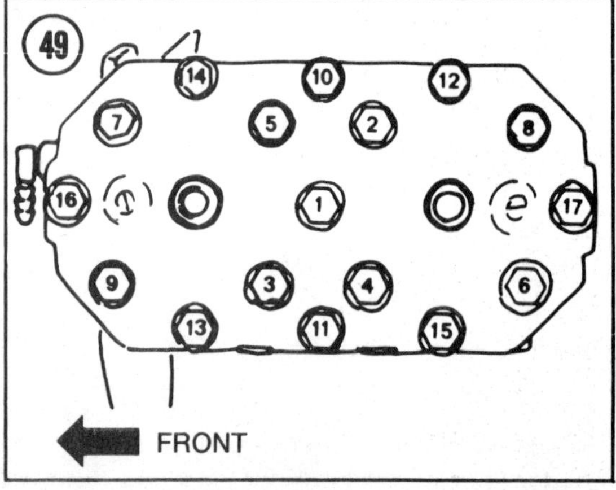

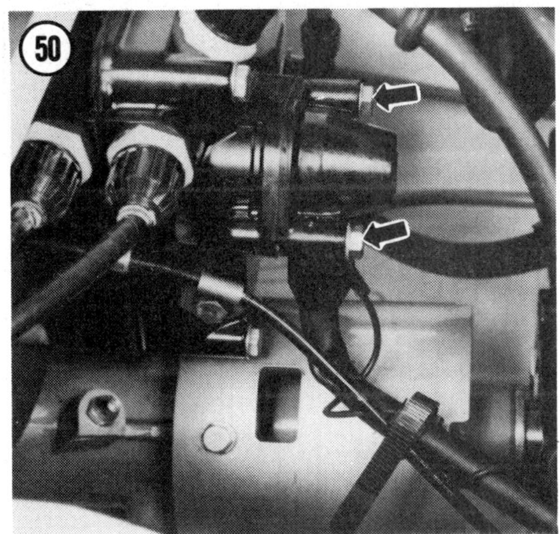

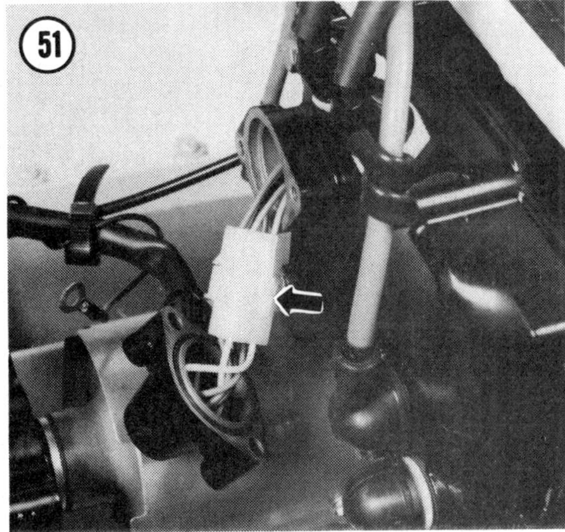

NOTE
On 1981 and later engines, nuts No. 10 and 11 in the sequence have been eliminated. Follow the indicated sequence, skipping No. 10 and 11.

9. Install the exhaust pipe/expansion chamber assembly. See *Exhaust Installation* in Chapter Six.

10. Connect the water hose from the exhaust pipe to the fitting at the front of the cylinder head. Tighten the clamp securely.

11. Install the intake cover bolts and the cover.

12. *On 1979 and later Jet Skis*: Connect the battery negative (-) ground cable at the engine.

13. *On 1976-1977 Jet Skis*: Connect the battery negative (-) ground cable at the battery.
14. Install the spark plugs and their caps.
15. Put the Jet Ski in water or connect a cooling water supply as described in *On-shore Cooling* in Chapter Three. Start the engine and check for coolant leaks.

> *WARNING*
> *The exhaust gases are poisonous. Do not run the engine in a closed area. Make sure there is plenty of ventilation.*

> *CAUTION*
> *Do not run the engine for more than 15 seconds without a supply of cooling water or the rubber parts of the exhaust system will be damaged. Prolonged running without coolant will cause serious engine damage. Do not operate the engine at maximum speed out of the water.*

ENGINE REMOVAL

Engine removal and crankcase separation is required for repair of the "bottom end" (crankshaft, connecting rod and bearings) and for removal of the drive shaft and bearing box. Although the "top end" can be left attached for engine removal, we recommend that you remove it first. It makes the engine much lighter and easier to handle.

Engine Removal

1. Remove the battery; see *Battery Removal* in Chapter Seven.
2. Remove the carburetor and the exhaust pipe/expansion chamber assembly as described in Chapter Six.
3. Remove the cylinder head, cylinder block (with intake and exhaust manifolds) and pistons; see *Top End Disassembly* in this chapter.
4. *On 440 cc Jet Skis*: Remove the 2 bolts securing the magneto wiring cap to the electric box (**Figure 50**). The connector is on the side of the box on 1977-1980 Jet Skis. Don't lose the O-ring between the cap and the box.
5. *On 440 cc engines*: Disconnect the 5-pin connector at the electric box (**Figure 51**).

6. Disconnect the starter cable at the starter (**Figure 52**).

7. Loosen the 4 engine bed bolts (**Figure 53**). Note any shims under each of the 4 engine bed corners so that the same shims can be installed later. Remove the bolts and shims.

8. Slide the engine to the front to disengage it from the coupler and lift it up out of the Jet Ski (**Figure 54**). Take it to a workbench for further disassembly.

CRANKCASE SEPARATION

The crankcases can be separated after the engine is removed from the hull.

1. Remove the 2 bolts at the rear of the starter (**Figure 55**). Note any shims between the starter and the crankcase so the same shims can be installed later.

2. Remove the 2 bolts at the front of the starter (**Figure 56**) and remove the starter.

3. Remove the 4 magneto cover bolts and the cover (**Figure 57**).

4. *On late 1980-on engines*: Hold the magneto rotor steady with a rotor holding tool (**Figure 1**) and unscrew the coupler half from the rear end of the crankshaft (**Figure 58**).

5. *On 1976-early 1980 Jet Skis*:

   a. Hold the magneto rotor steady with a rotor holding tool (**Figure 1**) and remove the coupler center bolt and washer from the rear end of the crankshaft.

   b. Insert a cap in the rear end of the crankshaft to protect the internal threads and pull the coupler half off of the crankshaft with a small universal gear puller (**Figure 59**).

   c. Remove the 4 rear oil seal housing bolts (**Figure 60**) and pull off the housing and gasket.

6. At the front of the engine, fold down the tabs on the rotor lockwasher (**Figure 61**), hold the rotor steady with a rotor holding tool and remove the rotor nut (**Figure 62**).

7. Loosen the rotor with a 4-bolt Kawasaki rotor puller (**Figure 63**). The Kawasaki puller tool is part No. T57001-259. Back out the puller center bolt, screw the 3 outer bolts into the rotor, then screw in the center bolt to pull the rotor off. You may have to alternate tapping on the center puller bolt sharply with a

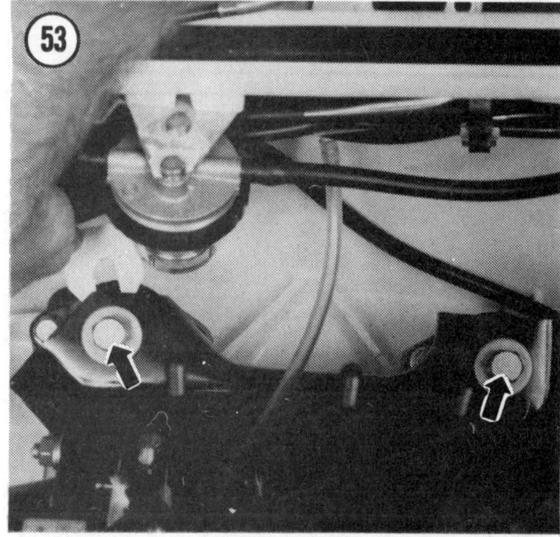

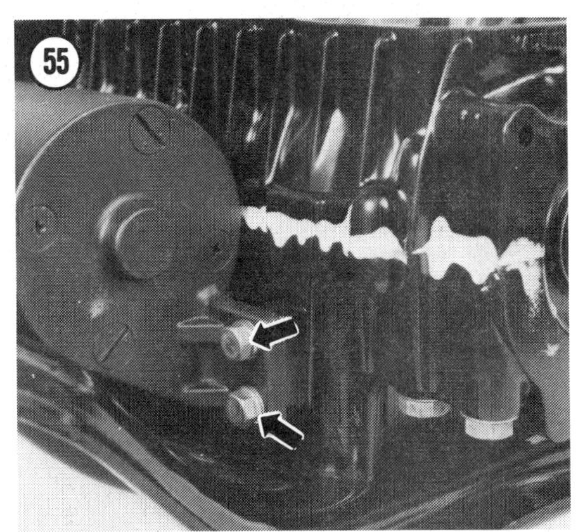

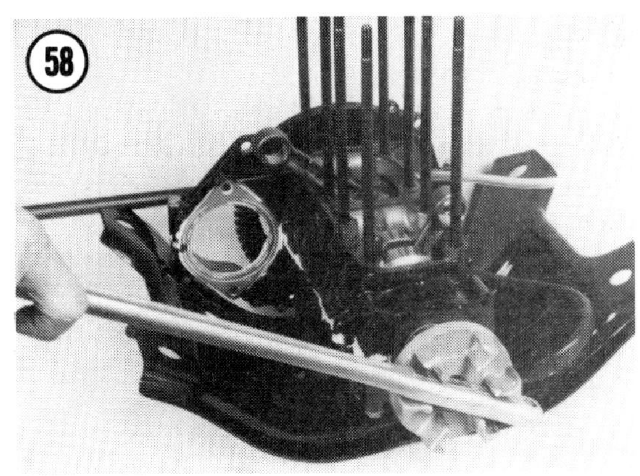

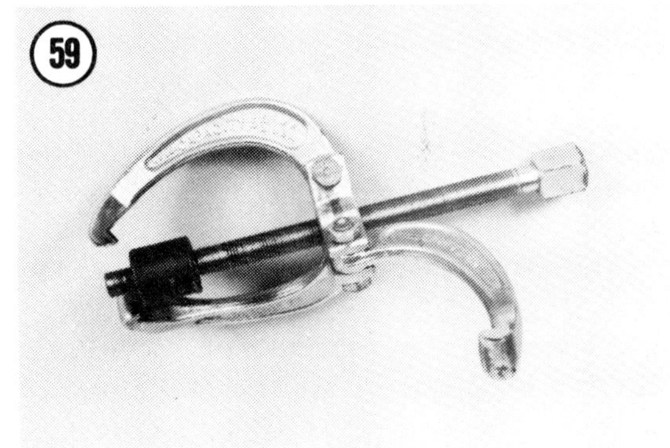

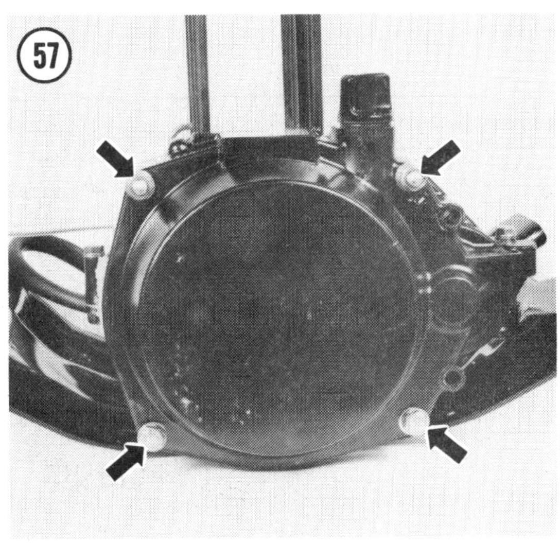

hammer and tightening the bolt some more, but don't hit the rotor.

CAUTION
Rotor removal requires a puller such as the one illustrated. Don't pry or hammer on the rotor itself. Damage is sure to result and you may also destroy the rotor's magnetism. You may be able to substitute an automotive steering wheel puller for the special Kawasaki puller.

8. Remove the rotor and pull the Woodruff key out of the end of the crankshaft so you don't lose it.

9. Remove the 2 stator screws and loosen the stator (**Figure 64**).

10. Turn the engine over, remove the 4 engine bed bolts from the bottom (**Figure 65**) and remove the engine bed.

11. Remove the 3 small bolts on the sides of the magneto housing (**Figure 66**). There is only one small bolt by the starter on the 400 cc engine.

12. Remove the 10 bolts or cap nuts that hold the crankcase halves together (**Figure 67**).

CAUTION
Make sure that you have removed all the fasteners. If the cases are hard to separate, check for any fasteners you may have missed.

13. Tap lightly on the ends of the crankcase studs with a hammer to separate the crankcase halves. On 1981 and later engines, screw an end case bolt 1/2 inch (10 mm) into the case and tap on it (**Figure 68**).

14. Remove the crankshaft assembly from the lower case half (**Figure 69**).

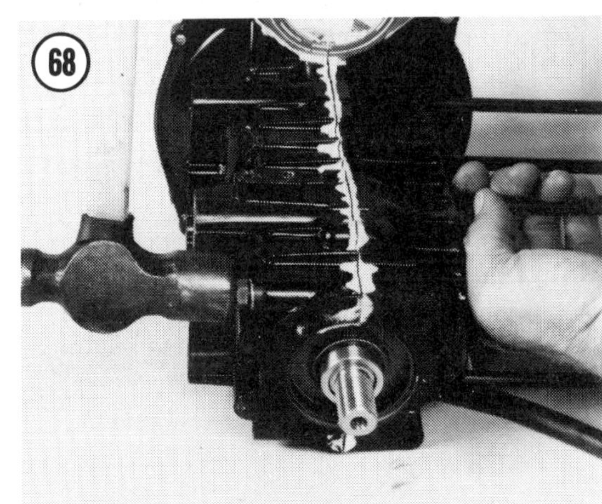

BOTTOM END INSPECTION

Crankcase Inspection

Check the crankcase halves for cracks or fractures in the stiffening webs, around the bearing bosses and at threaded holes. While the likelihood of such damage is rare, it should be checked for, particularly following a major failure (such as piston breakage or bearing failure).

If cracks or fractures are found, they should be repaired by a reputable shop experienced in and equipped to perform repairs on precision aluminum castings.

Crankshaft Inspection

Refer to **Figure 71** or **Figure 72**. The crankshaft and connecting rod assembly is pressed together. The bearings on the ends of the crankshaft can be replaced with little trouble, but the 2 center main bearings require crankshaft disassembly for their replacement. This is a job which should be entrusted to a shop equipped with a press capable of separating and reassembling the crankshaft halves and pins. Few shops are able to repair this kind of crankshaft, so in most cases you can inspect the crankshaft and rods but must replace the whole assembly if some part is faulty. See your Jet Ski dealer if you suspect crankshaft trouble.

1. Check connecting rod big-end radial clearance by supporting the crankshaft with the crankpin at top dead center. Grasp the connecting rod firmly and pull up on it. Tap sharply on the top of the rod with your free hand. If the bearing and crankpin are in good condition, there should be no movement felt in

the rod. If movement is felt, or if there is a sharp metallic click, the bearing may be unserviceable and the crankshaft should be replaced or rebuilt. If you measure clearance with a dial indicator (**Figure 73**), the radial clearance must not exceed the limit in **Table 1**.

2. Check connecting rod big-end side clearance with feeler gauges (**Figure 74**). If clearance exceeds the limit in **Table 1**, the crankshaft assembly should be replaced or rebuilt.

3. Carefully examine the condition of the crankshaft ball bearings. Clean the bearings in solvent and roll each bearing around by hand, checking that it turns quietly and smoothly and that there are no rough spots. There should be no apparent radial play. Defective end bearings can be replaced individually. The 2 center bearings must be replaced as an assembly with the crankshaft. Immediately after inspecting the bearings, oil them thoroughly to prevent rusting.

4. If these checks are satisfactory, take the crankshaft to your dealer or local machine shop for crankshaft runout and alignment inspection. Check against the measurements given in **Table 1** at the end of this chapter.

Main Bearing Installation
(Late 1980-on Engines)

These engines have cutaway crankshaft rotors; earlier engines have full circle rotors. When new outer crankshaft bearings are installed, they must be shimmed to achieve

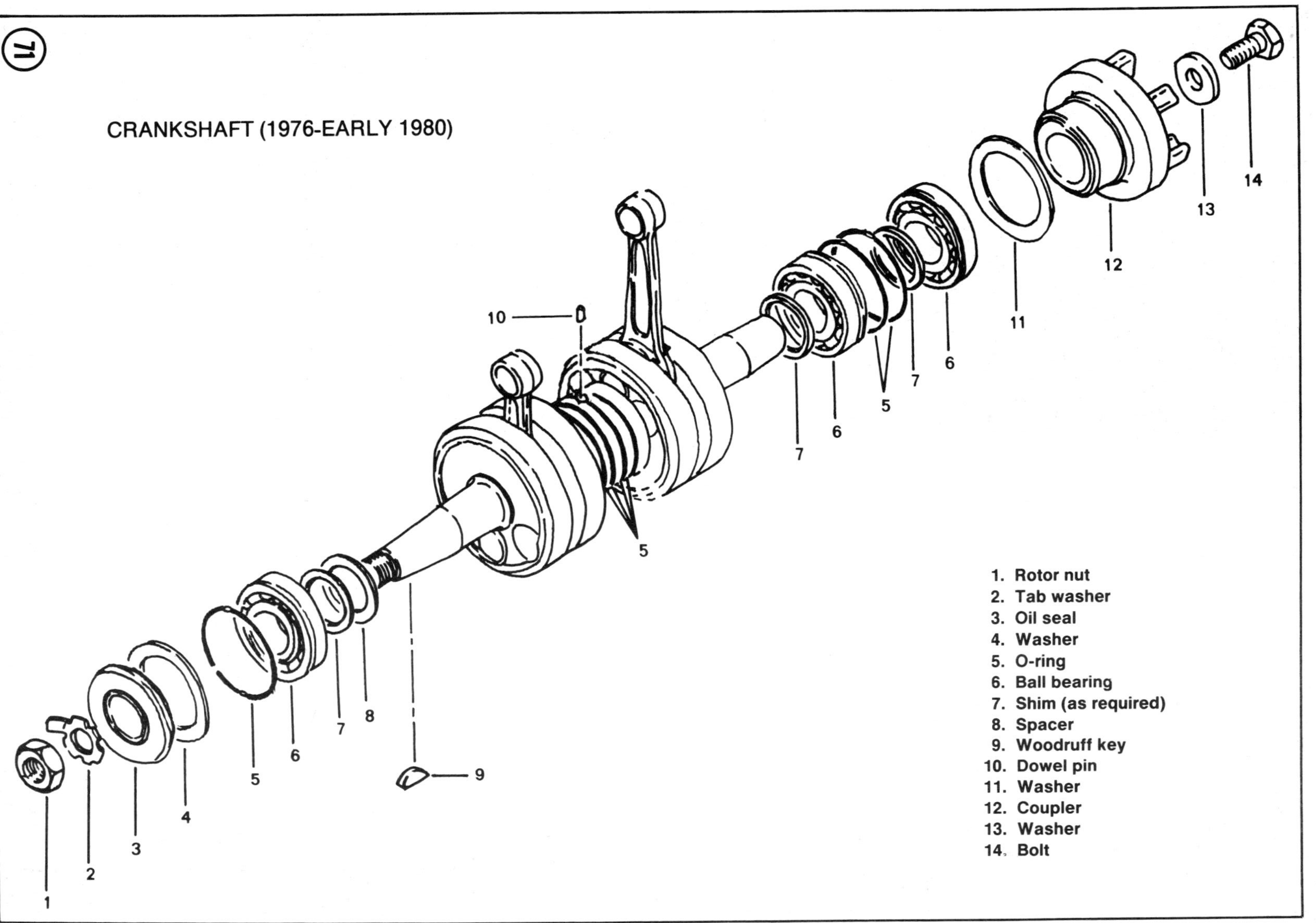
71
CRANKSHAFT (1976-EARLY 1980)
1. Rotor nut
2. Tab washer
3. Oil seal
4. Washer
5. O-ring
6. Ball bearing
7. Shim (as required)
8. Spacer
9. Woodruff key
10. Dowel pin
11. Washer
12. Coupler
13. Washer
14. Bolt

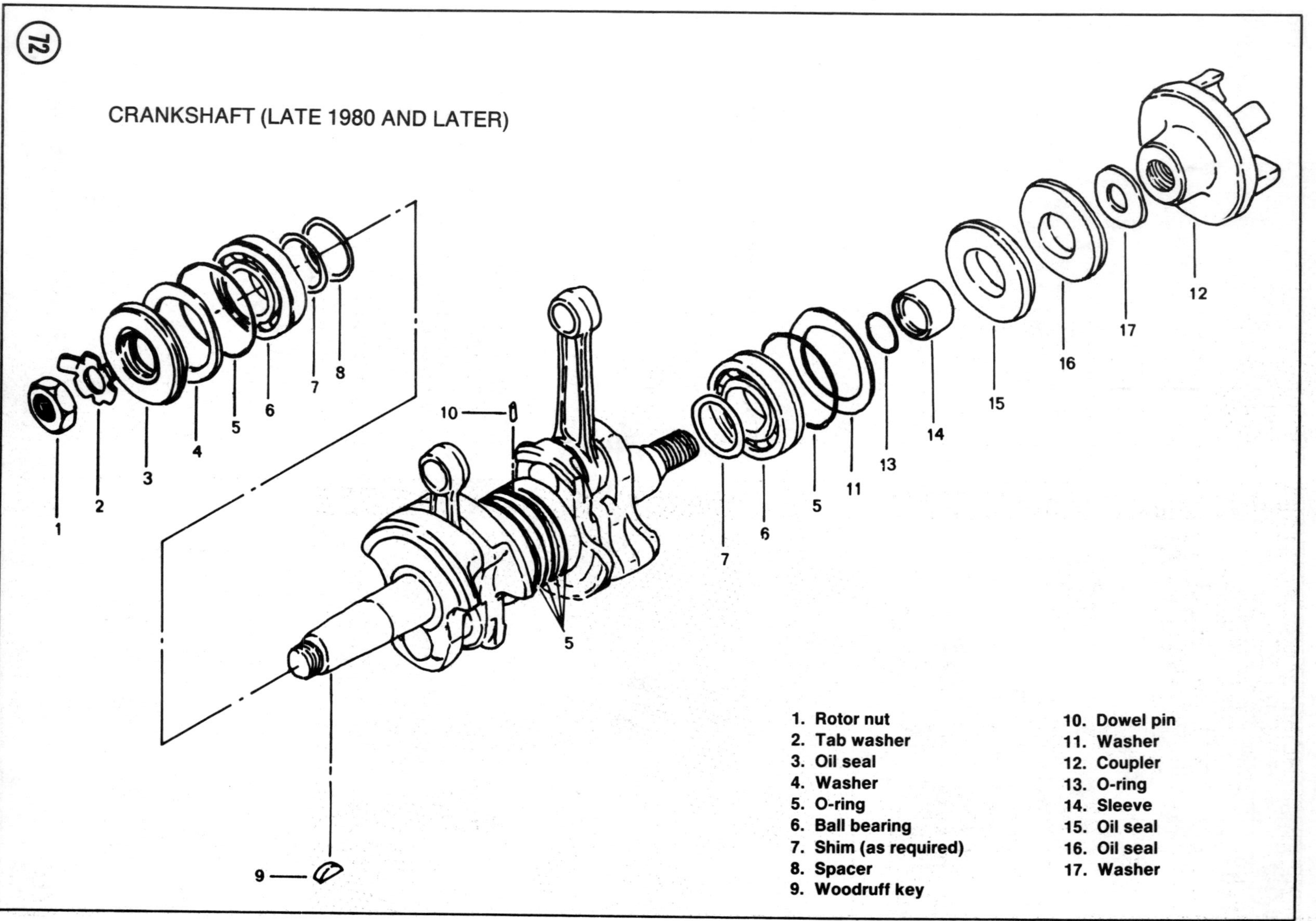

CRANKSHAFT (LATE 1980 AND LATER)

1. Rotor nut
2. Tab washer
3. Oil seal
4. Washer
5. O-ring
6. Ball bearing
7. Shim (as required)
8. Spacer
9. Woodruff key
10. Dowel pin
11. Washer
12. Coupler
13. O-ring
14. Sleeve
15. Oil seal
16. Oil seal
17. Washer

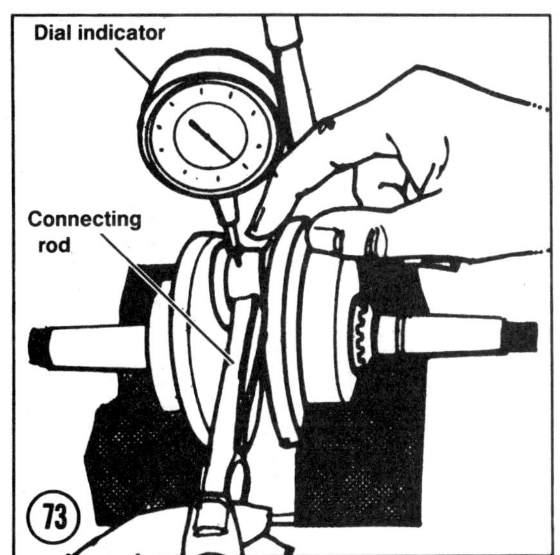

proper crankshaft end play at the front and rear ends of the crankshaft to avoid rapid crankshaft and bearing wear. Shims of different thicknesses are available from your Jet Ski dealer.

1. Measure the outside width across the forward cylinder rotors (A, **Figure 75**). If distance A is 1.955-1.963 in. (49.66-49.87 mm), no shim is required. If distance A is less than 1.955 in. (49.66 mm), add shims as required to total 1.959 +/-0.004 in. (49.75 +/-0.1 mm) when the bearing is installed. Slide the wide 1 mm thick spacer onto the crankshaft against the forward rotor, then add the selected shim and install the front bearing with its O-ring groove to the front.

2. Temporarily hold the rear bearing against the rear rotor and measure the distance between the forward face of the front bearing and the rear face of the rear bearing (B, **Figure 75**). If distance B is 7.440-7.432 in. (188.98-188.77 mm), no shim is required. If distance A is less than 7.432 in. (188.77 mm), add shims as required to total 7.434 +/-0.002 in. (188.82 +/-0.05 mm) when the bearing is installed. Place the selected shim against the rear rotor and install the rear bearing with its O-ring groove to the rear.

**Main Bearing Installation
(1976-early 1980 Engines)**

These engines have full circle crank rotors. When new outer crankshaft bearings are being installed, they must be shimmed to achieve

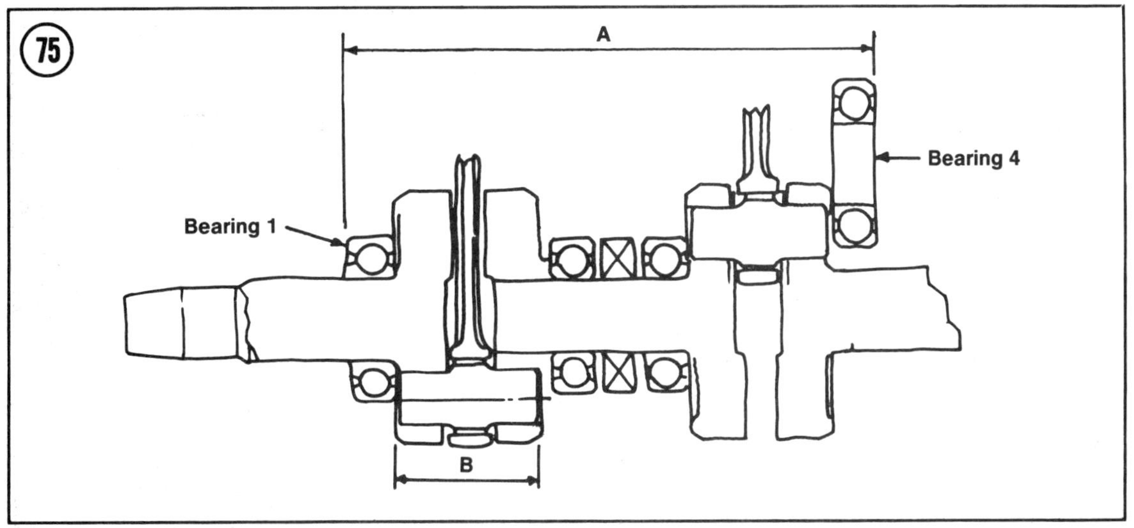

proper crankshaft end play at the front and rear ends of the crankshaft to avoid rapid crankshaft and bearing wear. Shims of different thicknesses are available from your Jet Ski dealer.

1. Measure the outside width across the front cylinder rotors (A, **Figure 76**). If distance A is 1.955-1.963 in. (49.66-49.87 mm), no shim is required. If distance A is less than 1.955 in. (49.66 mm), add shims as required to total 1.959 +/-0.004 in. (49.75 +/-0.1 mm) when the bearing is installed. Slide the wide 1 mm thick spacer onto the crankshaft against the front rotor, then add the selected shim and install the front bearing with its O-ring groove to the front.

2. Measure the outside width across the rear cylinder rotors (B, **Figure 76**). If distance B is 1.955-1.963 in. (49.66-49.87 mm), no shim is required. If distance B is less than 1.955 in. (49.66 mm), add shims as required to total 1.959 +/-0.004 in. (49.75 +/-0.1 mm) when the bearing is installed. Place the selected shim against the rear rotor and install the rear bearing with its O-ring groove to the rear.

3. Temporarily hold the second rear bearing next to the installed rear bearing and measure the distance between the front face of the front bearing and the rear face of the second rear bearing (C, **Figure 76**). If distance C is 8.061-8.179 in. (204.75-207.75 mm), no shim is required. If distance C is less than 8.061 in. (204.75 mm), add shims as required to total 8.063 +/-0.002 in. (204.80 +/-0.05 mm) when

the bearing is installed. Install the selected shim, then install the second rear bearing with its O-ring groove to the rear.

BOTTOM END ASSEMBLY

Crankshaft Installation

See **Figure 71** or **Figure 72**.

1. Oil the crankshaft bearings and check that each bearing's O-ring is in place (**Figure 77**).
2. Install the washer in front of the front main bearing, grease the front oil seal thoroughly with high temperature grease and install it on the front end of the crankshaft with the open side toward the connecting rod (**Figure 78**).
3. Install the washer to the rear of the rear main bearing.
4. *On late 1980-on engines*:
   a. Install the O-ring and sleeve on the rear end of the crankshaft (**Figure 79**). The recessed end of the sleeve faces the O-ring.
   b. Grease the 2 rear oil seals with high-temperature grease. Slide the oil seals onto the crankshaft as shown in **Figure 80**.
5. Turn the upper crankcase half upside down and fit the crankshaft assembly into place (**Figure 81**).
6. Turn the center seal's locating pin until it fits in its hole in the case.
7. Check that the bearing stop rings, the bearing O-rings and the oil seal ridges are located in their crankcase grooves (**Figure 82**).

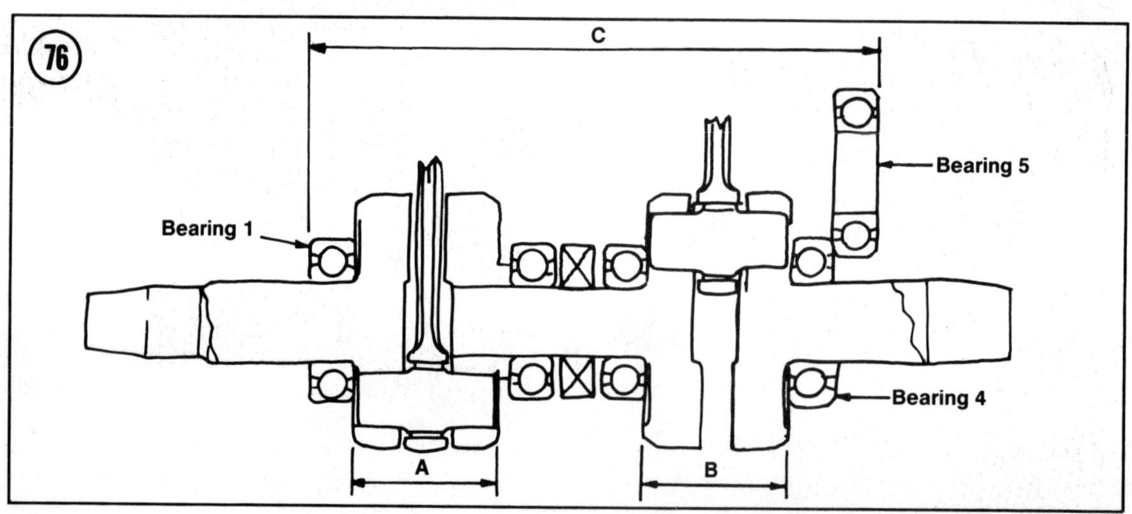

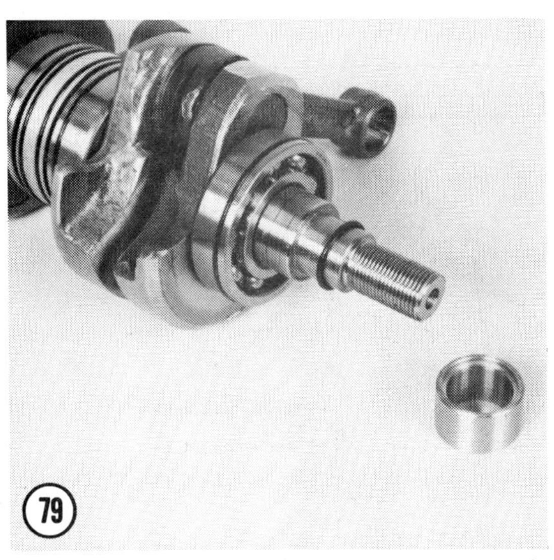

Crankcase Assembly

NOTE
The magneto stator leads pass through the lower crankcase half. If you removed the stator or its leads and connectors, see **Stator Installation** *in Chapter Seven.*

1. Install the crankshaft in the upper crankcase half.

2. Check that the 2 dowel pins are in place **(Figure 83)**.

3. Make sure the crankcase mating surfaces are completely clean and apply a light coat of sealant to the mating surfaces of one case half.

4. Put the lower case half onto the upper half, fitting the magneto stator over the end of the crankshaft.

5. Loosely install the 10 bolts or cap nuts and washers. Torque the fasteners gradually, in the sequence shown in **Figure 84**, to 16 ft.-lb. (2.2 mkg).

CAUTION
While tightening the crankcase fasteners, make frequent checks to

ensure that the crankshaft turns freely and that the crankshaft locating rings and crankcase dowel pins fit into place in the case halves.

6. Check again that the crankshaft turns freely. If it is binding, separate the crankcase halves and determine the cause of the problem.

7. Install the 3 small bolts on either side of the magneto housing (**Figure 66**) and torque them to 50 in.-lb. (0.6 mkg). There is only one small bolt by the starter on the 400 cc engines.

8. Position the magneto stator so that the mark on the stator plate lines up with the parting line of the crankcases (**Figure 85**). Put a small amount of silicone sealant on the threads of the 2 mounting screws (**Figure 64**), slip on their lockwashers and flat washers and tighten them securely.

9. Set the engine bed in position with the right-angle mounting tabs at the front and the 45° splayed tabs at the rear (**Figure 65**). Install the 4 engine mounting bolts with their lockwashers and flat washers and torque them to 35 ft.-lb. (4.8 mkg).

NOTE
Make sure you have the proper bolts. The engine bed bolts have a special 22 mm thread.

10. Turn the engine right side up. Clean any oil or grease from the front tapered end of the crankshaft. Apply a light coat of WD-40 to the taper and insert the Woodruff key (**Figure 85**).

11. Inspect the inside of the rotor carefully for any bits of metal or small parts that may have been picked up by the rotor magnets. Remove them to prevent damage when the engine starts.

12. Wipe the rotor hole clean, apply WD-40 to the crankshaft taper and then slide the rotor onto the crankshaft, aligning the Woodruff key with the slot in the rotor.

13. Install a new tabwasher with its tongue in the rotor hole (**Figure 86**).

14. Install the rotor nut. Hold the rotor steady with a rotor holding tool (**Figure 62**) and torque the nut to 115 ft.-lb. (16 mkg) on 440 cc engines or to 85 ft.-lb. (12 mkg) on 400 cc engines.

15. Bend the tabs on the washer up against the nut (**Figure 87**).

16. *On 1976-early 1980 engines*: Install the rear oil seal housing:

    a. Install new oil seals with their open sides facing out of the housing; the seals must be level with the face of the housing.

    b. Fill the inner oil seal with high temperature grease and the outer oil seal with a water-resistant grease such as Valvoline X-All.

    c. Install a new gasket and the oil seal housing on the crankcase (**Figure 60**). Install the 4 bolts with flat washers and lockwashers and torque them in a crisscross pattern to 12 ft.-lb. (1.6 mkg).

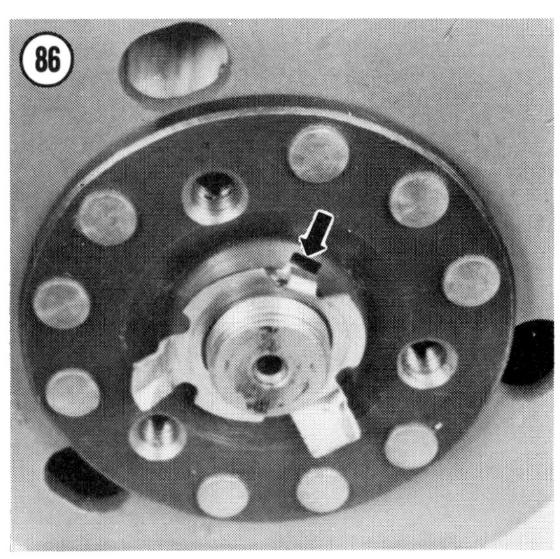

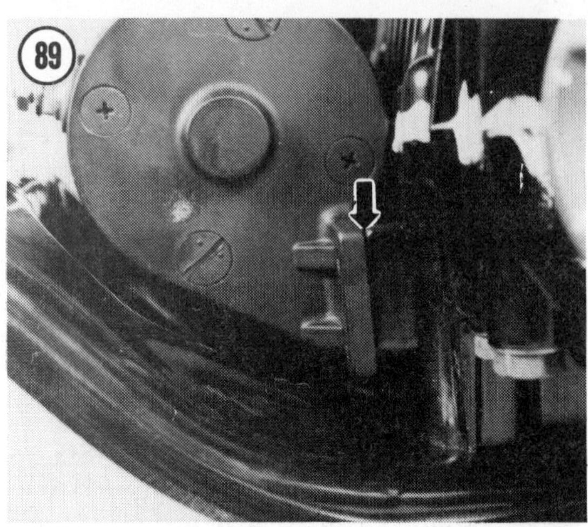

17. *On 1976-early 1980 engines*:
   a. Clean the tapered rear end of the crankshaft and the inside of the coupler with solvent, then apply a light coat of WD-40 to the taper.
   b. Slip the large coupler washer on the coupler, then slide the coupler over the crankshaft end (**Figure 71**).
   c. Install the coupler bolt and washer (**Figure 71**). Hold the crankshaft steady with a rotor holder as you torque the bolt to 45 ft.-lb. (6.2 mkg).

18. *On late 1980-on engines*: Coat the rear crankshaft threads with grease, install the coupler washer and hold the rotor steady with a rotor holding tool as you screw the coupler onto the crank (**Figure 58**). Torque the coupler to 20 ft.-lb. (2.7 mkg).

19. *On 1977 and later engines*: Check that the magneto cover O-ring is in good condition. Apply a light coat of waterproof grease such as Valvoline X-All.

20. *On 1976 engines*: Apply silicone sealant to both sides of the magneto cover gasket.

21. Install the magneto cover. Use a flat washer and lockwasher under each bolt head or nut.

22. Check the condition of the starter's O-ring, then grease it lightly and install it in the starter groove (**Figure 88**).

23. Loosely install the starter, using 2 bolts, lockwashers and flat washers at the front and 2 at the rear bracket. Torque the 2 front bolts to 12 ft.-lb. (1.6 mkg).

NOTE
On 1976-early 1980 Jet Skis, the battery ground cable must be attached to the upper front starter mount bolt before tightening.

24. Measure any space between the crankcase and the rear bracket of the starter (**Figure 89**). Install shims to take up any clearance, then torque the 2 rear bolts to 50 in.-lb. (0.6 mkg).

ENGINE INSTALLATION

To prepare the Jet Ski for engine installation, clean the bilge filter and check that the muffler is installed properly. Replace the muffler hold-down straps if they are cracked and make sure there is no debris or damage in the engine compartment and hull.

1. Examine the engine mounts and bolts (**Figure 90**). Replace any cracked mounts and check that the bolts are tight.

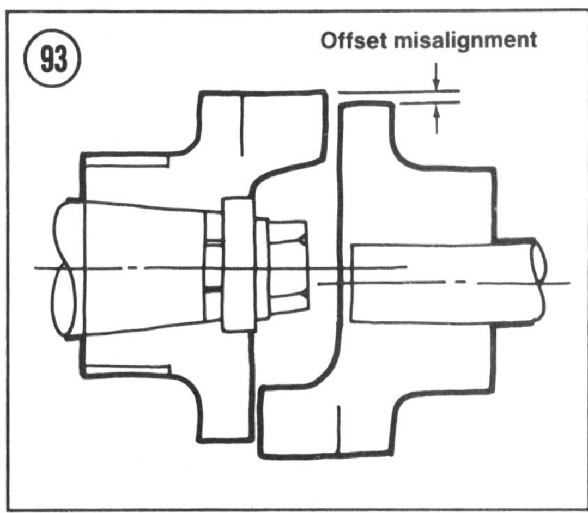

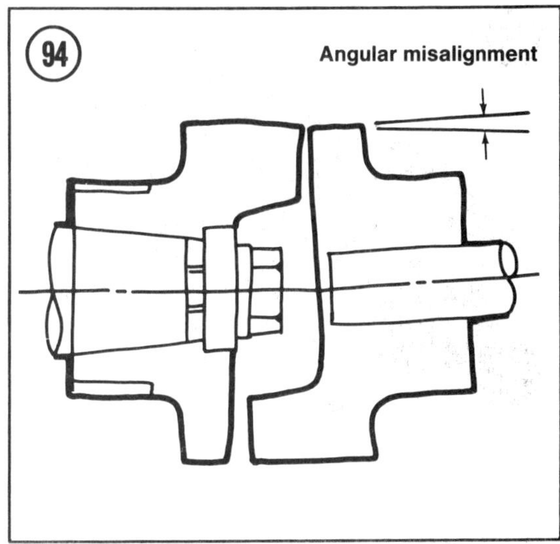

2. Check the coupling rubber for wear; see *Coupler Rubber Inspection* in Chapter Five. If it is worn, it must be replaced. Place the coupling rubber, hollow side forward, on the drive shaft coupler half.

3. Put the engine in the hull and slide it backward, meshing the engine coupler and driveshaft coupler into the coupler rubber.

4. Loosely install the 4 engine bed bolts and insert the original engine bed shims under the engine bed (**Figure 53**).

5. Slide the coupling rubber toward the front or rear and measure the gap between the front or rear face of the rubber and the coupling (**Figure 91**). If the gap exceeds 0.020 in. (0.5 mm), loosen all the bed bolts and push the engine toward the rear as necessary.

NOTE
Figure 91 *shows the starter cables incorrectly reversed at the electric box terminals.* ***Do not*** *connect the cables as shown.*

6. Check the coupler alignment as follows:
   a. Tighten the engine bed mounting bolts temporarily.
   b. Hold a straightedge against one side of the coupler halves (**Figure 92**). Push the straightedge against the flat sides of the couplers. If you can see a gap between one coupler flat and the straightedge or if you can feel the straightedge rock as you push against one coupler flat and then the

other, there is *offset* (**Figure 93**) or *angular* (**Figure 94**) misalignment. Repeat this check with the straightedge against the other side, and then on top of, the coupler halves.

c. To correct *offset* misalignment, loosen the bed bolts and slide the whole engine left or right. Shim it up or down at both the back and front as required to align the coupler halves. Tighten the bed bolts temporarily and recheck alignment with the straightedge.

d. To correct *angular* misalignment, loosen the bed bolts and twist the engine left or right. Shim it up or down at the front or rear as required to align the coupler halves. Tighten the bed bolts temporarily and recheck alignment with the straightedge.

CAUTION
It is important to align the coupler halves as closely as possible. Any significant degree of misalignment will cause vibration, damage to the coupling rubber and possible damage to the Jet Ski. Some Jet Skis will require quite a few shims to do the job.

6. After you have aligned the engine with the drive shaft, torque the engine bed bolts to 27 ft.-lb. (3.7 mkg).

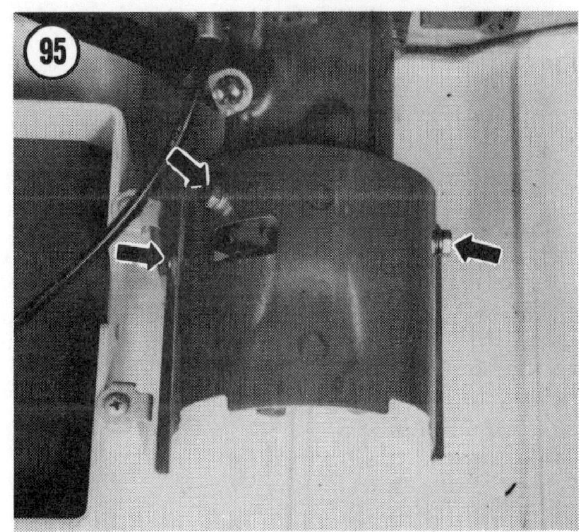

7. Install the coupler guard with 3 bolts, flat washers and lockwashers (**Figure 95**).
8. Install the starter cable on the starter and slide the boot down over the nut.
9. Attach the magneto wiring plug to the electric box connector (**Figure 51**). Grease the O-ring and install the cap. On 1981 and later models, the electric box ground wire attaches to one of the cap's bolts. The connector is on the side of the box on 1980 and earlier models.
10. Tie the ground wire, switch loom and magneto loom together with a cable tie (**Figure 50**).
11. Install the pistons, cylinder block (with intake and exhaust manifolds) and cylinder head; see *Top End Assembly* in this chapter.

Table 1   JS400/440 ENGINE WEAR LIMITS

Item	Wear Limit	Standard
Compression		
400 cc		115 psi (8.0 kg/cm^2)
440 cc		120 psi (8.4 kg/cm^2)
Connecting rod bend		
and twist per 4 in. (100 mm)	0.008 in. (0.20 mm)	
Connecting rod big-end clearance		
Radial	0.003 in. (0.08 mm)	0.0008-0.0012 in. (0.02-0.03 mm)
Side	0.028 in. (0.7 mm)	0.016-0.020 in. (0.4-0.5 mm)
Connecting rod		
small end ID	0.789 in. (20.05 mm)	
Crankshaft end play		Less than 0.030 in. (0.75 mm)
Crankshaft runout	0.003 in. (0.08 mm)	
Cylinder head warp	0.010 in. (0.25 mm)	
Cylinder bore ID (400 cc)		
Bore oversize at	2.585 in. (65.67 mm)	

(Continued)

Table 1   JS400/440 ENGINE WEAR LIMITS (Continued)

Item	Wear Limit	Standard
Cylinder bore ID (440 cc)		
Bore oversize at	2.704 in. (68.67 mm)	
Piston/cylinder clearance		0.0037-0.0052 in. (0.095-0.133 mm)
Piston OD (400 cc)	2.552 in. (64.82 mm)	
Piston OD (440 cc)	2.670 in. (67.82 mm)	
Piston pin bore ID	0.6331 in. (16.08 mm)	
Piston pin OD	0.6283 in. (15.96 mm)	
Piston ring/groove clearance (1976-1980)		
Top	0.010 in. (0.25 mm)	
Bottom	0.007 in. (0.19 mm)	
Piston ring thickness (1976-1980)	0.076 in. (1.92 mm)	
Piston ring groove width (1976-1980)		
Top	0.086 in. (2.18 mm)	
Second	0.083 in. (2.12 mm)	
Piston ring installed gap		0.008-0.027 in. (0.2-0.7 mm)

Table 2   JS400/440 ENGINE TORQUES

	Ft.-lb.	Mkg
Coupler		
Threaded coupler	20	(2.7)
Coupler bolt	45	(6.2)
Crankcase bolts		
Large (1981-on)	16	(2.2)
Small (all models)	50 in.-lb.	(0.6)
Crankcase nuts (1976-1980)	16	(2.2)
Cylinder head nuts	16	(2.2)
Engine mounting bolts (to bed)	35	(4.8)
Engine bed bolts (to mounts)	27	(3.7)
Engine mount bolts (to brackets)	16	(2.2)
Engine bracket bolts (to hull)	18	(2.5)
Exhaust manifold bolts	50 in.-lb.	(0.6)
Exhaust pipe flange nuts	12	(1.6)
Exhaust pipe/expansion chamber junction bolts	10	(1.4)
Expansion chamber bolts	10	(1.4)
Intake manifold bolts	50 in.-lb.	(0.6)
Magneto cover bolts	12	(1.6)
Oil seal housing bolts	12	(1.6)
Rotor nut		
400 cc	85	(12.0)
440 cc	115	(16.0)
Spark plugs	18	(2.5)
Starter mounting bolts		
Front	12	(1.6)
Rear	50 in.-lb.	(0.6)

NOTE: If you own a 1982 or 1983 model, first check the Supplement at the back of the book for any new service information.

CHAPTER FIVE

DRIVE TRAIN

The Jet Ski's drive train consists of the engine/drive shaft coupling, drive shaft, bearing box and jet pump.

Removal, installation and alignment of the engine/drive shaft coupling are described in Chapter Four; see *Engine Installation*.

Table 1 and **Table 2** are at the end of the chapter.

COUPLER

The coupler (**Figure 1**) transmits power from the engine to the drive shaft. It acts somewhat like a "universal joint" to accommodate stresses caused by minor misalignment between the crankshaft axis and the drive shaft axis and by drive shaft runout and hull flexing.

Alignment of the coupler is adjusted by moving the engine left, right, up and down by means of shims placed under the engine bed. Refer to *Engine Installation* in Chapter Four.

> *CAUTION*
> *Always keep the original factory-installed shims between the bearing box and the hull bulkhead. These shims affect alignment of the drive shaft with the jet pump, as well as alignment with the crankshaft.*

The coupler rubber cushion should be inspected for wear according to the maintenance schedule in Chapter Three and replaced if excessively worn.

Coupler Rubber Inspection

Check the coupling rubber for wear on the round outer knobs as shown in **Figure 2**. Replace it if worn so much that any rotational play exists between the engine coupler half and the drive shaft coupler half.

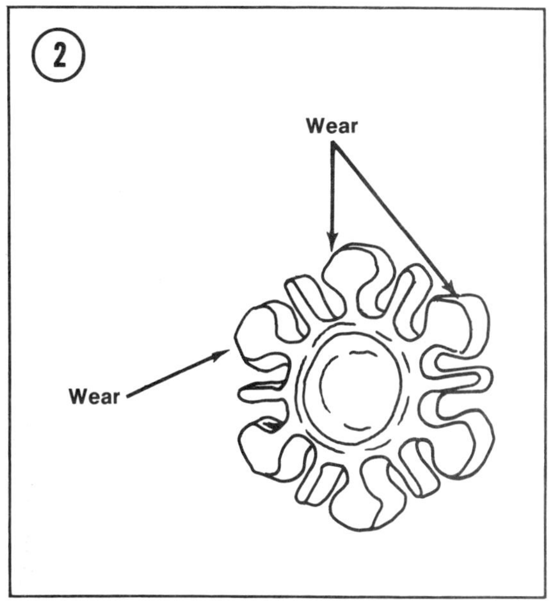

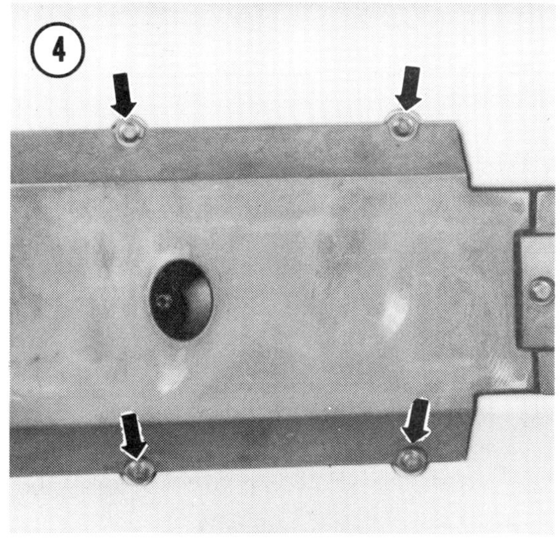

JET PUMP

The jet pump case contains the impeller (propeller) mounted on the drive shaft. The end of the drive shaft rides in a bushing at the tail end of the pump case. A grease fitting is provided at the pump outlet for regular lubrication.

The pump is carefully manufactured so that there is very little clearance between the impeller and the case. As the pump wears from normal use, the clearance between the impeller and case will increase and so pump thrust will decrease. The impeller and case should be inspected according to the maintenance schedule in Chapter Three and replaced when excessively worn.

With extended use, the drive shaft bushing in the tail end of the pump case will wear and may cause inaccurate impeller/case clearance.

Positioning of the impeller inside the case is controlled by the pump case bushing and by shims placed under the pump case; refer to *Jet Pump Installation* in this chapter.

NOTE
Do not change the original factory installed shims between the jet pump and the hull, unless you want to reposition the impeller within the pump case. This may be required after installing new bearings in the bearing box or after replacing the bushing in the tail end of the pump case.

Jet Pump/Impeller Removal

1. Remove the battery to prevent acid spillage; see *Battery Removal* in Chapter Seven.
2. Disconnect the spark plug leads to prevent accidental engine startup.
3. Put a towel or pad under the left side of the hull to protect the finish, then turn the Jet Ski onto its left side and prop it up.
4. Take out the 3 bolts holding the water intake grate and remove the grate (**Figure 3**).
5. Take out the 4 bolts on the jet pump cover and remove the cover (**Figure 4**).
6. Detach the steering cable/nozzle ball-joint from the pump nozzle; slide its spring-loaded sleeve forward and pull the connector off of the ball (A, **Figure 5**).

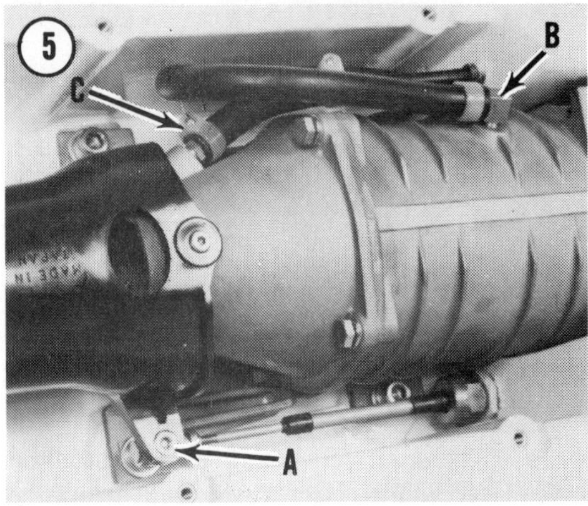

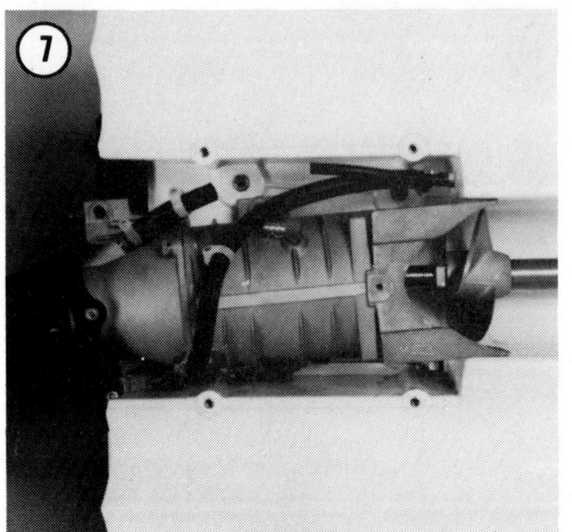

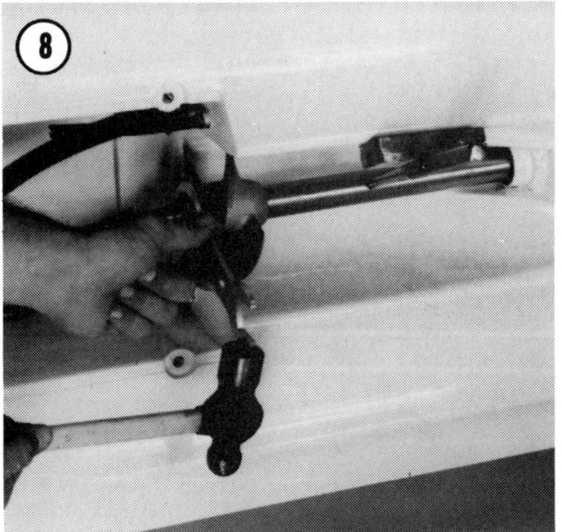

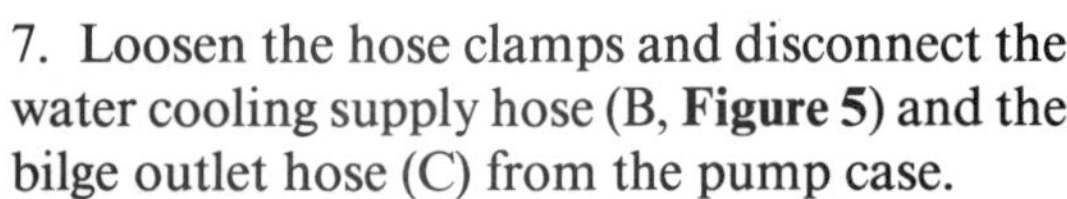

7. Loosen the hose clamps and disconnect the water cooling supply hose (B, **Figure 5**) and the bilge outlet hose (C) from the pump case.

8. Remove the 4 Allen bolts that hold the jet pump to the hull (**Figure 6**).

> *NOTE*
> *While removing the jet pump, pay attention to the number and position of alignment shims under each pump mounting lug (A, **Figure 6**). These shims will have to be reinstalled in exactly the same position for the pump and impeller to align properly.*

9. Remove the jet pump by pulling it to the rear and tapping it lightly with a soft mallet if necessary (**Figure 7**).

10. Hold the drive shaft steady by inserting a rod through the hole in the shaft. Prop the rod against a pad to protect the hull, then loosen the impeller with a 32 mm wrench or a large

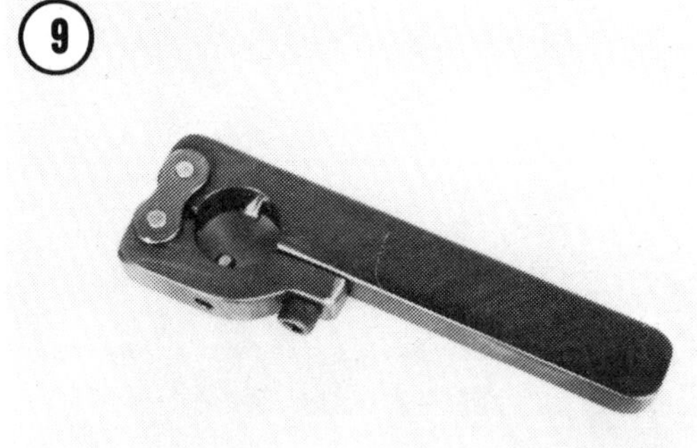

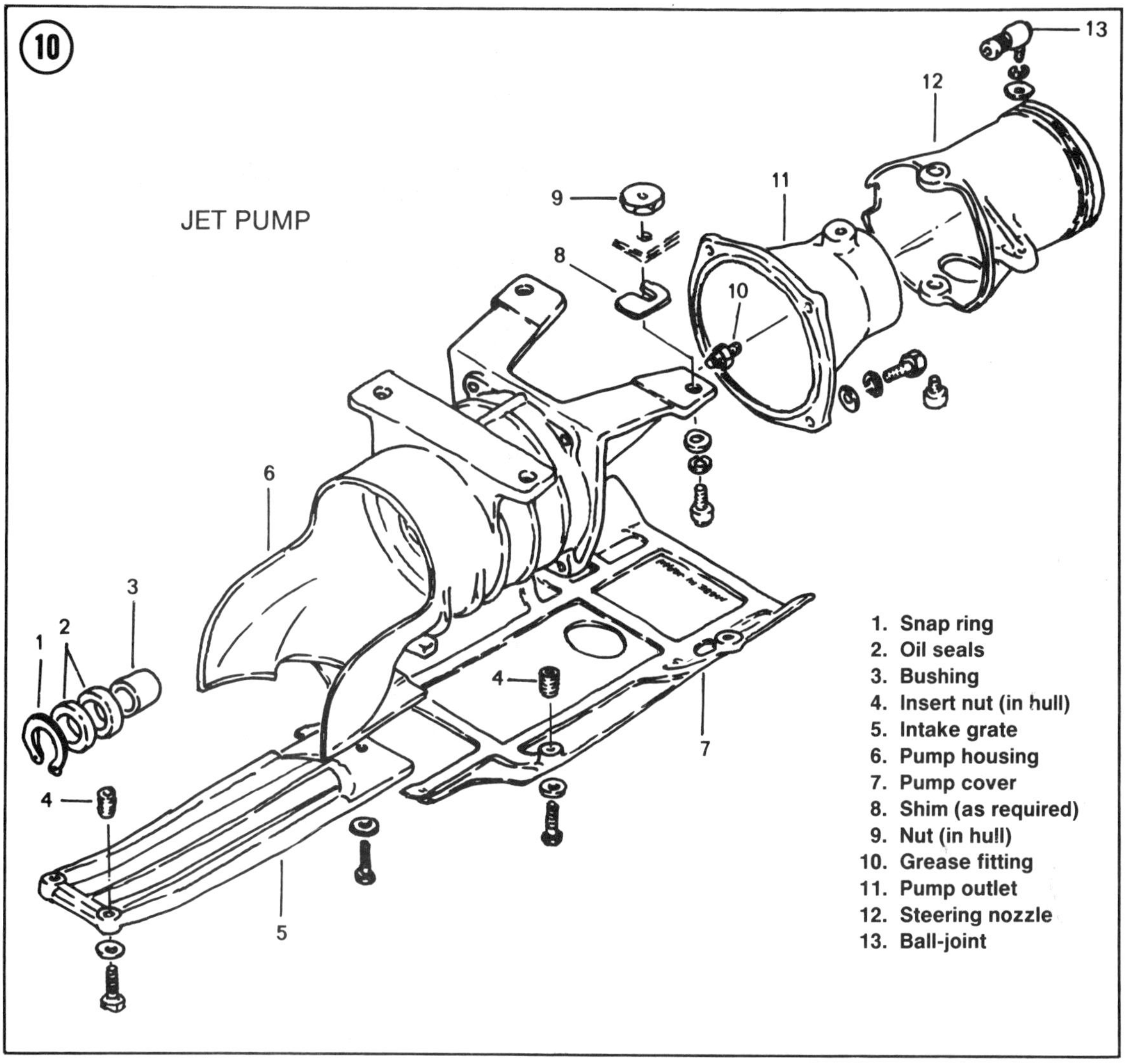

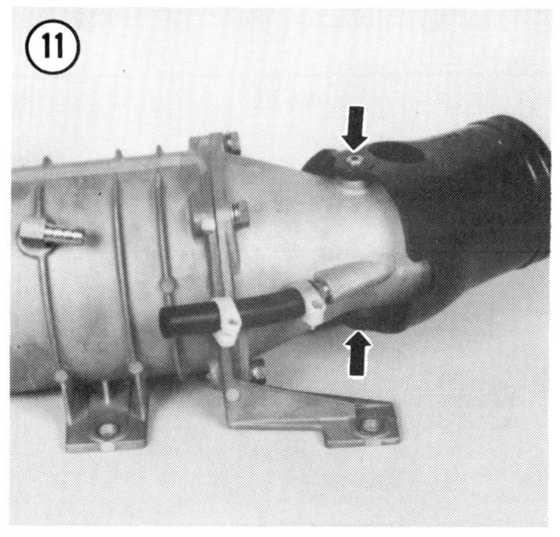

⑩

⑪

crescent wrench on the hex section of the impeller (**Figure 8**).

> *NOTE*
> *Kawasaki makes a drive shaft holding tool specifically for the Jet Ski (**Figure 9**), Part No. W56019-003.*

Pump Case Disassembly

See **Figure 10**.

> *NOTE*
> *Do not remove the seals and bushing in the jet pump unless you intend to install new ones. They will be damaged during removal.*

1. Remove the 2 Allen bolts out of the steering nozzle pivots and take off the steering nozzle (**Figure 11**).

2. Remove the 4 bolts that attach the pump outlet to the pump case (**Figure 12**) and tap the outlet free with a soft mallet.

Jet Pump/Impeller Inspection

Normal wear of the pump case and impeller can reduce jet pump thrust and top speed, even when the engine is running perfectly, but more often the problem is caused by obstructions in the pump or damaged pump case and impeller blades.

1. Check for nicks and gouges in the impeller blades and the pump case blades. If they are minor, they can be smoothed out with abrasive paper or carefully filed away. It is especially important for the blade edges to be smooth. If there is major damage to the impeller or pump case blades, replace the parts.

2. Measure the outside diameter (OD) of the impeller (**Figure 13**). If it is smaller than the limit in **Table 1** at the end of the chapter, replace the impeller.

3. Check the inside of the jet pump case for deep scratches and measure the inside diameter (ID) of the section that houses the impeller. If it is damaged or the diameter is larger than the limit in **Table 1**, replace the pump case.

4. Wash the bushing in the tail end with solvent (**Figure 14**) and check it for scratches and uneven wear. Measure the bushing's inside diameter (I D) and replace it if the diameter is larger than specified in **Table 1**.

Bushing and Seal Removal/Installation

> *CAUTION*
> *The bushing and seals will be damaged by removal. Do not remove them unless you intend to install new ones. If the bushing and/or seals are hard to remove or install, don't take a chance on expensive case damage. Have the work done by a Jet Ski dealer.*

1. Remove the snap ring from the jet pump case with snap ring pliers (**Figure 15**).
2. Pull the 2 grease seals out with a hook.
3. Heat the pump case to about 212° F (100° C) in an oven.

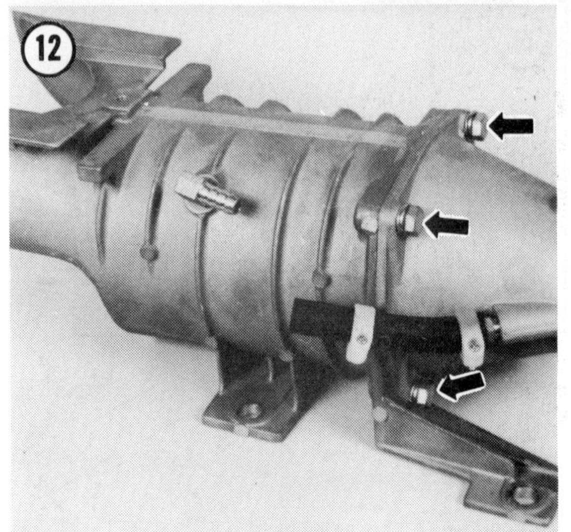

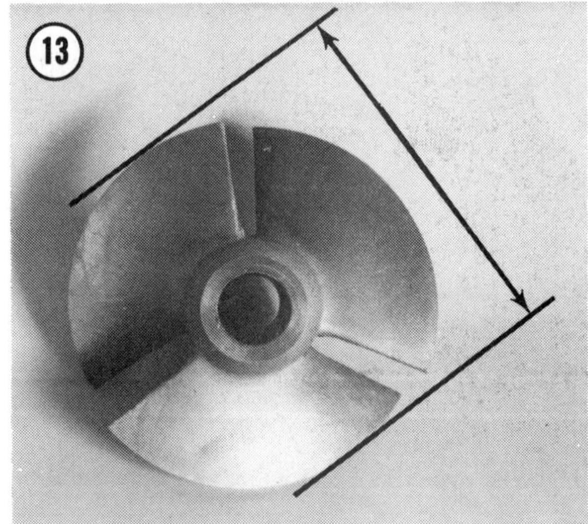

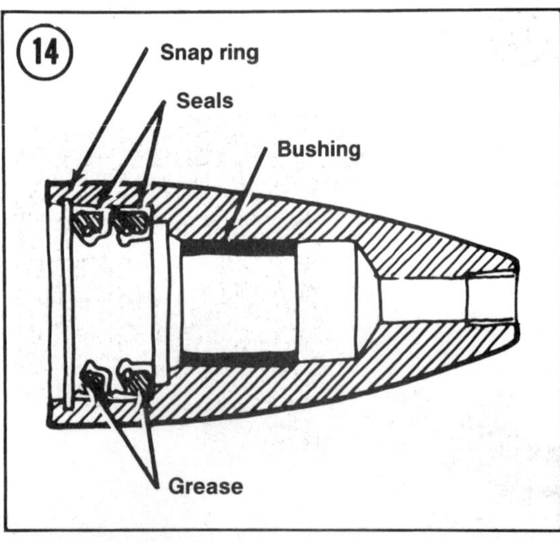

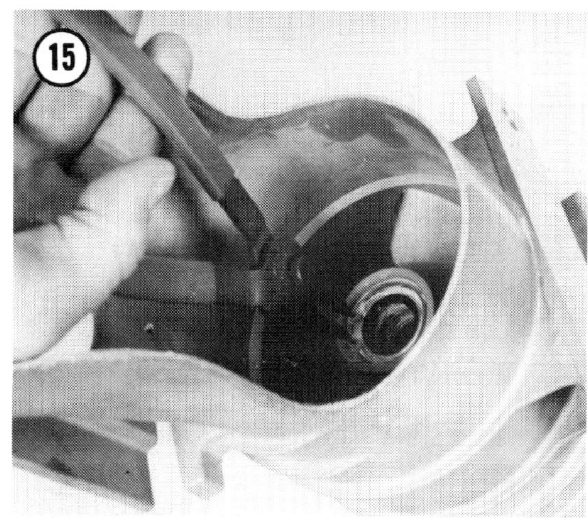

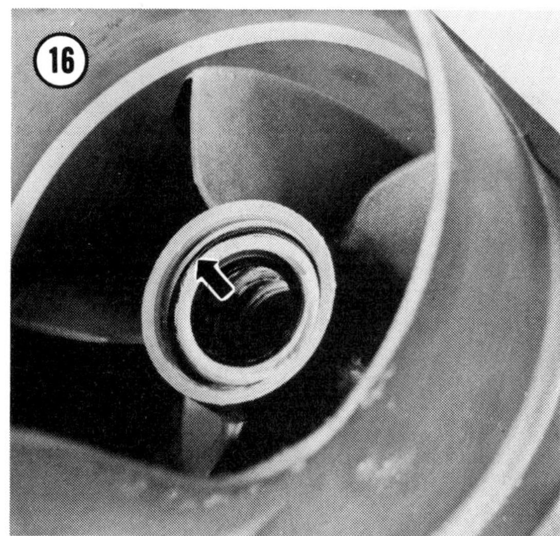

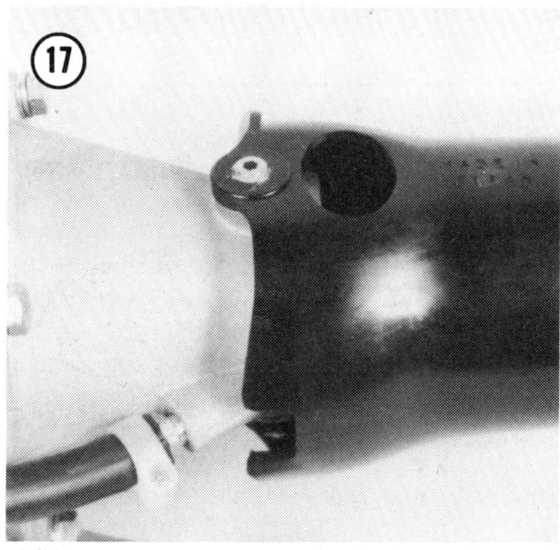

4. Insert a brass or aluminum rod into the tail end of the pump case and find the edge of the bushing (**Figure 14**). Move the rod around the bushing edge as you tap the end of the rod with a hammer until the bushing is forced out.

5. Place the new bushing in a freezer while reheating the jet pump case.

6. Grease the new bushing and push it into the pump case as far as it will go. If the bushing will not seat all the way into the pump case, do not try to hammer it in or you will probably damage the bushing; have the job done by a Jet Ski dealer with the proper bushing installation tool (Kawasaki part No. W56019-004).

7. Grease 2 new oil seals and install them with their open side facing the front of the Jet Ski (**Figure 14**). Butt a wrench socket of the same diameter as the seal against the seals and tap them in with a hammer until the face of the outer seal is just below the snap ring groove on the inside of the tail piece (**Figure 16**). Make sure that the seals are not cocked in the hole.

8. Install the snap ring, checking that it is fully seated in the case groove.

Pump Case Assembly

See **Figure 10**.

1. Lightly coat the mating surface of the jet pump outlet with silicone sealant such as GE RTV 108. Mount the pump outlet to the pump case with the 4 bolts, lockwashers and flat washers (**Figure 12**). Torque the bolts in a crisscross pattern to 12 ft.-lb. (1.6 mkg).

> *NOTE*
> *The hose fitting on the outlet must be on the same side as the one on the pump case (**Figure 12**).*

2. Fit the steering nozzle onto the pump case with its ball-joint on the side opposite the pump case water hose fittings (**Figure 17**). Install the 2 pivot bolts and tighten them securely. Check that the nozzle swings smoothly by hand.

Impeller/Jet Pump Installation

1. Grease the threaded end of the drive shaft, then hold the drive shaft steady and screw the impeller onto the drive shaft. Use a 32 mm

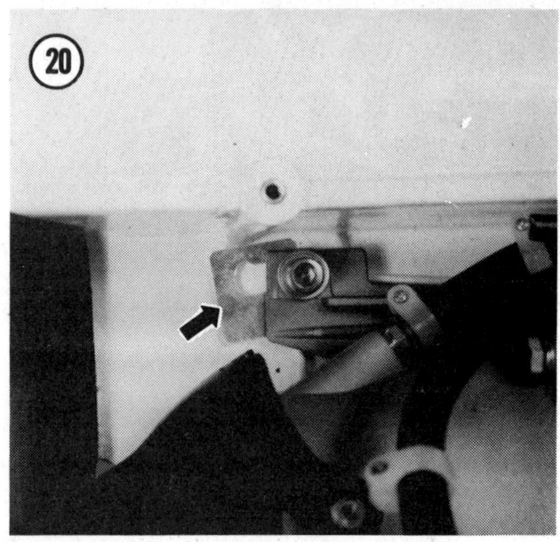

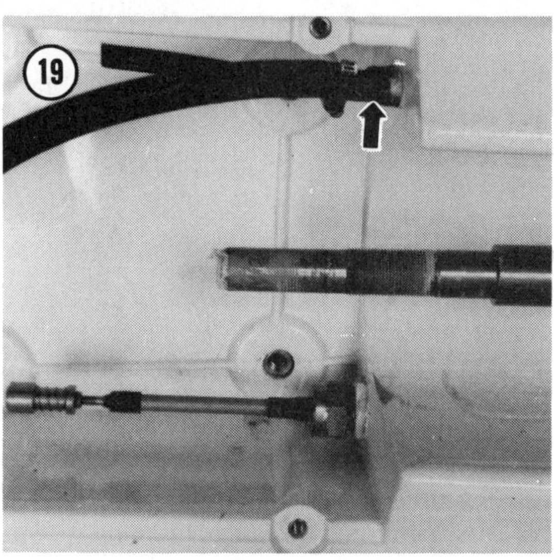

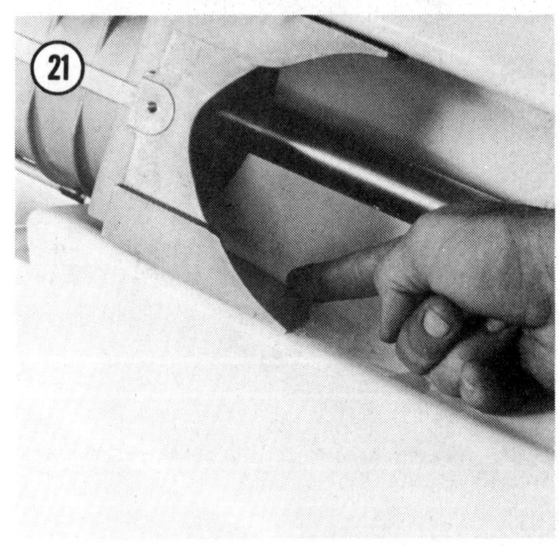

wrench or a large crescent wrench on the hex section of the impeller (**Figure 8**). Torque the impeller to 45 in.-lb. (0.5 mkg).

2. To prevent a hydraulic lock when installing the pump on the drive shaft, remove the grease fitting from the tail end of the pump case (**Figure 18**).

3. Check that the cooling intake and bilge outlet hoses are in position in the pump cavity (**Figure 19**).

4. Grease the end of the drive shaft lightly. Being careful not to damage the oil seals, gently slide the pump case over the shaft and the impeller.

5. Loosely install the 4 pump mounting bolts with flat washers and lockwashers.

6. Put the alignment shims back on the pump mounting bolts exactly the way they were originally installed (**Figure 20**).

7. Tighten the pump mounting bolts temporarily and check that there is an even gap of at least 0.004 in. (0.1 mm) all around the impeller circumference. If there is not, change shims on the pump mounting bolts as required to get an even gap all around the impeller.

8. When the clearance around the impeller is correct, torque the 4 mounting bolts to 2.2 ft.-lb. (16 mkg) and then check the gap around

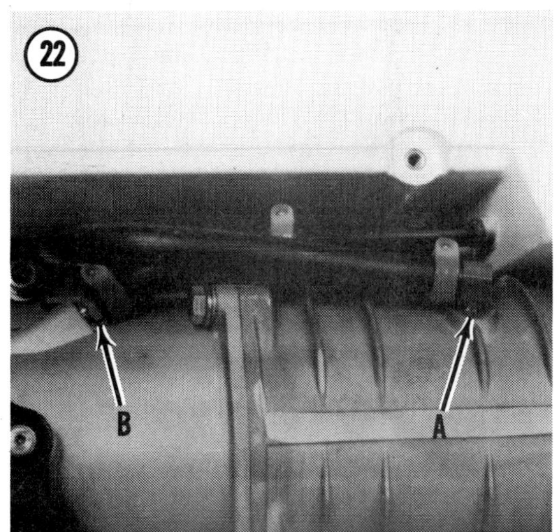

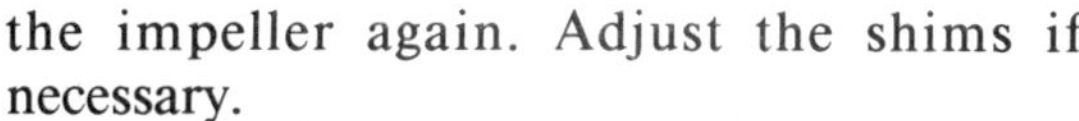

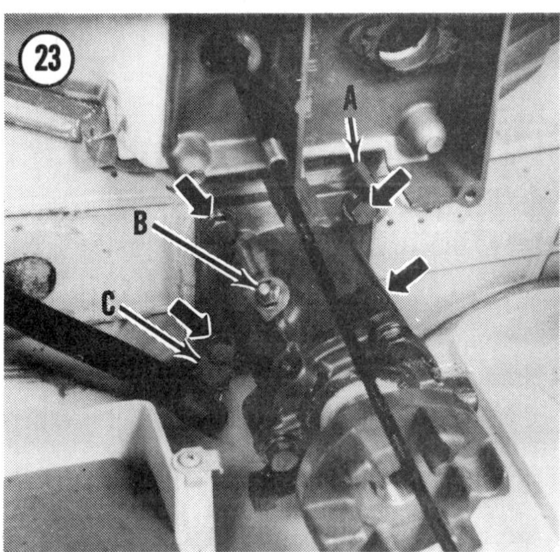

the impeller again. Adjust the shims if necessary.

9. Seal the gap between the hull and the edge of the pump intake area with silicone sealant such as GE RTV 108 (**Figure 21**). Be sure that all excess sealant is removed from inside the pump intake or it will cause water cavitation and reduced thrust.

10. Install the grease fitting in the pump outlet (**Figure 18**). Lubricate the bearing with waterproof bearing grease until resistance is felt.

11. Connect the steering cable at the nozzle.

12. Hook up the engine cooling and bilge drain hoses; the cooling supply hose goes to the fitting toward the front of the pump case (A, **Figure 22**) and the bilge hose goes to the fitting at the tail end of the pump (B). Tighten the hose clamps.

> *CAUTION*
> *If the hoses are connected incorrectly, the engine will get no cooling water and the engine compartment will fill with water.*

13. Pivot the steering nozzle to make sure there is no binding or pinching of the hoses.

14. Install the pump cover plate and torque its 4 bolts with washers to 7 ft.-lb. (1.0 mkg).

15. Install the intake grate and torque its 3 bolts with washers to 7 ft.-lb. (1.0 mkg).

16. Turn the Jet Ski upright and install the battery; see *Battery Installation* in Chapter Seven.

17. Connect the spark plug leads.

DRIVE SHAFT

The stainless steel drive shaft is supported by 2 ball bearings in the bearing box at the hull bulkhead and by the pump case bushing at the rear.

Grease fittings are provided at the bearing box and at the pump tail piece for periodic lubrication.

Drive Shaft Removal

1. Remove the engine; see *Engine Removal* in Chapter Four.

2. Remove the jet pump and impeller as described in this chapter.

3. Remove the 4 bearing box mounting bolts (**Figure 23**).

> *CAUTION*
> *Always keep any original factory-installed shims between the bearing box and the hull bulkhead (A, **Figure 23**). These shims affect alignment of the drive shaft with the jet pump as well as alignment with the engine.*

4. Loosen the bearing box by wiggling the rear end of the drive shaft back and forth to loosen the seal at the bulkhead.

5. Remove the bearing box and drive shaft from the hull (**Figure 24**).

Bearing Box Disassembly

See **Figure 25**.

1. If you are going to disassemble the bearing box, hold the drive shaft steady and unscrew the coupler half from the front end of the drive shaft (**Figure 26**).

2. Remove the 3 bearing box cover bolts (**Figure 27**) and tap the cover free with a soft mallet.

3. Remove any bearing shim(s) if installed between the cover and the bearing.

4. Wrap a cloth around the shaft to protect it and hold it in a vise. With a soft mallet, gently tap the bearing box toward the rear, off the bearings on the shaft (**Figure 28**).

CAUTION
Do not tighten the vise so much that you damage the drive shaft.

5. Wash the bearings in solvent, allow them to dry, then roll each bearing around by hand and check that it turns smoothly and quietly and has no rough spots. If any problem is found, the bearings must be replaced. Immediately after inspecting the bearings, lubricate them with a waterproof grease such as Valvoline X-All to prevent rusting.

6. Remove the bearings if desired. Since the bearings are installed with an interference fit, if possible heat the end of the shaft holding the bearings in an oven to about 212° F to aid bearing removal. Then, use a bearing puller to pull the bearings and sleeve off the shaft. You may be able to remove the bearings by slamming the front end of the heated drive shaft down on a piece of wood.

CAUTION
If bearings and/or seals are hard to remove or install, don't take a chance on expensive damage. Have the work done by a Jet Ski dealer.

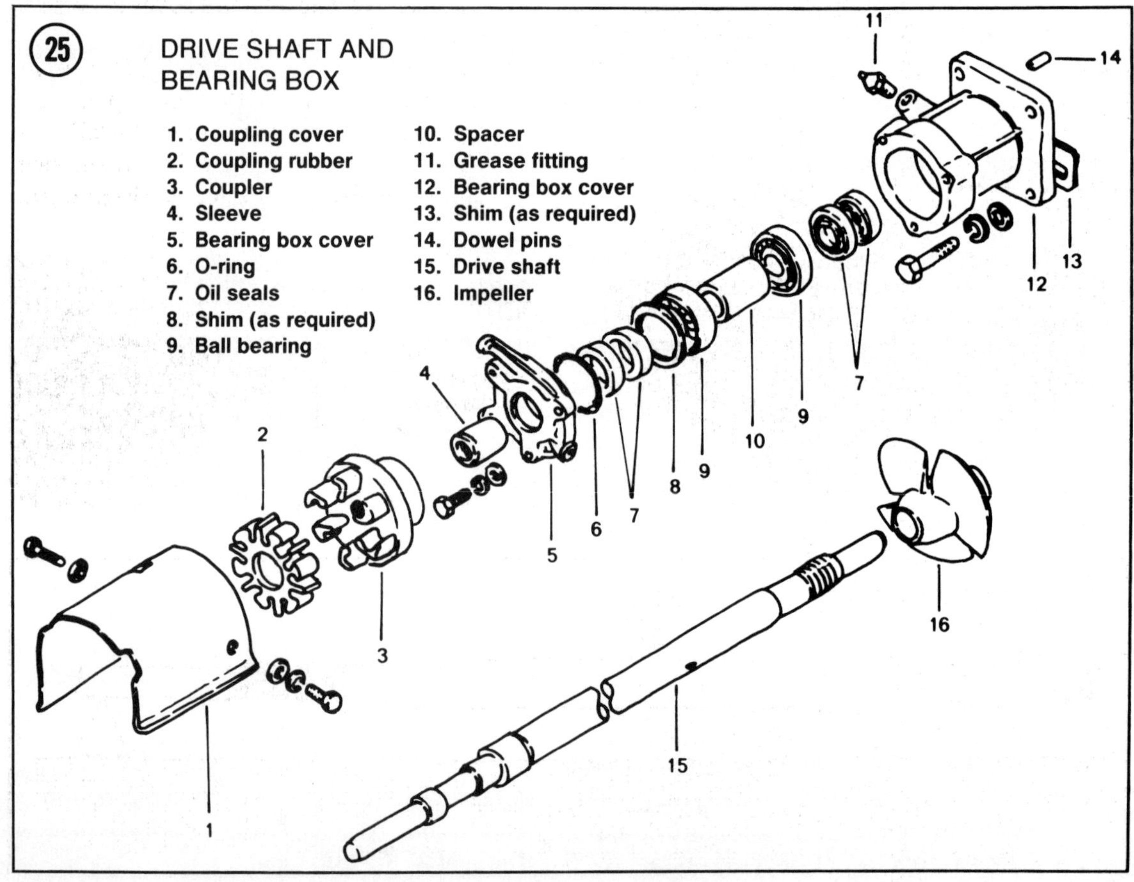

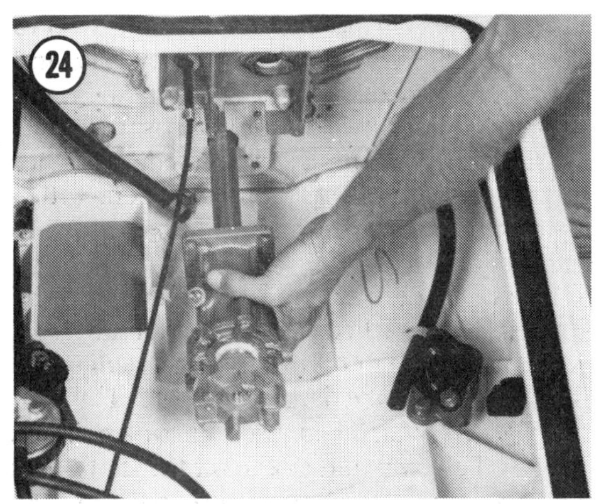

7. If the 2 oil seals in the bearing box cover are to be replaced, pry them out with a screwdriver.

Drive Shaft/Bearing Box Inspection

1. Check the drive shaft runout; refer to **Figure 29**. Mount a dial gauge at each point shown while slowly turning the drive shaft. The runout is the difference between the highest and lowest dial gauge reading. Replace the shaft if the runout is greater than the limit specified in **Table 1**.

2. At the impeller (rear) end of the drive shaft, measure the outside diameter (OD) of the shaft where it runs in the jet pump bushing. Replace the shaft if the measurement is less than the limit specified in **Table 1**.

Bearing Box Assembly

See **Figure 25**.

1. If the oil seals were removed from the bearing box and cover:

   a. Heat the bearing box and cover in an oven to about 212° F (100° C).

   b. Grease 4 new oil seals. Install 2 of them in the bearing box with their open side facing the rear of the Jet Ski. Install 2 of them in the cover with their open side facing the front of the Jet Ski (**Figure 30**).

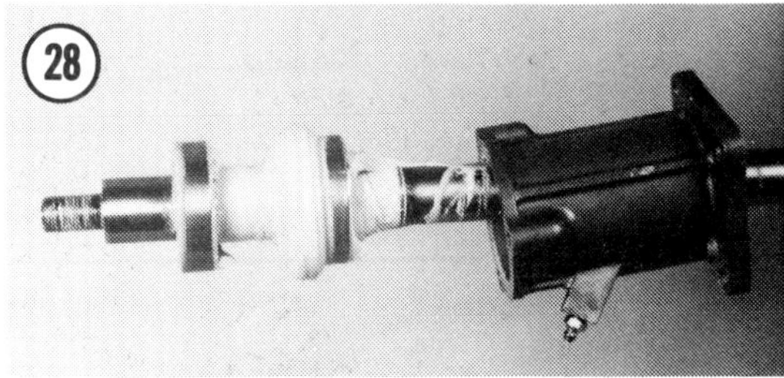

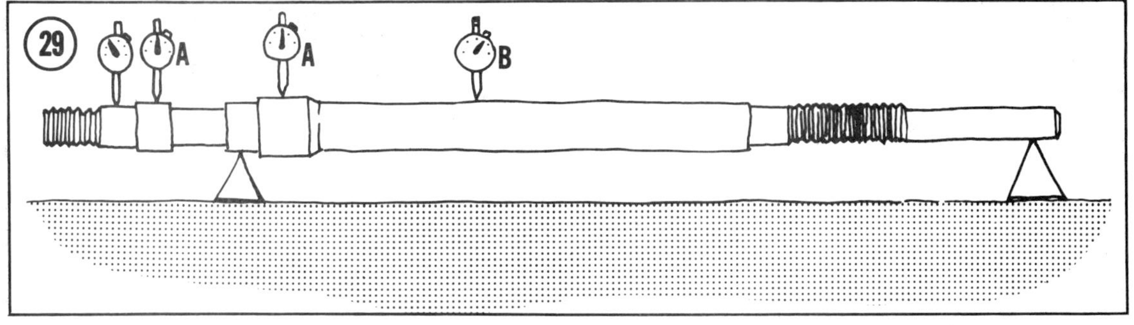

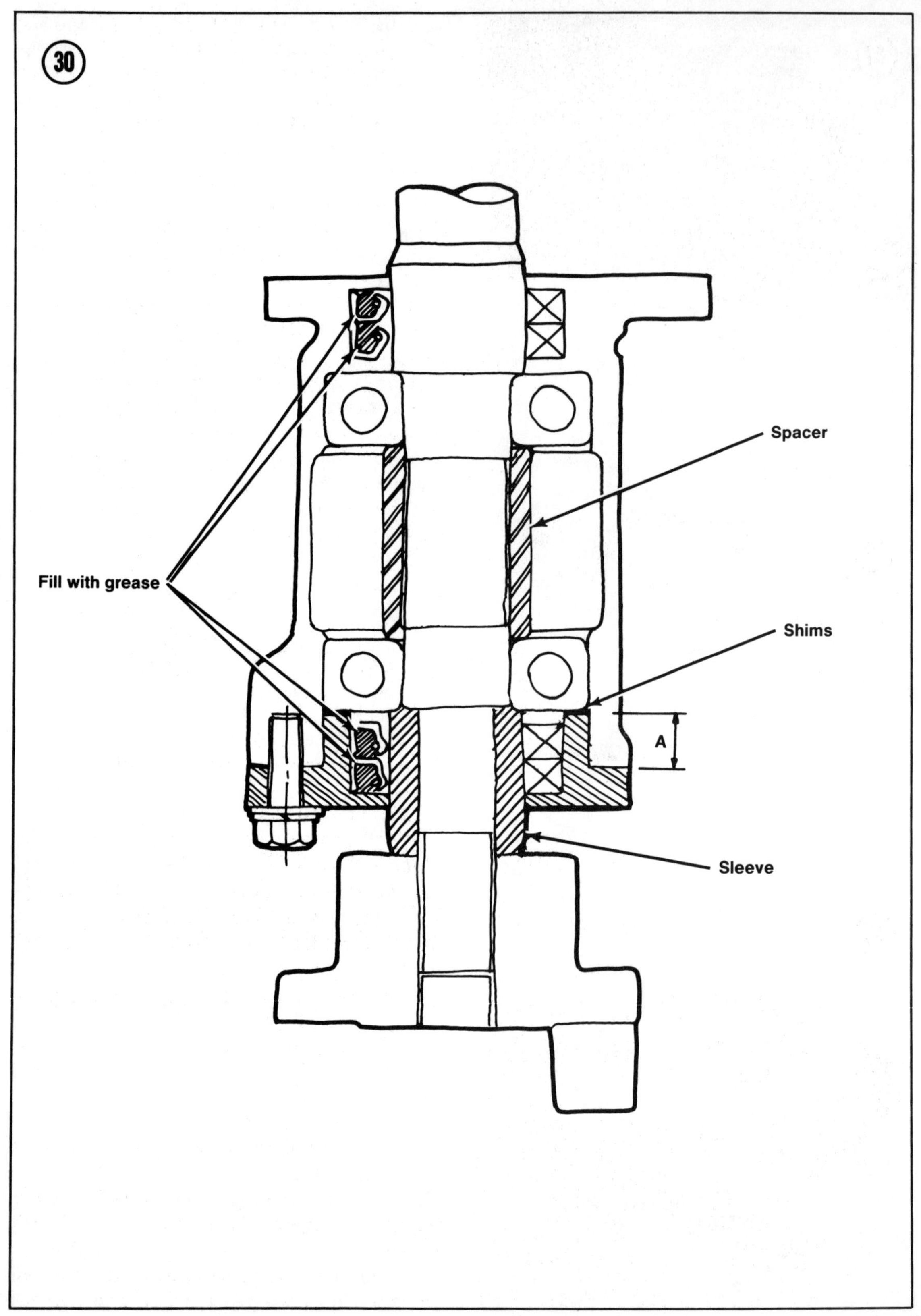
30
Fill with grease
Spacer
Shims
A
Sleeve

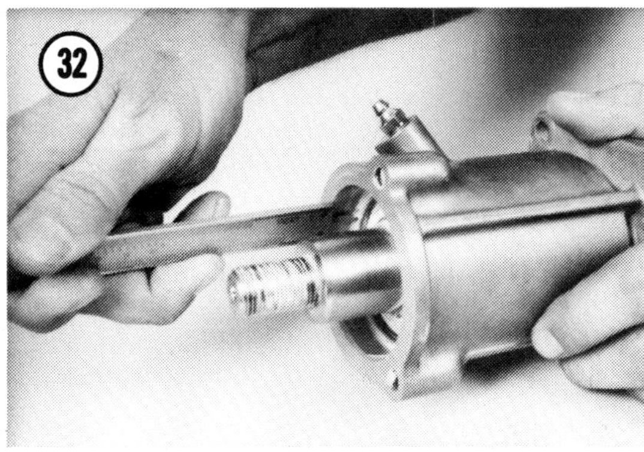

Butt a wrench socket of the same diameter as the seal against the seals and tap them in with a hammer until seals "bottom out" in the bearing box and the cover. Make sure that the seals are not cocked in the hole.

2. Fill the cavities of the seals with grease.

3. Heat the bearings in an oven to about 212° F (100° C). Tap the rear bearing into place with a socket or pipe of the same diameter as the bearing's outer race.

4. Install the spacer against the rear bearing and tap the front bearing into place against the spacer (**Figure 30**).

5. Push the front sleeve onto the drive shaft.

6. Lubricate the bearings thoroughly with a waterproof grease such as Valvoline X-All.

7. Wrap a cloth around the shaft to protect it and hold it in a vise. With a soft mallet, gently tap the bearing box toward the front, over bearings on the shaft.

> *CAUTION*
> *Do not tighten the vise so much that you damage the drive shaft. Do not strike the bearings; be sure they are not cocked as they enter the holder.*

8. If no bearings have been replaced, install the original shims outside the outer bearing (**Figure 31**).

9. If any bearing has been replaced, calculate which shims are required between the outer bearing and the box cover. With the bearings fully seated in the box, measure the distance from the end face of the box to the outer face of the bearing as shown in **Figure 32**:

   a. If the distance is 0.508-0.514 in. (12.9-13.05 mm), no shim is required.

   b. If the distance is 0.514-0.520 in. (13.05-13.2 mm), use a 0.006 in. (0.15 mm) shim.

   c. If the distance is 0.520-0.524 in. (13.2-13.32 mm), install a 0.012 in. (0.30 mm) shim.

10. Check that the end cover O-ring is in good condition (**Figure 33**) and lubricate it with grease.

11. Coat the mating surfaces of the bearing box and the end cover with a silicone sealant

such as GE RTV 108 and install the end cover on the box as shown in **Figure 27**.

12. Install the 3 bearing box cover bolts with lockwashers and flatwashers and torque them to 12 ft.-lb. (1.6 mkg).

13. Using a hand grease gun, pack the bearing box with grease until resistance is felt.

14. Hold the drive shaft steady and grease the threads at the front. Install the coupler half and torque to 45 in.-lb. (0.5 mkg).

NOTE
Be careful not to tighten the impeller too much. Normal engine rotation tends to tighten the impeller even more and too much initial tightening may make impeller removal very difficult.

Drive Shaft Installation

1. Coat the mounting surface of the bearing box with silicone sealant such as GE RTV 108 and slide the holder and drive shaft into position in the hull. The dowel pins in the back of the box (**Figure 34**) fit into holes in the bulkhead. The grease fitting must be on the upper right side of the box (B, **Figure 23**).

2. Loosely install the 4 bearing box bolts with their lockwashers and flat washers. The lower right bolt also holds the bilge filter clamp (C, **Figure 23**).

3. Reinstall any shims in the same location they were in at disassembly (A, **Figure 23**). Torque the bolts to 12 ft.-lb. (1.6 mkg).

CAUTION
Always keep the original factory-installed shims between the bearing box and the hull bulkhead. These shims affect alignment of the drive shaft with the jet pump as well as alignment with the crankshaft.

4. Install the impeller and jet pump as described in this chapter.

5. Install the coupling rubber.

6. Install the engine as described in *Engine Installation* in Chapter Four.

Table 1   JS400/440 DRIVE TRAIN WEAR LIMITS

Item	Wear Limit	Standard
Drive shaft OD (at bearings)	0.783 in. (19.9 mm)	
Drive shaft runout		
At A, Figure 29	0.004 in. (0.1 mm)	
At B, Figure 29	0.020 in. (0.5 mm)	
Impeller OD	4.724 in. (120 mm)	4.744 in. (120.05 mm)
Impeller/pump clearance	0.034 in. (0.87 mm)	0.014-0.018 in. (0.35-0.45 mm)
Jet pump housing ID	4.831 in. (122.7 mm)	4.793 in. (121.75 mm)
Jet pump bushing ID	0.795 in. (20.2 mm)	
Jet pump bushing/drive shaft clearance		0.001-0.005 in. (0.025-0.137 mm)

Table 2   JS400/440 DRIVE TRAIN TORQUES

	Ft.-lb.	Mkg
Bearing box cover bolts	12	(1.6)
Bearing box mounting bolts	12	(1.6)
Coupler	20	(2.7)
Handle pole bracket bolts	16	(2.2)
Handle pole pivot bolt	10	(1.4)
Handle pole pivot nut	25	(3.5)
Impeller	45 in.-lb.	(0.5)
Intake grate bolts	7	(1.0)
Jet pump cover bolts	7	(1.0)
Jet pump mounting bolts	16	(2.2)
Jet pump outlet mounting bolts	12	(1.6)

5

NOTE: If you own a 1982 or 1983 model, first check the Supplement at the back of the book for any new service information.

CHAPTER SIX

FUEL AND EXHAUST SYSTEMS

This chapter includes removal and repair procedures for the carburetor, fuel tank and exhaust system. See Chapter Three for idle speed and mixture adjustment.

CARBURETOR OPERATION

The following paragraphs explain the basic operation of the carburetor, which may be helpful in troubleshooting a problem you suspect is caused by carburetion.

The carburetor's purpose is to supply and atomize fuel and mix it in correct proportions with air that is drawn in through the air intake. The Jet Ski uses a diaphragm regulated carburetor. **Figure 1** is a schematic drawing of the carburetor. This type of carburetor has a rotating butterfly throttle valve and an engine vacuum-controlled diaphragm that controls the fuel inlet needle. The regulator diaphragm and its fuel reservoir take the place of the float bowl and float used in other types of carburetors. Both the idle mixture and the high-speed mixture are adjustable on this carburetor.

Since the Jet Ski fuel tank is positioned lower than the carburetor, a fuel pump is required. The fuel pump is attached to the side of the carburetor. It is powered by crankcase pressure pulses.

Fuel Pump

See **Figure 1**. The side of the fuel pump diaphragm toward the carburetor bore is exposed to crankcase pressure pulses, conducted by the external pulse line. As the diaphragm moves back and forth, fuel is drawn from the fuel line through a filter screen, through 2 reed valves and into the fuel reservoir chamber.

Inlet Needle

See **Figure 1**. To assure an adequate supply of fuel, the carburetor is equipped with an inlet needle valve through which fuel flows from the carburetor's fuel reservoir into the regulator chamber. Inside the chamber is a flow regulator diaphragm that contacts one end of a spring-loaded control arm. The other end of the control arm contacts the inlet needle.

The side of the regulator diaphragm toward the carburetor is exposed to engine intake vacuum through the low speed fuel passage. The other side of the diaphragm is vented to atmospheric pressure. When air flow and engine intake vacuum are low, the vacuum pulls the regulator diaphragm in slightly toward the carburetor; the diaphragm pushes on one end of the inlet control arm, compressing the control spring a little and

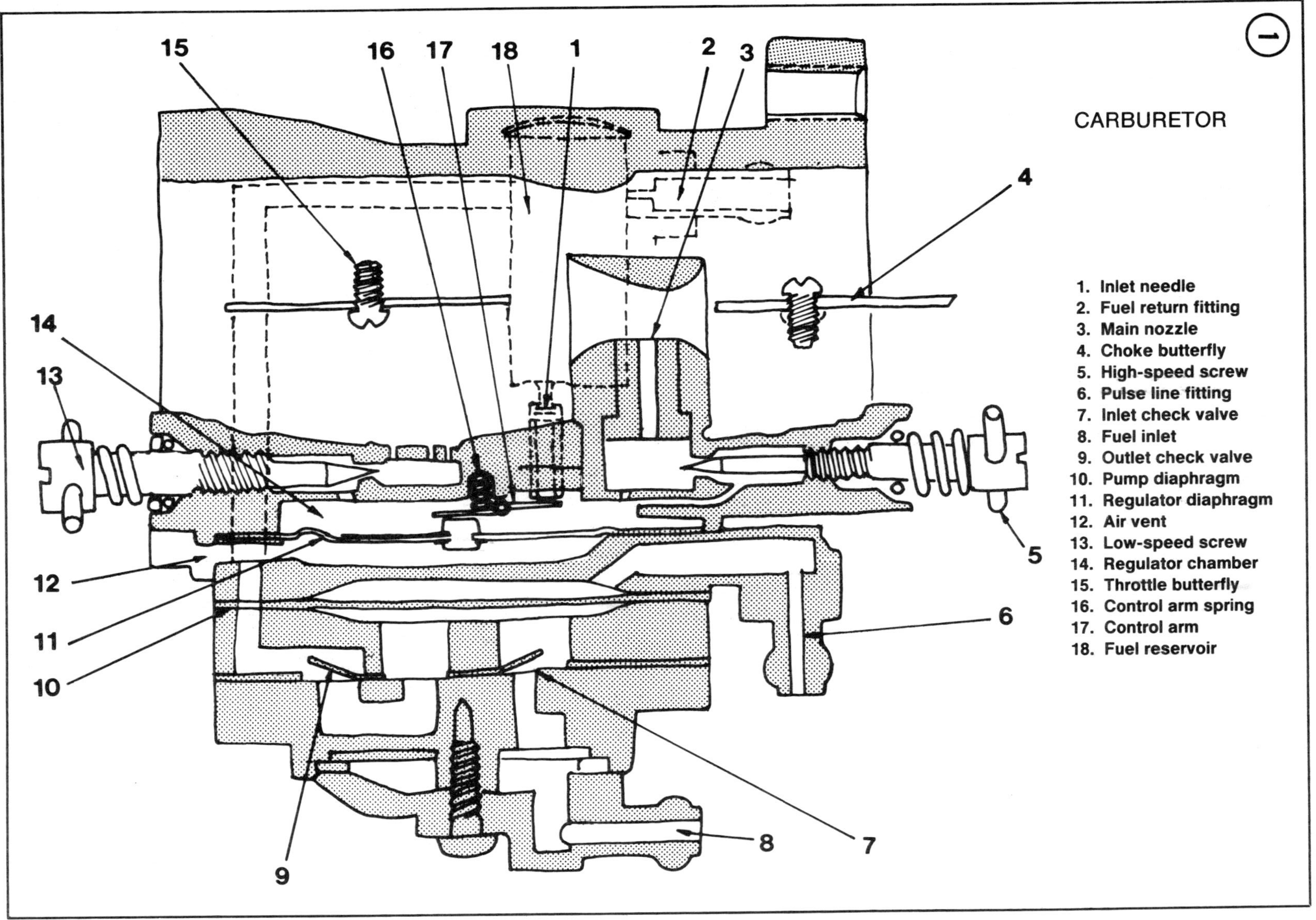
CARBURETOR

1. Inlet needle
2. Fuel return fitting
3. Main nozzle
4. Choke butterfly
5. High-speed screw
6. Pulse line fitting
7. Inlet check valve
8. Fuel inlet
9. Outlet check valve
10. Pump diaphragm
11. Regulator diaphragm
12. Air vent
13. Low-speed screw
14. Regulator chamber
15. Throttle butterfly
16. Control arm spring
17. Control arm
18. Fuel reservoir

6

opening the inlet needle just enough to allow an adequate fuel flow. As air flow and engine intake vacuum rise, the vacuum pulls the diaphragm closer to the carburetor, pivoting the control arm more and opening the inlet needle further to allow more fuel to enter the carburetor bore.

Because the fuel flow is regulated by a diaphragm that balances intake vacuum against atmospheric pressure, this carburetor is less sensitive to changes in altitude than most other types of carburetors. The carburetor also operates well when it is tilted at an angle.

Low-speed Circuit

See **Figure 2**. At small throttle openings (from idle to about 1/5 throttle), a small amount of fuel is siphoned through the opening around the tip of the low-speed screw by suction from air flowing past the throttle valve. The size of the opening around the low-speed screw can be adjusted by turning the screw in or out, allowing less or more fuel to mix with a given air flow.

The bypass ports allow air to mix with the fuel before it enters the carburetor bore at idle. As the throttle opens, fuel flows out of the bypass ports into the carburetor bore.

High-speed Circuit

See **Figure 3**. At large throttle openings (from about 1/5 throttle to full throttle) air flowing through the high-speed venturi siphons a large amount of fuel through the passage from the regulator chamber directly to the high-speed chamber. Fuel is also siphoned through the opening around the tip of the high-speed screw. The size of the opening around the high-speed screw can be adjusted by turning the screw in or out, allowing less or more fuel to mix with a given air flow.

The high-speed fuel flow will not be less than that allowed by the passage from the regulator chamber directly to the high-speed chamber, but it can be increased with the high-speed screw. In this way the passage from the regulator chamber to the high-speed chamber acts as a minimum "jet," preventing an extremely lean high-speed mixture.

The passage from the regulator chamber to the high-speed chamber has a check valve that keeps the high-speed chamber from draining back into the regulator chamber when the throttle is closed. This prevents hesitation when the throttle is next opened.

Choke

See **Figure 1**. The choke is a rotating butterfly valve. When the choke valve closes the carburetor opening it causes a very high vacuum in the carburetor bore. A large quantity of fuel flows through both the high- and low-speed fuel passages to mix with the small amount of air coming through the carburetor. This provides a very rich mixture for cold starting.

CARBURETOR TROUBLESHOOTING

If the mixture is too lean at any or all throttle settings, the engine may overheat. It may stutter at high rpm. The performance (acceleration and top speed) will fall off. You may be able to confirm this by checking the spark plugs. If the mixture is too lean across the rpm scale, the spark plugs will be white and their electrodes may be rounded. While riding the Jet Ski, pull the choke knob out to see if the performance improves with what would normally be an overrich mixture. If so, the mixture is too lean.

If the mixture is too rich at any or all throttle settings, the engine may be sluggish and blubbery. It may generate black exhaust smoke. It may perform best while still cold. If the mixture is too rich across the rpm scale, the spark plugs may be black and sooty.

Diagnosing the Problem

The fact that the mixture being burned is too rich or too lean does not necessarily indicate that the carburetion is at fault. The engine may as easily have an ignition or compression problem.

If the mixture cannot be corrected with the mixture adjustment screws, check the obvious fuel system components. For example, if the mixture is too rich, check that the choke butterfly valve is fully open. If the mixture is too lean, check the sediment bowl filter and the

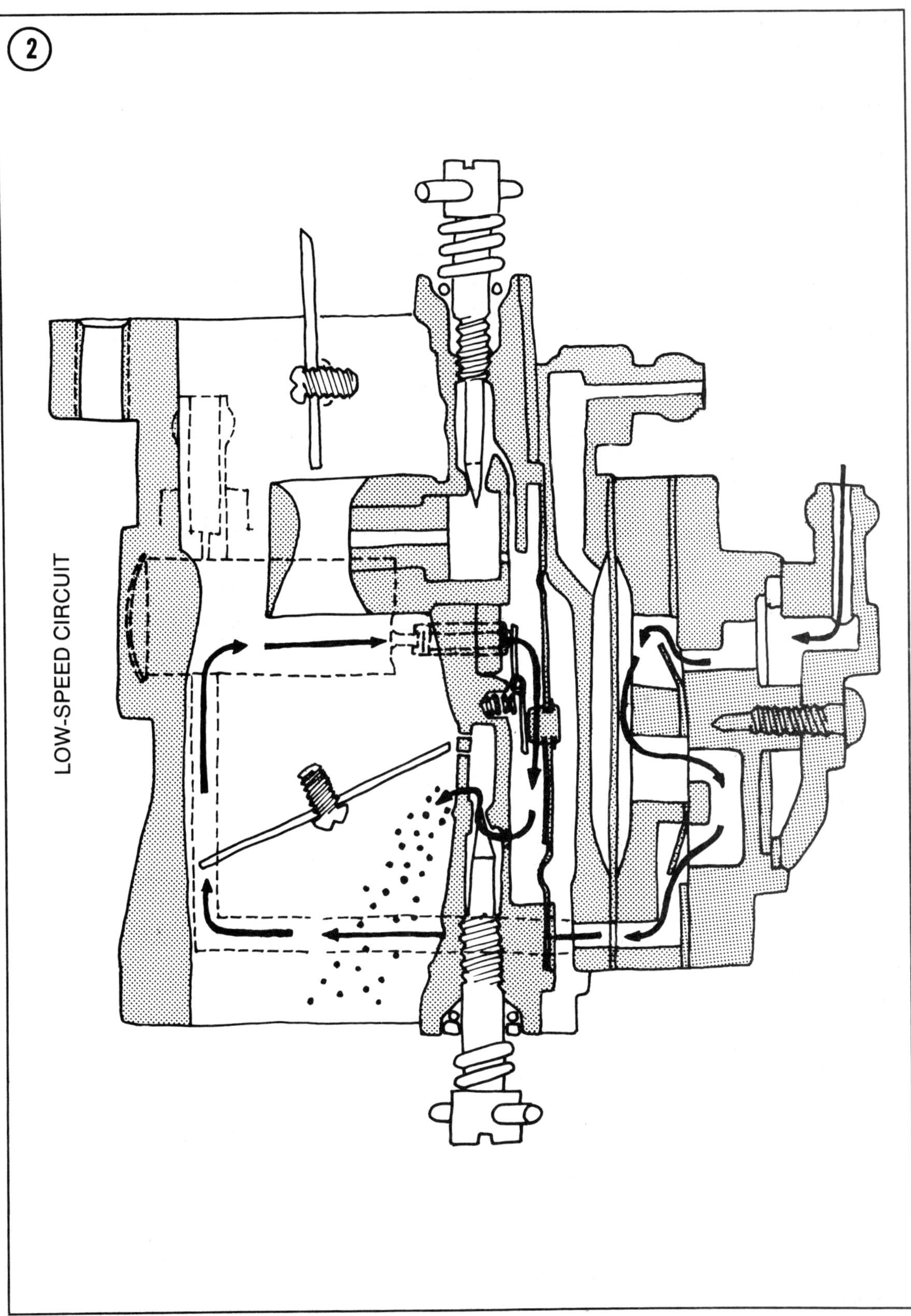
2
LOW-SPEED CIRCUIT

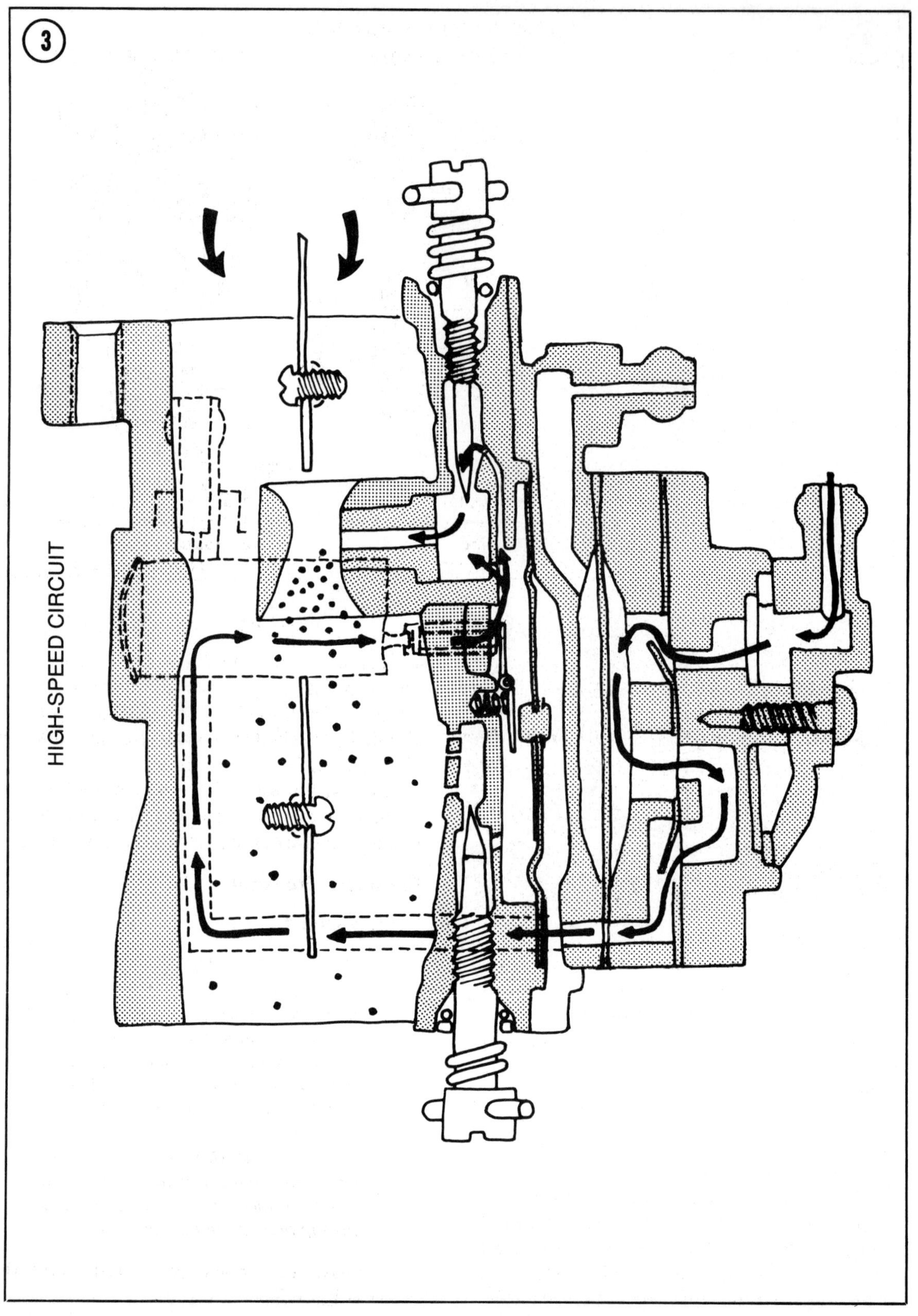
3
HIGH-SPEED CIRCUIT

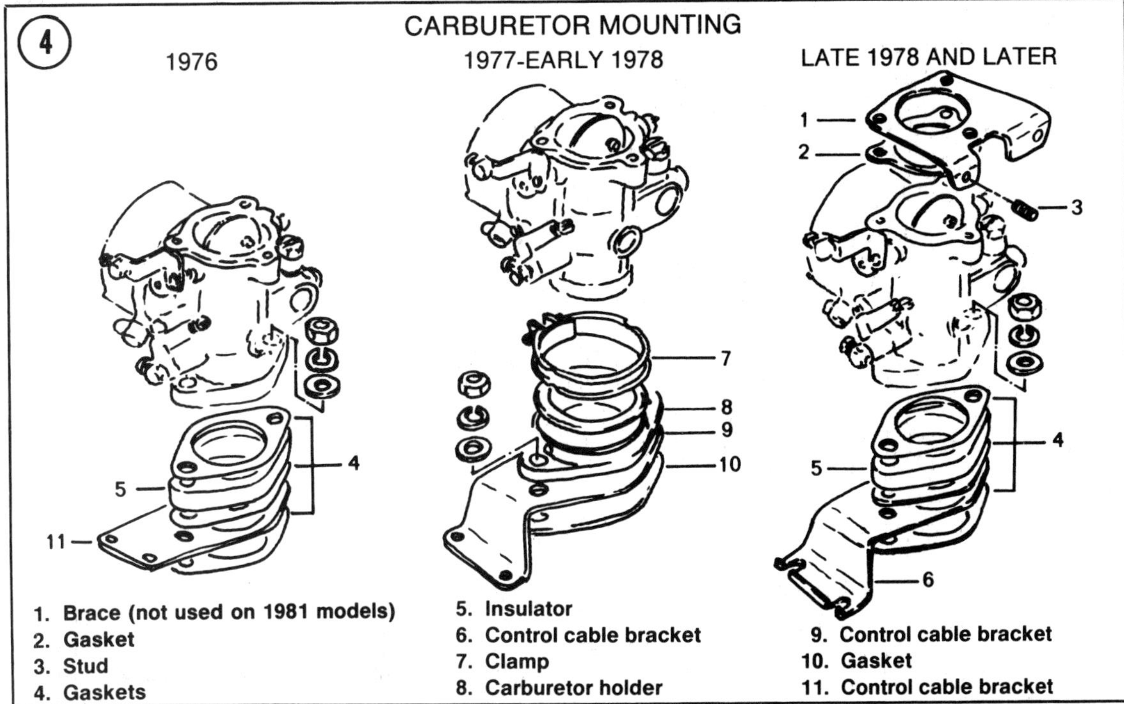

4

1. Brace (not used on 1981 models)
2. Gasket
3. Stud
4. Gaskets
5. Insulator
6. Control cable bracket
7. Clamp
8. Carburetor holder
9. Control cable bracket
10. Gasket
11. Control cable bracket

fuel lines for blockage; also check for air leakage at the sediment bowl or carburetor/intake manifold junction.

Dirt in the fuel may lodge in the inlet needle and cause an overrich mixture. As a temporary measure, tap the carburetor lightly to dislodge the dirt. Clean the fuel tank, fuel valve, fuel lines and carburetor at the first opportunity should this occur.

Before taking apart the carburetor, you should first check out the spark plugs and ignition timing and the cylinder compression. If none of the possible troubles listed above exist, disassemble and inspect the carburetor.

CARBURETOR SERVICE

Carburetor overhaul intervals depend on type and frequency of use. A carburetor on a Jet Ski that is used weekly in rigorous competition should be checked frequently to ensure that it is always in top working order.

Slight variations exist among models so it is important to pay particular attention to the location and order of parts during disassembly.

Carburetor Removal

See **Figure 4**.

WARNING
Some fuel may spill during these procedures. Work in a well-ventilated area at least 50 feet from any sparks or flames, including gas appliance pilot lights. Do not smoke in the area. Keep a BC rated fire extinguisher handy.

WARNING
Before disconnecting any fuel lines, loosen the fuel filler cap to relieve any built-up pressure in the fuel tank.

1. Remove the intake cover bolts and the cover (**Figure 5**).

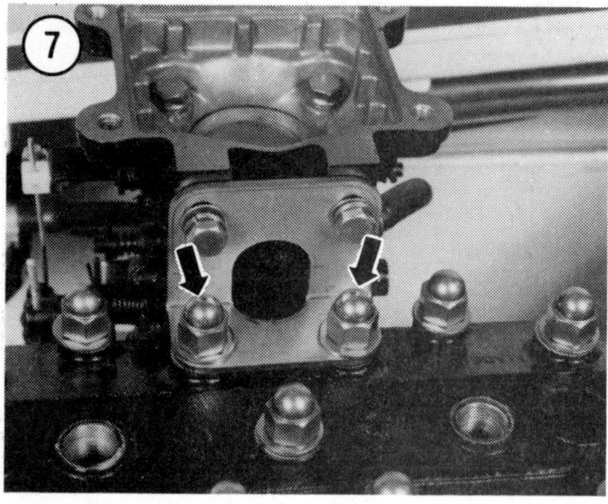

2. *On 1981 and later models* : Remove the flame arrestor element (**Figure 6**). Handle the element carefully to prevent damage.

3. *On 1978 and later models* : Remove the cylinder head nuts holding the carburetor brace to the cylinder head (**Figure 7**).

4. Remove the fuel tank outlet hose assembly from the tank to keep fuel from siphoning into the engine compartment.

5. Disconnect the fuel lines at the carburetor (**Figure 8**).

6. Disconnect the crankcase pulse line at the carburetor (A, **Figure 9**).

7. Loosen the control cable set screws (B, **Figure 9**) and pull the inner cables out of their fittings.

8. *On 1976, 1978 and later models* : Remove the carburetor base flange nuts (**Figure 4**) and remove the carburetor.

9. *On 1977 models* : Loosen the carburetor clamp screw and remove the carburetor (**Figure 4**).

10. After the carburetor has been removed, pack the carburetor holder opening with a clean rag to keep dirt and parts from falling into the intake manifold.

Flame Arrestor Removal/Installation (1976-1980 Models)

See **Figure 10A** or **Figure 10B**.

1. Remove the intake cover bolts, cover and flame arrestor plate.

2. Carefully remove the 4 corrugated springs from the sides of the flame arrestor element. Remove the flame arrestor element.

3. When installing the flame arrestor on 1976 models, tighten the intake cover bolts until the bolt head bottoms against the collar inside the rubber damper.

Flame Arrestor Removal/Installation (1981 Models)

Remove the intake cover bolts, cover and flame arrestor. See **Figure 11**. Install by reversing these steps.

10 A   FLAME ARRESTOR (1977-1980)

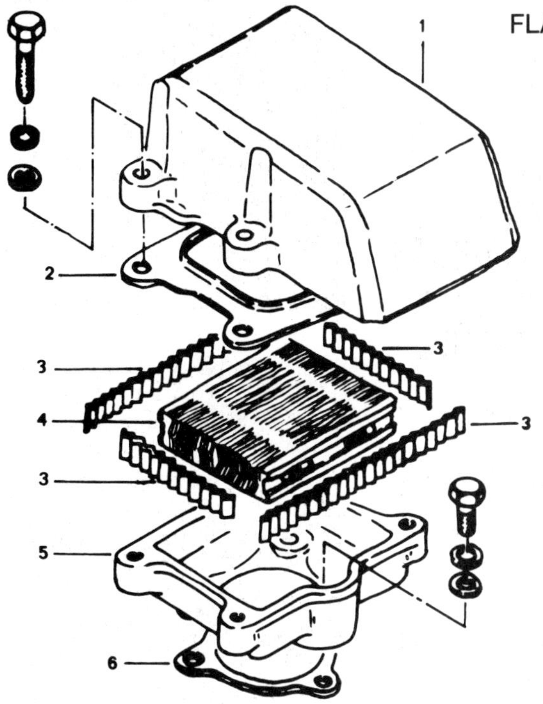

1. Intake cover
2. Plate
3. Spring
4. Flame arrestor
5. Flame arrestor holder
6. Gasket

10 B   FLAME ARRESTOR (1976)

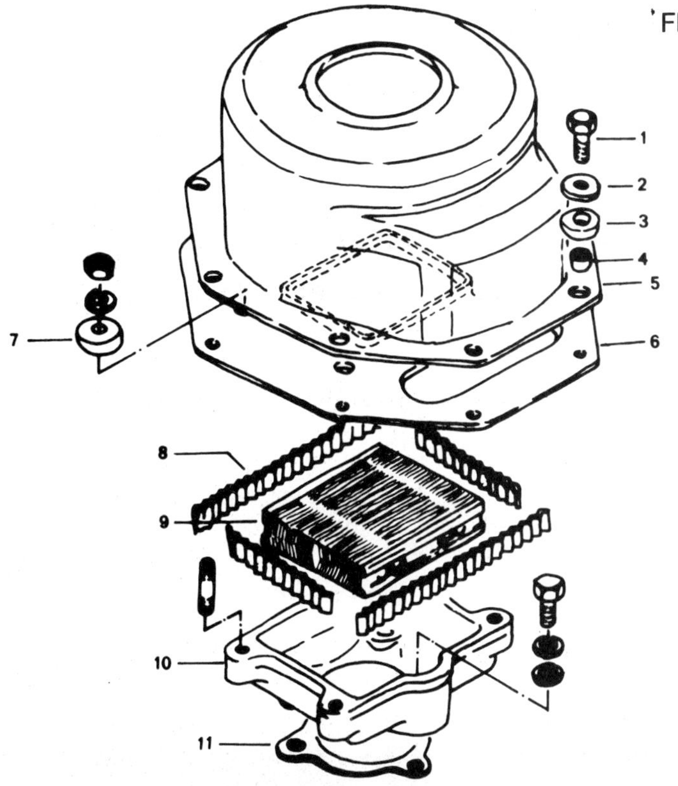

1. Bolt
2. Washer
3. Rubber damper
4. Collar
5. Intake cover
6. Flame arrestor plate
7. Plate washer
8. Spring
9. Flame arrestor
10. Flame arrestor holder
11. Gasket

Fuel Pump Disassembly

The fuel pump can be disassembled without removing the carburetor from the engine.

NOTE
Do not disassemble the fuel pump body unless necessary. There are many gaskets that should be replaced whenever the fuel pump is disassembled. Get replacement gaskets before you take the fuel pump apart.

1. Remove the center screw securing the fuel fitting to the fuel pump and carefully take off the cover and the gasket underneath it (A, **Figure 12**). There is also a filter screen on 1976-1980 models.
2. Remove the 6 screws that hold the fuel pump to the carburetor (B, **Figure 12**) and pry the pump assembly off of the carburetor (**Figure 13**).
3. Gently separate the pump assembly into individual parts: 3 body castings, 4 gaskets and 3 diaphragms. Since the assembly may be stuck together, take special care to avoid damaging the diaphragms and castings.

CAUTION
The diaphragms are delicate. Handle them carefully and avoid setting them on rough or dirty surfaces.

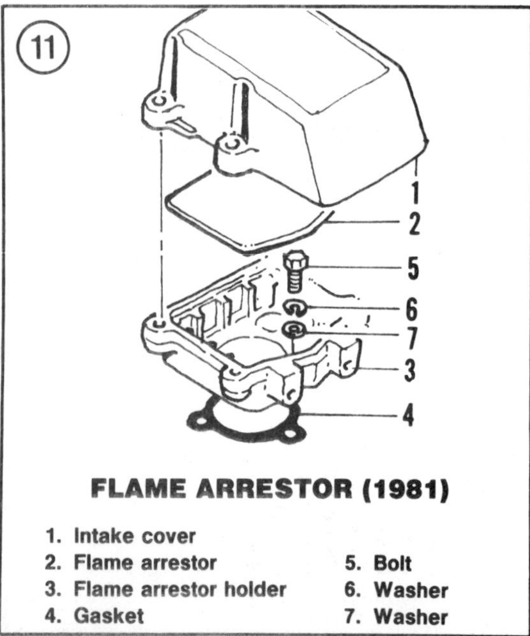

FLAME ARRESTOR (1981)

1. Intake cover
2. Flame arrestor
3. Flame arrestor holder
4. Gasket
5. Bolt
6. Washer
7. Washer

Carburetor Body Disassembly

See **Figure 14**.

1. Remove the fuel pump as described in this chapter.
2. Remove the screw that holds the carburetor's control arm pivot pin (A, **Figure 15**) and remove the arm, its pin and spring.
3. Turn the carburetor over so the inlet needle falls out. Remove the seat and its gasket (A,

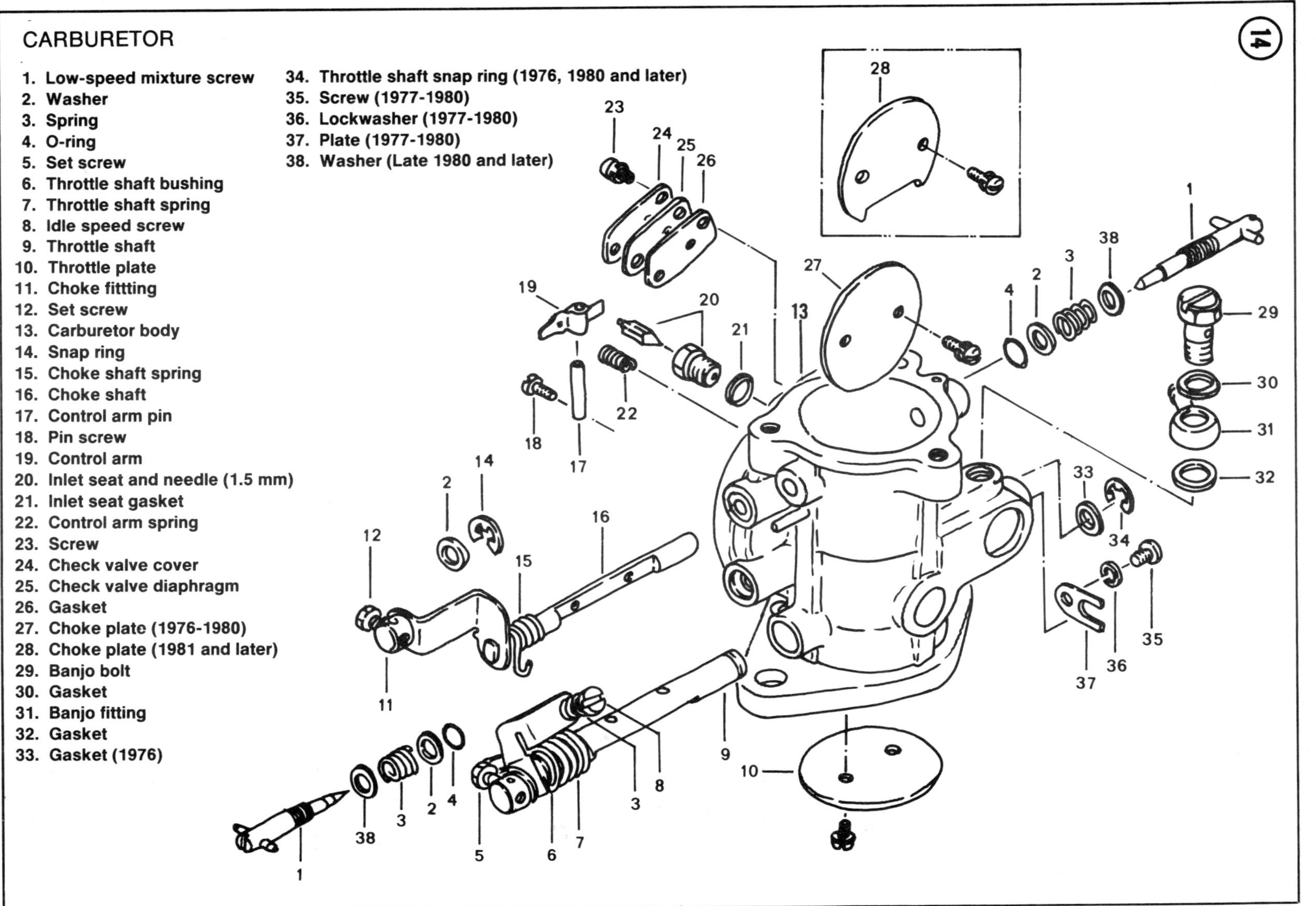

CARBURETOR

1. Low-speed mixture screw
2. Washer
3. Spring
4. O-ring
5. Set screw
6. Throttle shaft bushing
7. Throttle shaft spring
8. Idle speed screw
9. Throttle shaft
10. Throttle plate
11. Choke fittting
12. Set screw
13. Carburetor body
14. Snap ring
15. Choke shaft spring
16. Choke shaft
17. Control arm pin
18. Pin screw
19. Control arm
20. Inlet seat and needle (1.5 mm)
21. Inlet seat gasket
22. Control arm spring
23. Screw
24. Check valve cover
25. Check valve diaphragm
26. Gasket
27. Choke plate (1976-1980)
28. Choke plate (1981 and later)
29. Banjo bolt
30. Gasket
31. Banjo fitting
32. Gasket
33. Gasket (1976)
34. Throttle shaft snap ring (1976, 1980 and later)
35. Screw (1977-1980)
36. Lockwasher (1977-1980)
37. Plate (1977-1980)
38. Washer (Late 1980 and later)

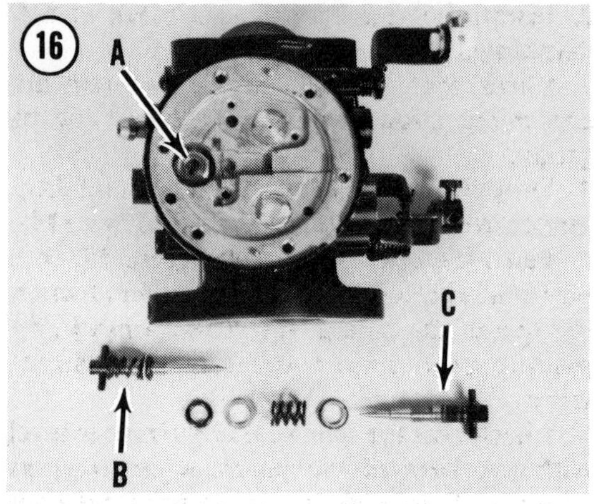

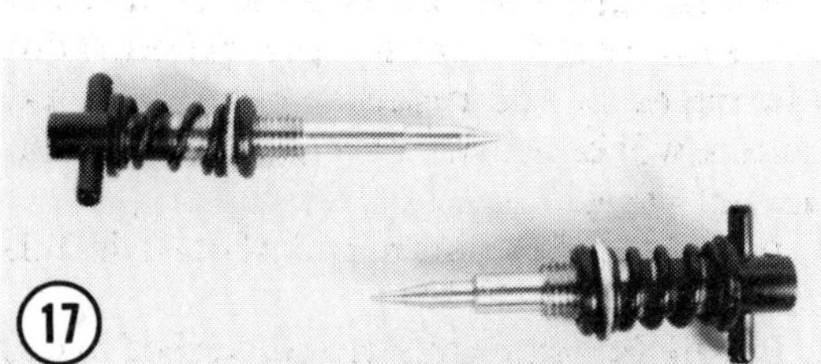

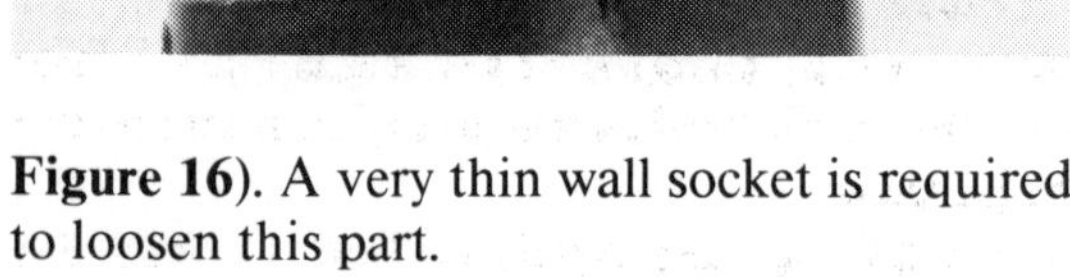

Figure 16). A very thin wall socket is required to loosen this part.

4. Remove the 2 screws (B, **Figure 15**) and the high-speed check valve plate, diaphragm and gasket.

5. Remove the high- (B, **Figure 16**) and low-speed (C) mixture screws and their springs, washers and O-rings.

Carburetor Cleaning and Inspection

1. Thoroughly clean and dry all parts. If a special carburetor cleaning solution is used, all non-metal parts must be removed (gaskets, O-rings, etc.).

2. Remove any old gasket material and check that all fuel and vent passages are clear. Blow them clean with compressed air, if necessary. Don't use wire to clean any of the orifices; wire will enlarge them and change fuel flow rates .

3. Clean the fuel pump filter screen with a toothbrush. If there is much residue in the inlet cavity, the carburetor body should be cleaned thoroughly in a special carburetor cleaning solvent available at auto parts stores.

4. Inspect the rubber gasket that fits between the fuel pump filter screen and the end cover. Replace it if damaged.

5. Replace all 4 fiber fuel pump gaskets.

6. Check the fuel pump diaphragm and regulator diaphragm for tears or pin holes. Replace any damaged diaphragms.

7. Inspect the carburetor control arm and replace it if excessively worn. Replace the spring if it is damaged or weakened.

8. Check the inlet seat and the taper on the inlet needle for wear, scratches or other damage. Replace the seat and needle as a set if either part is defective.

9. Inspect the high-speed check valve diaphragm and gasket. Replace them if worn or damaged.

10. Check the tapered ends of the high- and low-speed screws (**Figure 17**) for grooves or roughness and replace if any is found. Inspect the O-rings and replace if damaged or mis-shapen.

11. Check the throttle return spring and shaft bushing (**Figure 14**) for wear. Replace if necessary.

Carburetor Body Assembly

See **Figure 14**.

1. Install the high- and low-speed screws with their springs, washers and O-rings. The shorter (low-speed) screw is on the side with the control linkage.

2. Install the high-speed check valve gasket, diaphragm and plate (**Figure 18**).

3. Check that the inlet needle and seat are completely clean. Install the inlet seat and its gasket.

4. Drop the inlet needle into its seat and drop the control arm spring in its hole (A, **Figure 19**).

5. Place the control arm (B, **Figure 19**) into position with the rounded projection down in the top of the spring. Insert the control arm pivot through the arm and install its retaining screw.

6. Check that the long side of the arm is level with the base of the regulator chamber as shown in **Figure 20**. If it is not level, take out the arm and bend it carefully as required. If this adjustment is not made correctly, the fuel mixture will be too rich or too lean throughout the rpm range.

7. Install the fuel pump as described in this chapter.

8. Install the flame arrestor as described in this chapter.

Fuel Pump Assembly

NOTE
As you assemble the fuel pump body, make sure that all locating pegs on the carburetor body pieces and their corresponding holes in gaskets and diaphragms line up and that the rounded projection in the outer edge of each piece is lined up as shown in Figure 21. If they are not aligned correctly, the pump will not function properly.

1. Place the black regulator diaphragm and gasket on the carburetor (A, **Figure 22**). Make sure the perforated metal plate faces toward the carburetor.

2. Install the cast regulator body. It has the crankcase pulse line fitting (B, **Figure 22**).

3. *On 1977 and later models*: Place an open-center gasket on the regulator body, then the open-center ring.

4. Install the solid pump diaphragm.

5. Fit the center pump casting over the assembly (**Figure 23**).

6. Install an open-center gasket, then the reed valve diaphragm with cut-outs in its center (**Figure 24**).

7. Install the outer casting and tighten its 6 screws.

> *CAUTION*
> *Be careful not to crossthread or strip the fuel pump screws. The aluminum threads in the carburetor are easily damaged, resulting in air or fuel leaks.*

8. Position the screen (1976-1980 models only), gasket and cover fitting on the cast pump cover. Be sure the fitting is properly seated or an air leak will result. Install the center screw.

Carburetor Installation

1. Check that the control cable bracket, gasket(s) and insulator or carburetor holder and clamp are in place (**Figure 25**).

2. *On 1979 and later models:*
   a. Fit the carburetor assembly onto the intake manifold studs and install the washers, lockwashers and nuts. Torque the carburetor base flange nuts to 7 ft.-lb. (1.0 mkg).

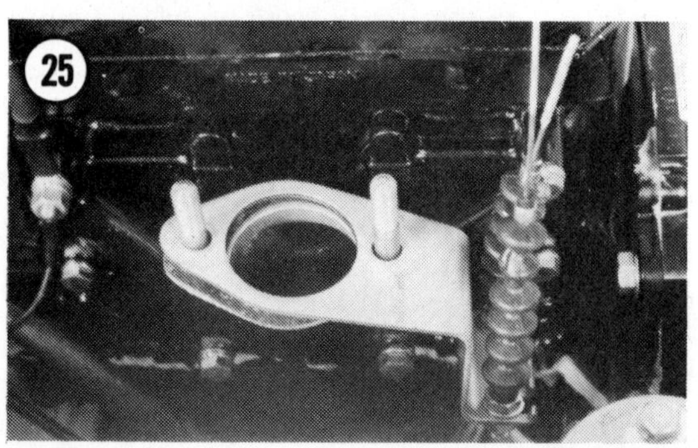

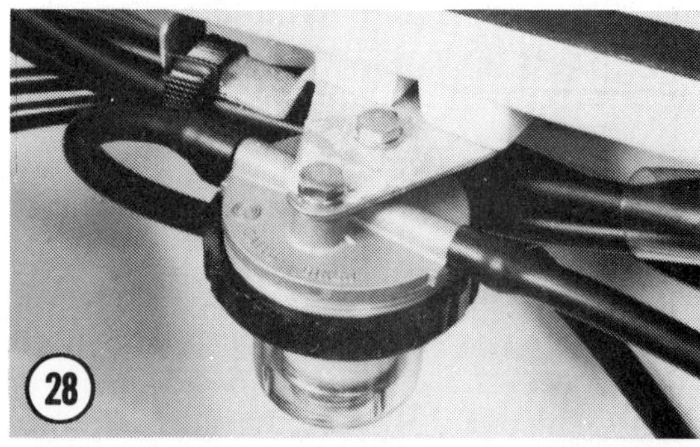

b. To mount the carburetor brace, remove 2 cylinder head nuts and install the brace (**Figure 26**). Do not tighten the cylinder head nuts yet.

c. Install the 2 bolts (or nuts), flat washers and lockwashers that hold the cylinder head brace to the carburetor (or carburetor top bracket). Tighten them securely.

d. Torque the 2 cylinder head nuts (**Figure 26**) to 16 ft.-lb. (2.2 mkg).

3. *On 1977-1978 models*: Fit the carburetor assembly into the rubber carburetor holder and tighten the clamp screw until the ends of the clamp are about 1/8 in. (3 mm) apart.

4. *On 400 cc engines*: Fit the carburetor assembly onto the intake manifold studs and install the washers, lockwashers and nuts (**Figure 4**). Torque the carburetor base flange nuts to 7 ft.-lb. (1.0 mkg).

5. If the cables have been removed from the bracket, install one adjuster nut on each control cable and insert the cable through the cable bracket. Install the upper cable adjuster nut and the rubber cable boot on 1978 and later models.

NOTE
If you have an early boat without rubber cable boots, ask your Jet Ski dealer for a set. They keep water, sand and dirt out of the control cable housing.

6. Insert the control cables in their fittings, tighten the set screws (B, **Figure 9**) and adjust the throttle and choke cables as described in Chapter Three.

7. If there are rubber boots on the control cables, position them as follows:

a. Apply full choke or throttle and hold it.

b. Push the boot all the way down the cable until it is fully compressed (**Figure 27**).

c. When the choke knob or the throttle is released, the boot will be in the correct position.

8. Connect the crankcase pulse line (A, **Figure 9**) and the fuel lines at the carburetor (**Figure 8**).

9. Install the fuel tank outlet hose assembly at the tank.

FUEL FILTER

The fuel filter (and sediment bowl on 1977 and later models) keeps dirt or water from getting into the carburetor (**Figure 28**). Fuel flows from the tank through the fuel valve into the sediment bowl, where water and other contaminants settle to the bottom and a filter strains out dirt. Filtered fuel from the top of the bowl is drawn into the fuel pump.

The 400cc engine has a simple fuel filter mounted on top of the fuel tank (**Figure 29**).

The sediment bowl and filter should be cleaned in accordance with the maintenance schedule and the *Fuel Filter* procedure in Chapter Three.

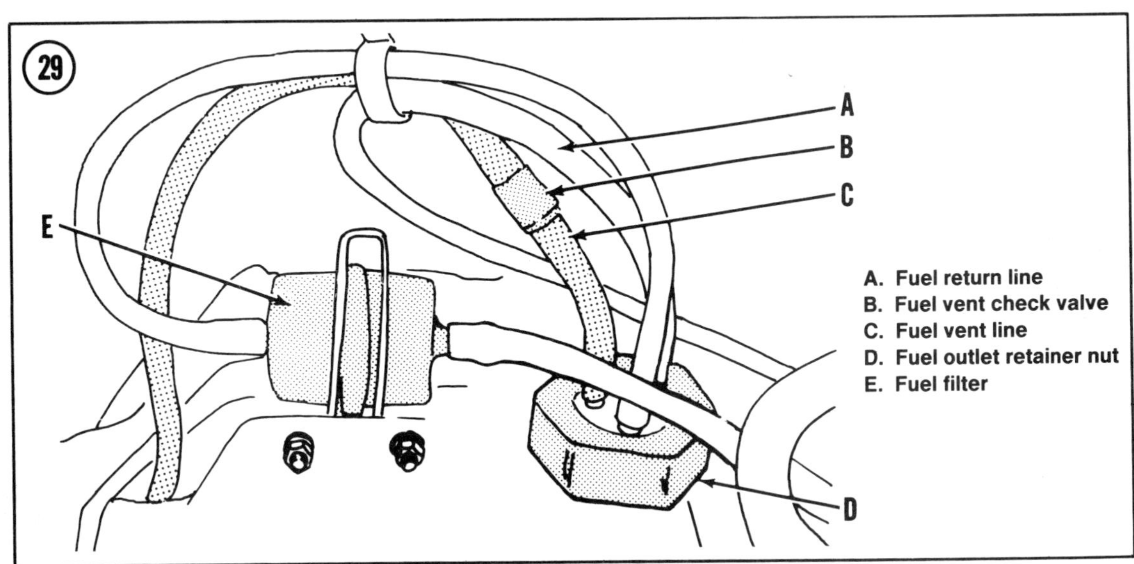

FUEL TANK

If water and dirt accumulate in the fuel tank, engine performance will deteriorate. Clean the fuel system when the engine is cold.

The fuel tank must be removed to inspect the ignition timing and to service the magneto when the engine is mounted in the Jet Ski.

Fuel Tank Removal/Installation

> *WARNING*
> *Some fuel may spill during these procedures. Work in a well-ventilated area at least 50 feet from any sparks or flames, including gas appliance pilot lights. Do not smoke in the area. Keep a BC rated fire extinguisher handy.*

1. Siphon the contents of the tank into a safe container.
2. Unhook the fuel tank's rubber straps from the clips on the hull (**Figure 30**).
3. Unscrew the outlet retainer nut (A, **Figure 31**) and remove the fuel outlet assembly and fuel tubes.
4. Loosen the hose clamp at the front of the tank (**Figure 32**) and pull the tank free from the filler hose. Lift the tank out of the hull.
5. Discard any fuel in the tank and pour about a pint of clean fuel into the tank. Install the cap, slosh the fuel around for about a minute and pour it into a safe container.
6. To install, reverse the removal steps. Note the following:
   a. Check that the fuel tank damper pads (**Figure 33**) are in good condition. Install new pads if necessary, using a waterproof contact cement such as Goodyear Pliobond.
   b. When installing the tank retainer straps, position the strap ends with their tabs toward the tank (**Figure 30**) to keep the hooks from chafing the tank.
   c. Make sure the filler hose clamp and tank outlet connections are tight.

FUEL VENT CHECK VALVE

There is a rubber vent hose on the fuel tank that runs to the lower section of the handle pole. This line contains a small plastic one-way check valve which allows air to enter the tank

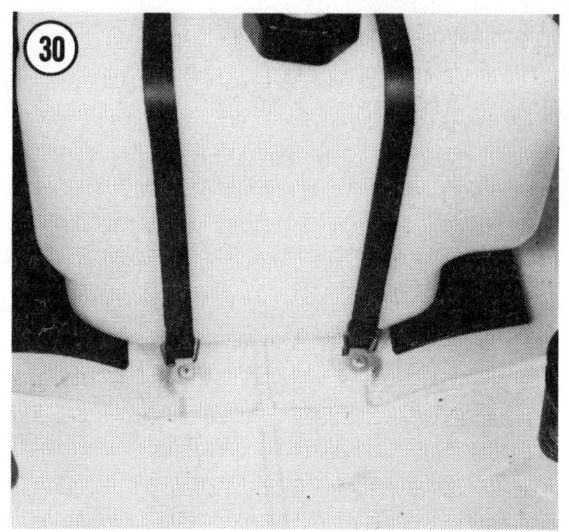

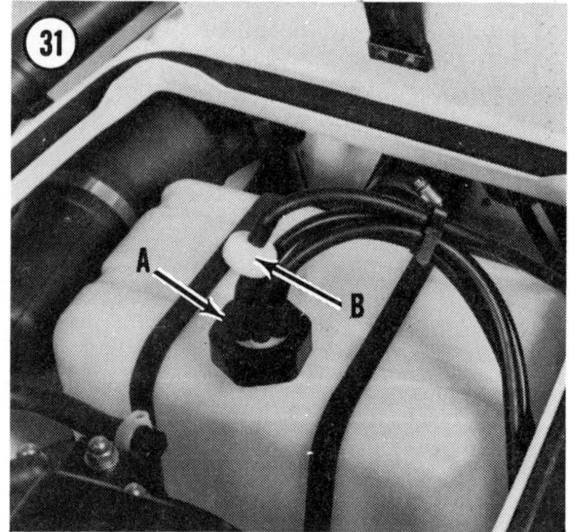

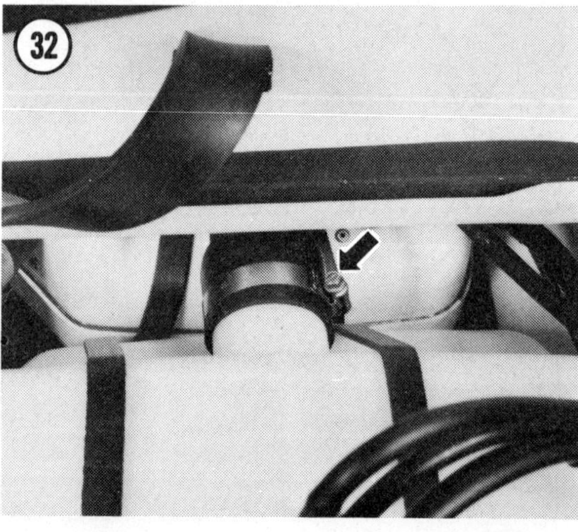

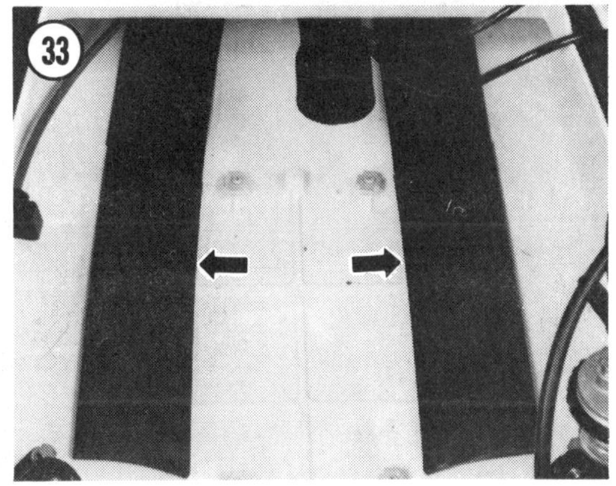

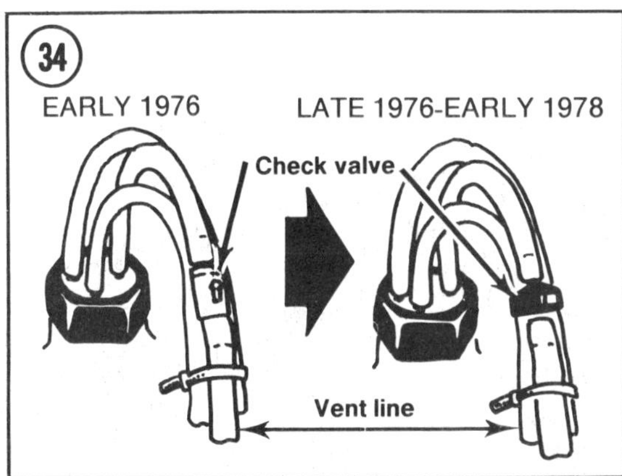

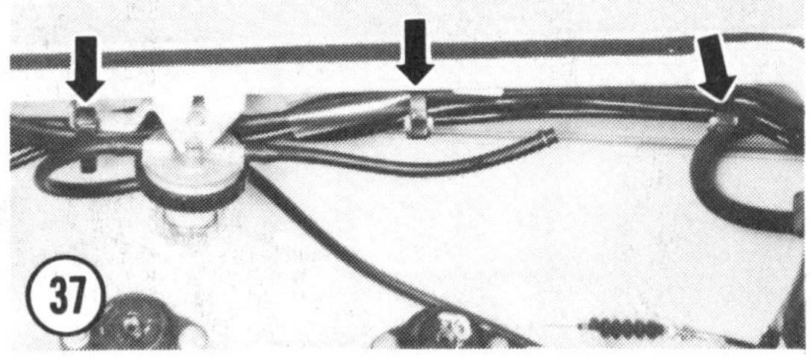

when the engine is running, but keeps fuel from spilling out of the tank when the boat is tipped over.

Inspect the check valve in accordance with the maintenance schedule in Chapter Three and the following procedure.

> *WARNING*
> *Before disconnecting any fuel lines, loosen the fuel filler cap to relieve any built-up pressure in the fuel tank.*

Check Valve Inspection

1. Pull the check valve out of the vent line to the handle pole (B, **Figure 31**).
2. Blow through each end of the check valve. Air should pass through the valve into the fuel tank, but air must not pass through the valve out of the fuel tank. If the valve is faulty, install a new one.
3. Insert the check valve back into the vent line:
   a. *On late 1978-on models:* Install the valve with the arrow toward the fuel tank; the off-center fitting must be turned to the bottom as shown in **Figure 31**.
   b. *On late 1976-early 1978 models:* Install the valve with the cone-shaped side toward the fuel tank; see **Figure 34**.
   c. *On early 1976 models:* Install the valve with the arrow toward the fuel tank; see **Figure 34**.

FUEL VALVE AND LINES

The 1977 and later models have a fuel valve mounted on the control panel that switches on the reserve fuel supply. The valve (**Figure 35**) can be replaced after removing the electric box; see *Electric Box Removal* in Chapter Seven. **Figure 36** shows fuel line routing and connections for late 1977-on models. The line at the rear of the fuel filter goes to the carburetor.

On 1976-early 1977 models, the fuel line routing is similar, but the carburetor's fuel line attaches to the front of the fuel filter. These filters have an arrow on top of the filter indicating the direction of fuel flow.

When installing the fuel lines, be sure to secure the lines with cable ties as shown in **Figure 37**.

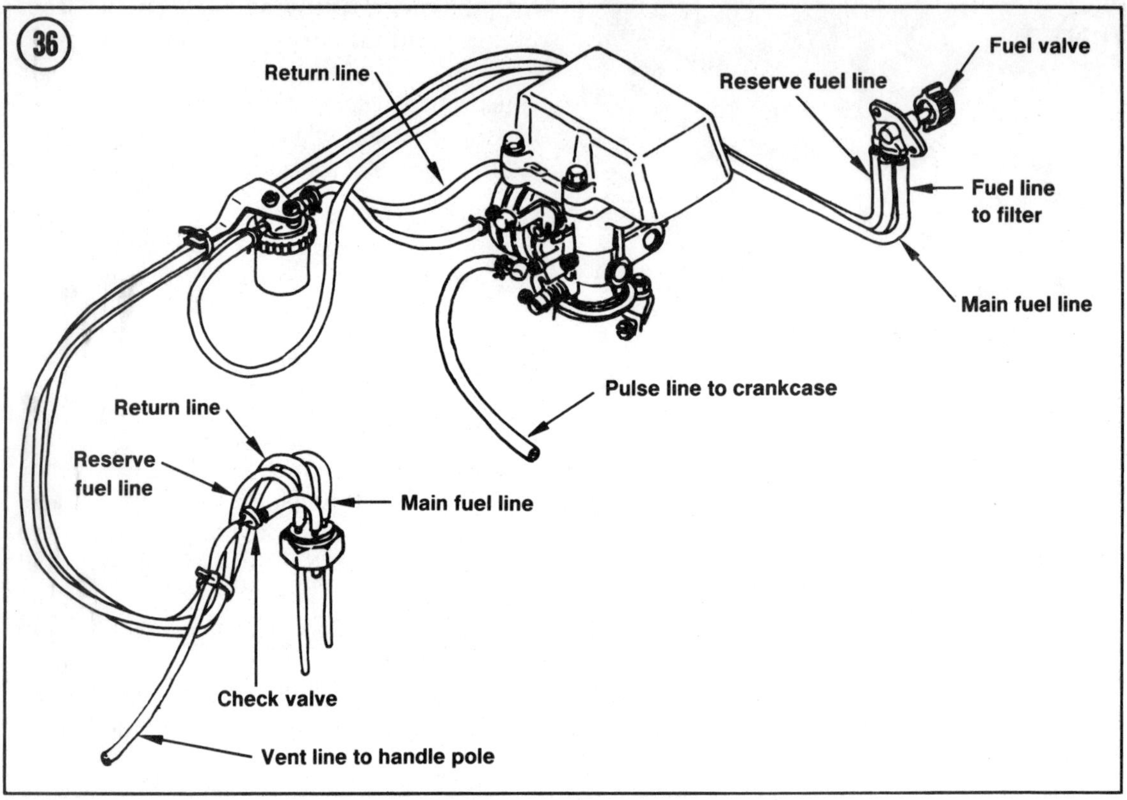

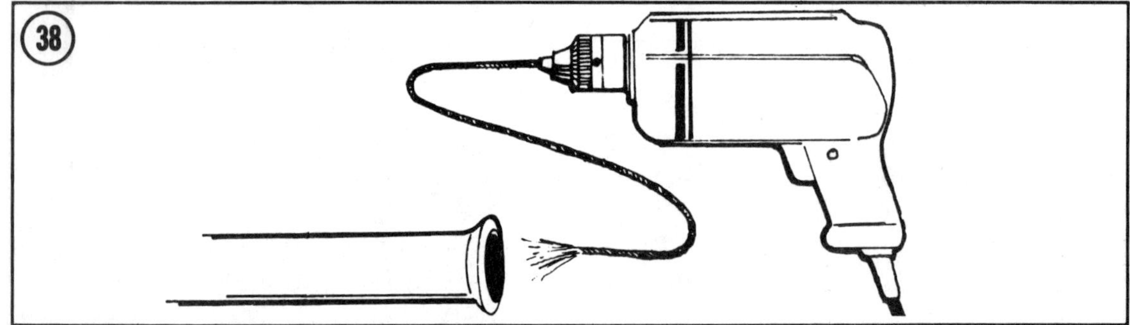

EXHAUST

The exhaust system on a Jet Ski engine is much more than a means of routing exhaust gases to the rear of the Jet Ski. It's a vital performance component.

Periodically remove the resonator and clean any carbon that accumulates inside the resonator core. The expansion chamber itself may also require decarbonizing.

> *NOTE*
> *You can clean the expansion chamber with a piece of stranded cable in an electric drill (**Figure 38**). Fray the loose end of the cable and run the drill while moving the cable back and forth inside the chamber.*

Check the expansion chamber for cracks and check the entire exhaust system for loose bolts and clamps. If the rubber resonator is worn out it must be replaced.

Exhaust Removal

See **Figure 39**. When removing the exhaust pipe and expansion chamber for access to other

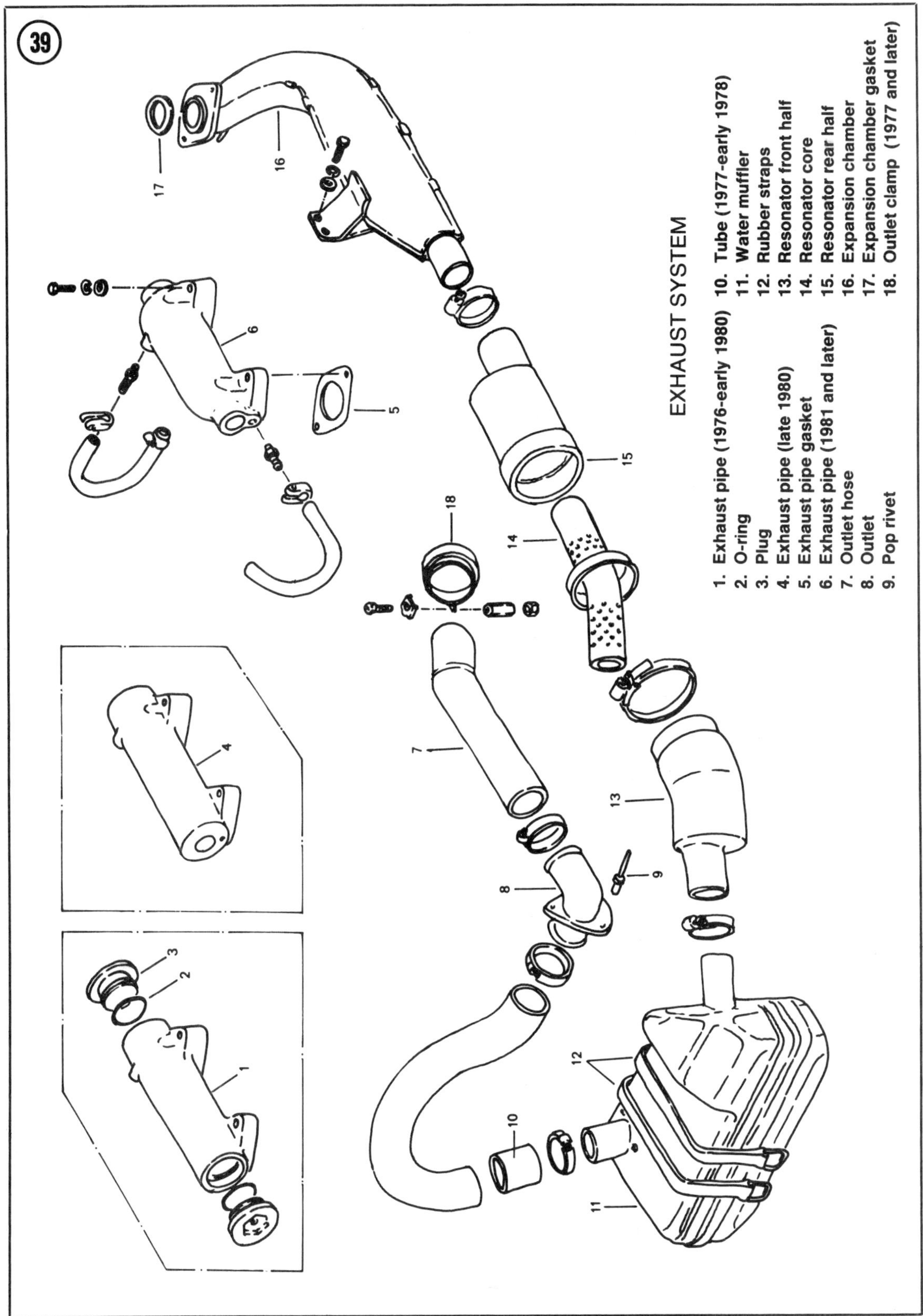

39
EXHAUST SYSTEM
1. Exhaust pipe (1976-early 1980)
2. O-ring
3. Plug
4. Exhaust pipe (late 1980)
5. Exhaust pipe gasket
6. Exhaust pipe (1981 and later)
7. Outlet hose
8. Outlet
9. Pop rivet
10. Tube (1977-early 1978)
11. Water muffler
12. Rubber straps
13. Resonator front half
14. Resonator core
15. Resonator rear half
16. Expansion chamber
17. Expansion chamber gasket
18. Outlet clamp (1977 and later)

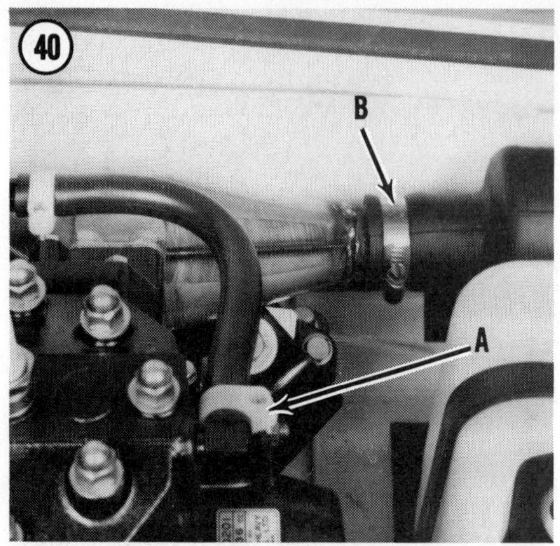

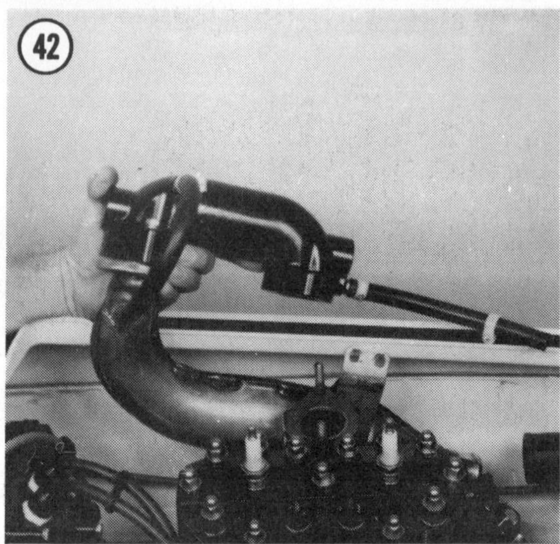

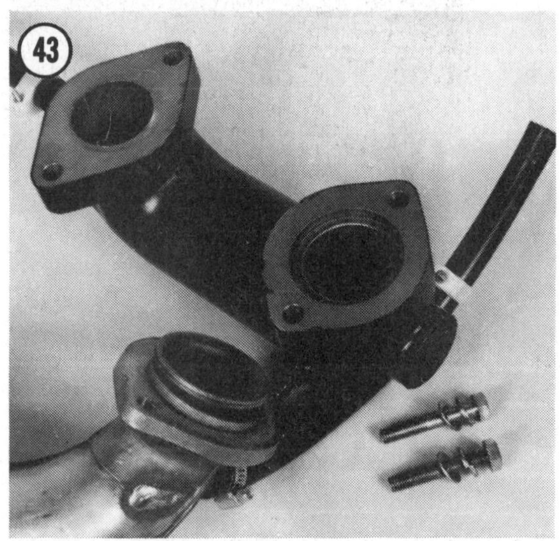

parts, it is best to remove them in one piece so you don't disturb the gasket seal between the 2 pieces.

1. Loosen the clamp at the front of the cylinder head and disconnect the water hose (A, **Figure 40**).

2. Loosen the clamp holding the exhaust resonator to the expansion chamber (B, **Figure 40**).

3. Remove the 2 expansion chamber brace bolts (A, **Figure 41**) and the 2 exhaust pipe flange nuts (B).

4. Remove the exhaust pipe and expansion chamber in one piece (**Figure 42**).

5. *To separate the exhaust pipe from the expansion chamber:* Remove the 2 bolts, lockwashers and flat washers holding the exhaust pipe to the expansion chamber, then remove the exhaust pipe (**Figure 43**). Make sure the round copper/asbestos gasket for the expansion chamber is not lost or damaged.

6. Loosen the front resonator clamp (**Figure 44**) and pull the resonator free from the water muffler. To disassemble the resonator, loosen the middle clamp and pull the rubber halves off of the metal core.

7. Release the rubber straps holding the water muffler in place (A, **Figure 45**) and loosen the

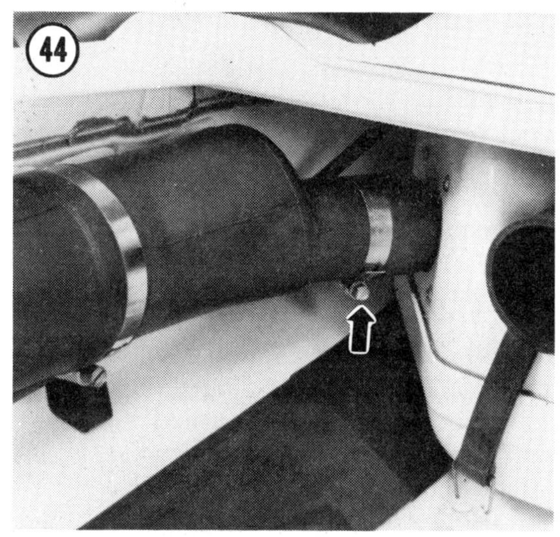
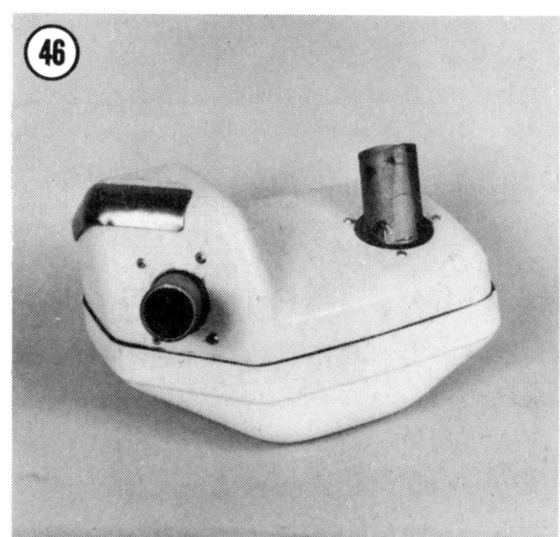
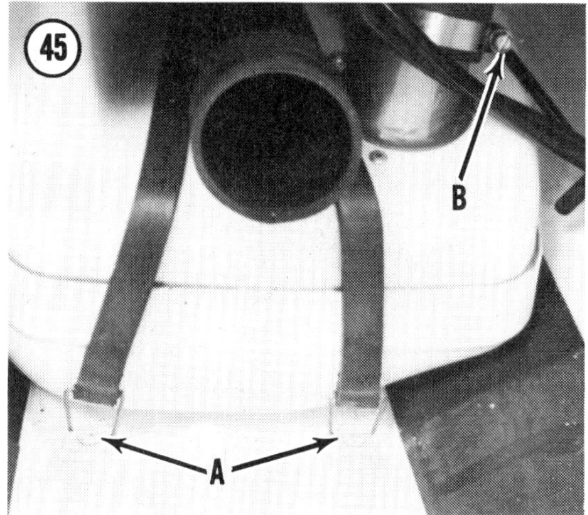

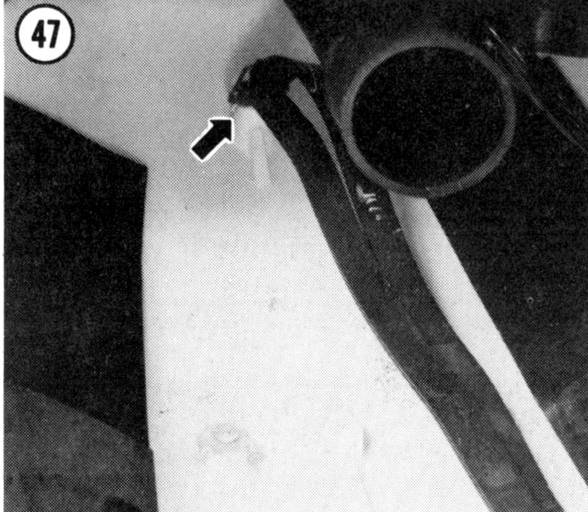

clamp that holds the muffler to the outlet hose
(B). Pull the muffler free.

8. Inspect the water muffler for cracks or holes
(**Figure 46**). If necessary, replace it or repair it
using the hull repair kit described in Chapter
Seven.

Exhaust Installation

See **Figure 39**.

1. Hook the rubber water muffler straps onto
their hooks in the front of the boat (**Figure 47**).
There is only one strap on 1976 models.
2. Push the water muffler outlet into its hose
and tighten the hose clamp.
3. Hook the muffler straps onto the retainers
to the rear of the muffler.

4. If you disassembled the resonator, assemble
it with the core cutout at the bottom and align
the arrows on the rubber halves at the top. The
front half fits inside the rear half. Position the
middle clamp so it won't chafe at the fuel tank.
5. If you separated the exhaust pipe from the
expansion chamber, use a new gasket at the
junction and *loosely* install the 2 bolts with
lockwashers and flat washers.

NOTE
*Do not tighten the junction bolts until
after the pipe and chamber are securely
mounted on the engine.*

6. Install a new gasket on the exhaust manifold
and fit the expansion chamber/exhaust pipe
into place. Place the flat washers, lockwashers

and exhaust pipe flange nuts on the manifold studs (B, **Figure 41**); do not tighten them yet.

7. Loosely install the 2 expansion chamber brace bolts (A, **Figure 41**). Torque the exhaust pipe flange nuts to 12 ft.-lb. (1.6 mkg) and then torque the expansion chamber brace bolts to 10 ft.-lb. (1.4 mkg).

8. *If you separated the exhaust pipe from the expansion chamber:* Torque the 2 junction bolts evenly to 10 ft.-lb. (1.4 mkg). Tighten the bolts again after a day's riding.

9. Tighten the exhaust resonator clamp onto the expansion chamber outlet.

10. After the job is complete, run the motor and check for exhaust leaks.

> *CAUTION*
> *Do not run the engine for more than 15 seconds without a supply of cooling water or the rubber parts of the exhaust system will be damaged. Prolonged running without coolant will cause serious engine damage. Do not operate the engine at maximum speed out of the water.*

VENTILATION SYSTEM OPERATION

As the Jet Ski is ridden through water, air is let in through the holes in the front and the air scoop on top of the engine cover. The air then flows through a plenum chamber, through a short pipe and into the engine compartment as shown in **Figure 48**.

The pipe that carries air into the engine extends above the plenum chamber floor. This minimizes water entry through the intake. Any water that enters runs down the floor of the plenum and out the drain holes in the front of the engine cover. When air enters the engine compartment, some is drawn into the carburetor and consumed. The air that is left over, along with any gas vapor, is forced into a long pipe that pulls it from the engine compartment into another plenum chamber. From there, the air and vapor exit through holes in the rear of the engine cover. This system complies with Coast Guard regulations requiring that the engine compartments of inboard boats be ventilated to prevent the accumulation of potentially hazardous gas vapor.

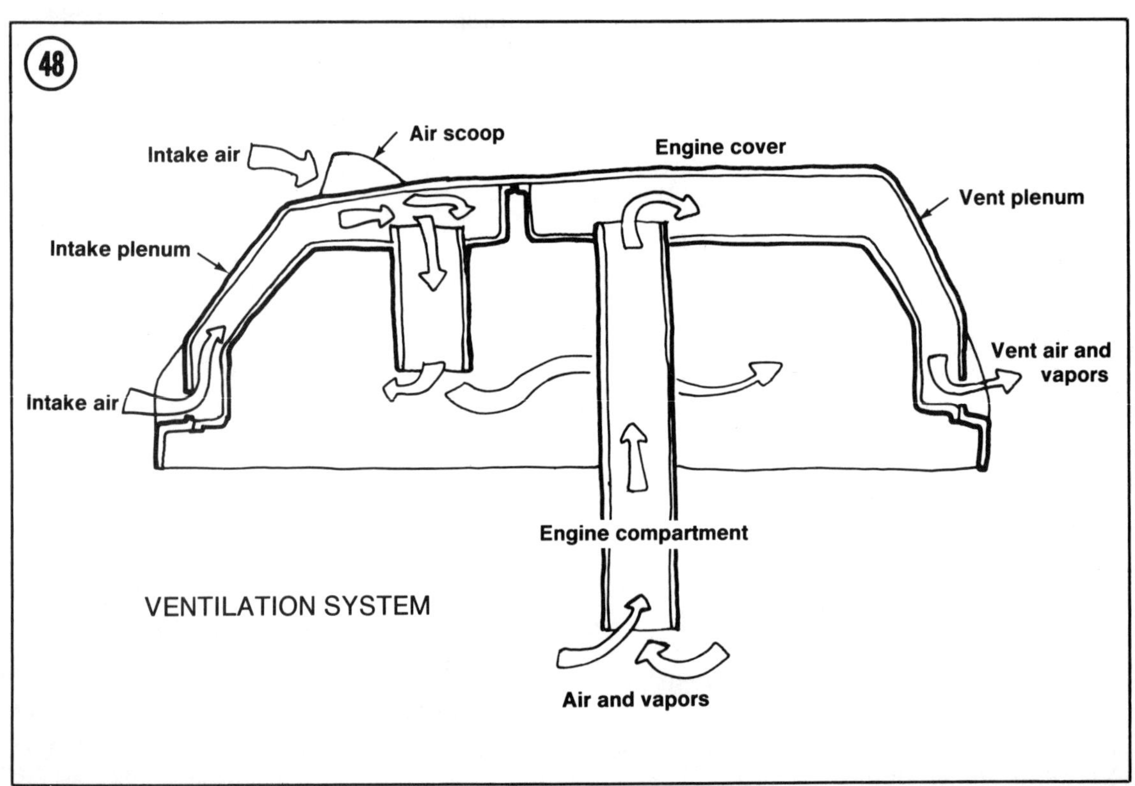

NOTE: If you own a 1982 or 1983 model, first check the Supplement at the back of the book for any new service information.

CHAPTER SEVEN

ELECTRICAL SYSTEMS

The Jet Ski electrical system includes the battery, ignition system, charging system and starting system. Detailed electrical specifications are given in **Table 1**. **Table 1** and **Table 2** are at the end of the chapter.

WIRING DIAGRAMS

Full color wiring diagrams are located at the end of the book.

TOOLS

Several specialized tools will be helpful in the disassembly and inspection procedures in this chapter.

Removal of the magneto rotor requires a means of locking the engine when loosening and tightening the rotor nut. A very handy tool for this purpose is a universal rotor holder (**Figure 1**). To remove the rotor from the crankshaft, a special Kawasaki 4-bolt rotor puller (**Figure 2**) will be required. Your Jet Ski

dealer, or any Kawasaki motorcycle dealer, should be able to provide you with these tools.

If you want to check ignition timing at exactly the specified rpm, you will need a tachometer suited for use on electronic ignition systems. Sun Instruments makes an Inductive Tach-Dwell Meter with a sensor lead that clips onto a spark plug lead. The meter is available at well-stocked auto parts stores.

BATTERY

The Jet Ski is equipped with a 12 volt, 16 ampere-hour battery with an electrolyte specific gravity of 1.280 at 68° F when fully charged.

NOTE
In very warm climates an electrolyte with a specific gravity of 1.260 is used. With such a battery, you should subtract 0.020 for all specified test readings of

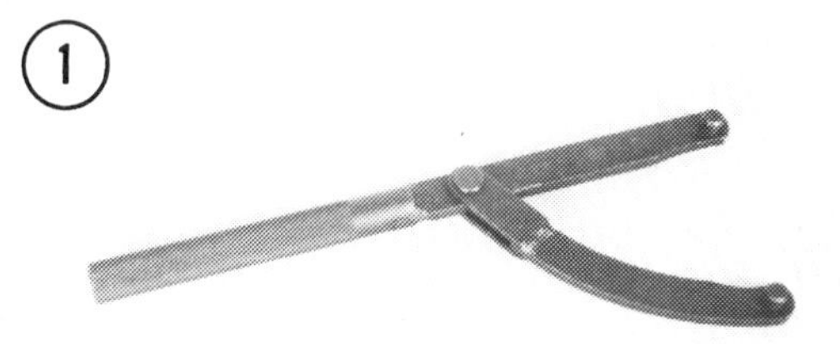

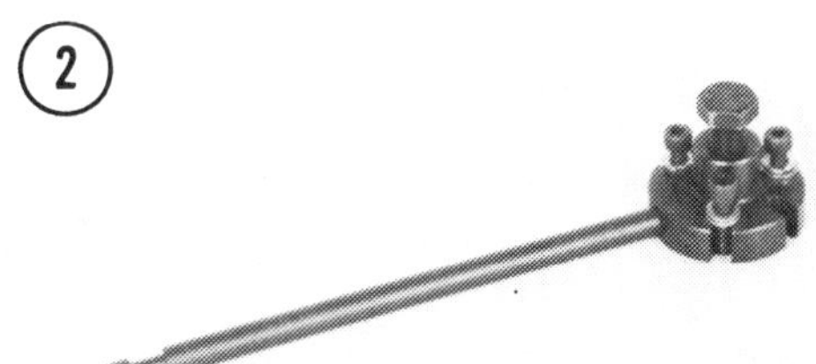

specific gravity. If you are uncertain of the electrolyte installed in the battery, any local dealer should be able to tell you from the label of the acid container he uses to initially service batteries.

Battery electrolyte testing and battery charging may be required after long periods (more than a month) of inactivity, or when starter trouble arises.

More water evaporates from batteries in warmer climates, but excessive use of water may be an indication that the battery is being overcharged. Check the voltage regulator if this situation exists.

If the Jet Ski will not be used for an extended period, remove the battery from the machine, charge it fully and store it in a cool, dry place. Recharge the battery every 2 months while it is in storage and again before it is put back into service.

> *WARNING*
> *Study the **Safety Precautions** before servicing the battery.*

Safety Precautions

While working with batteries, use care to avoid spilling or splashing the electrolyte. The electrolyte is a sulfuric acid solution which can destroy clothing and cause serious chemical burns. If you get any electrolyte on your clothing, body or any other surface, neutralize it immediately with a solution of baking soda and water, then flush with plenty of clean water.

> *WARNING*
> *Electrolyte splashed into the eyes is extremely dangerous. Wear safety glasses while working with batteries. If electrolyte is splashed into the eye, call a doctor immediately, force the eye open and flood it with cool water for at least 5 minutes.*

When batteries are being charged, highly explosive hydrogen gas forms in the cells of the battery. Some of this gas escapes through the filler openings and may form an explosive atmosphere around the battery. Sparks, flames or a lighted cigarette can ignite the gas, causing a battery explosion and possible serious

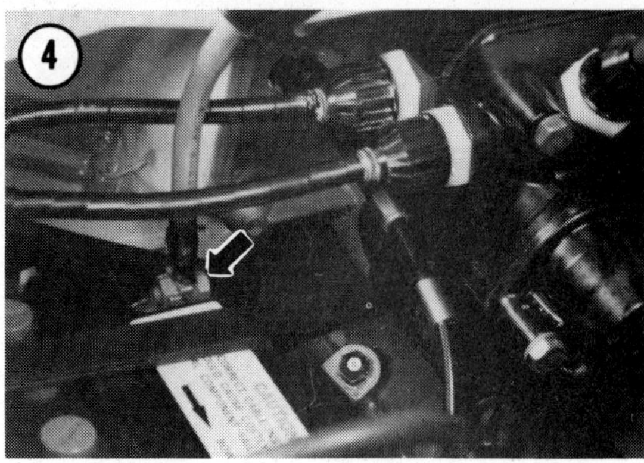

personal injury. Follow these precautions to help prevent accidents.

1. Do not smoke or permit any flame near a battery being charged or which has been charged recently. Keep the battery away from gas appliances too.

2. When using a battery charger, don't plug the charger in until the battery clips have been securely attached. Unplug the charger before you remove the clips from the battery.

Battery Removal

Disconnect the negative (-) ground cable first, then the positive (+) cable. This minimizes the chance of a tool shorting to ground when disconnecting the "hot" positive cable.

1. *On 1979 and later models*: Disconnect the negative (-) ground cable at the engine (**Figure 3**).

2. *On 1976-1978 models*: Disconnect the negative (-) ground cable at the battery.

3. Disconnect the positive (+) cable at the battery (**Figure 4**).

2. Connect the positive (+) terminal from the electric box first, then the negative (-) ground. Don't overtighten the clamps. Slide the rubber boot over the terminal.

3. Connect the battery's red lead to the positive (+) terminal, and its ground lead to the negative (-) terminal. Coat the inside of the battery terminal rubber boots with a water-resistant grease such as Valvoline X-All and slide the boots over the battery terminals.

Specific Gravity Testing

Hydrometer testing is the best way to check battery condition. A hydrometer with numbered graduations from 1.100 to 1.300 is better than one with color-coded bands.

To use the hydrometer, squeeze the rubber ball, insert the tip into the cell and release the ball. Draw enough electrolyte to float the weighted float inside the hydrometer. Note the number in line with surface of the electrolyte (**Figure 6**); this is the specific gravity for this cell. Return the electrolyte to the cell from which it came.

The specific gravity of the electrolyte in each battery cell is an excellent indication of that cell's condition. A fully charged cell will read 1.275-1.280, while a cell in good condition reads from 1.225-1.250 and anything below 1.225 is practically dead.

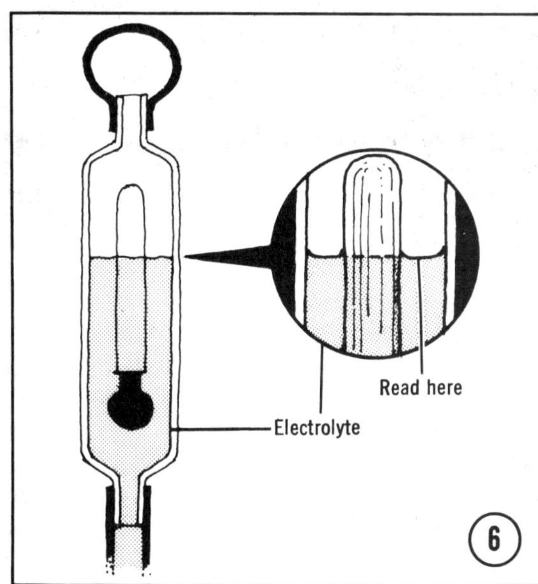

> *NOTE*
> *Remember that some batteries originally sold in warm climates have a fully charged specific gravity of 1.260.*

Specific gravity varies with temperature. For each 10° that electrolyte temperature exceeds 80° F, add 0.004 to the reading indicated on the hydrometer. Subtract 0.004 for each 10° below 80° F.

Repeat this measurement for each battery cell. If there is more than 0.050 difference between cells, battery condition is questionable.

If the cells test in the poor range, the battery requires recharging. The hydrometer is useful for checking the progress of the charging operation. **Figure 7** shows the approximate state of charge.

4. Detach the rubber hold-down straps and remove the battery.

Battery Installation

Be very careful while installing the battery to connect it properly. If the battery is installed backward, the electrical system may be damaged.

1. Clean the battery terminals and tray. Coat the terminals with Vaseline or WD-40 spray to retard corrosion of the terminals. Make sure the cushion and support plate are in place under the battery (**Figure 5**).

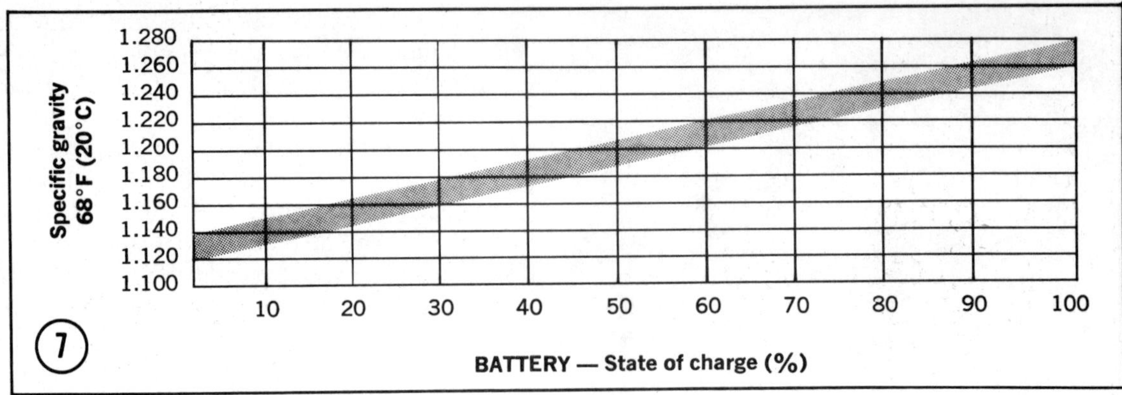

It is most important to keep the battery fully charged during cold weather. A fully charged battery freezes at a much lower temperature than one which is partially discharged. Freezing temperature depends on specific gravity, as shown in **Table 2** at the end of the chapter.

Battery Charging

> *WARNING*
> *Do not smoke or permit any open flame in any area where batteries are being charged or immediately after charging. Highly explosive hydrogen and oxygen gases are formed during the charging process. Be sure to reread **Safety Precautions** at the beginning of this section.*

> *CAUTION*
> *Always disconnect the battery cables before connecting charging equipment or you may damage part of the Jet Ski's charging system. It is best to remove the battery from the boat.*

The Jet Ski battery is not designed for high charge or discharge rates. It should be charged at a rate not exceeding 10 percent of its ampere-hour capacity. That is, do not exceed 1.6 amperes for a 16 ampere-hour battery. This charge rate should continue for about 10 hours if the battery is completely discharged or until the specific gravity of each cell is up to 1.260-1.280, corrected for temperature.

Some temperature rise is normal as a battery is being charged. Do not allow the electrolyte temperature to exceed 110° F. Should the temperature reach that figure, discontinue charging until the battery cools, then resume charging at a lower rate.

1. Remove the battery from the Jet Ski.
2. Before you switch on or plug in the charger, connect the positive charger lead to the positive battery terminal and the negative charger lead to the negative battery terminal.
3. Remove all vent caps from the battery, set the charger at 12 volts and switch it on. If the output of the charger is variable, it is best to select a setting that doesn't exceed 10% of the battery's ampere-hour capacity.
4. When you want to check the state of charge, turn the charger off or unplug it, disconnect the leads and check the specific gravity. It should be within the limits specified in **Figure 7**. If it is, and remains stable for one hour, the battery is charged.
5. Install the battery.

ELECTRIC BOX

The CDI unit, ignition coil, regulator and starter solenoid (and stop relay on 1980 and later models) are sealed inside the metal electric box to protect them from corrosion. The electric box is in the engine compartment, mounted on the bulkhead in front of the control panel. Removal procedures differ, depending on the model year.

Electric Box Removal/Installation (1981 and Later Models)

See **Figure 8**.

1. Remove the battery as described in this chapter and disconnect the electric box ground wire at the engine (**Figure 3**).

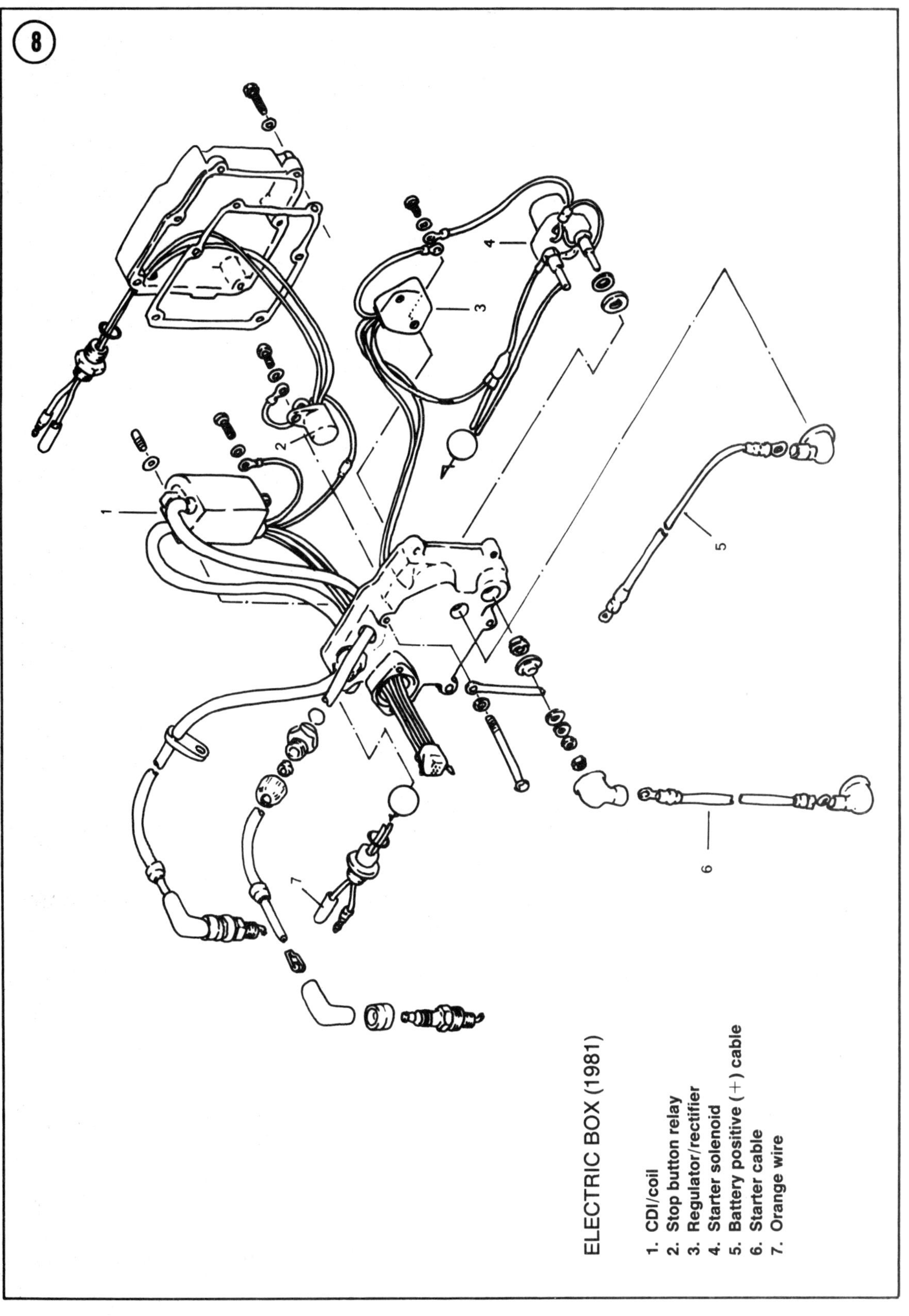

ELECTRIC BOX (1981)

1. CDI/coil
2. Stop button relay
3. Regulator/rectifier
4. Starter solenoid
5. Battery positive (+) cable
6. Starter cable
7. Orange wire

2. Disconnect the spark plug leads at the plugs.

3. Remove the exhaust pipe and expansion chamber as one piece; see *Exhaust Removal* in Chapter Six.

4. Disconnect the starter cable (**Figure 9**).

5. Remove the choke cable clamp from the electric box (A, **Figure 10**).

6. Remove the 2 bolts with washers securing the magneto wiring connector cap (B, **Figure 10**). The electric box ground lead is attached to one of the bolts.

7. Remove the cap and detach the connector from the electric box (**Figure 11**).

8. Spray the start and stop switch grommet caps with WD-40 to lubricate the rubber and unscrew the caps (C, **Figure 10**).

9. Pull the switch leads out of the electric box carefully, one at a time, until their connectors show (**Figure 12**) and disconnect them.

10. Remove the 4 bolts with washers that attach the electric box to the control panel (**Figure 13**). One upper bolt has a battery cable strap attached.

11. Remove the electric box from the hull.

12. To separate the electric box halves, remove the 2 bolts with washers from the back of the box (**Figure 14**).

13. To install, reverse the removal procedure. Note the following:

   a. Make sure the start and stop switch leads are sticking out of their case openings. If they are inside the box, separate the halves and thread the leads out the openings. The *orange* and *white* leads go out the hole in the front half of the box and the *black* and *blue* leads go out the hole in the cover (**Figure 15**). Connect the color-coded wires to wires of the same color.

   b. Coat the electric box gasket with silicone sealant on both sides. Install a new gasket if the old one is damaged. Make sure that none of the wires are pinched between the electric box halves.

   c. Apply a light coat of water-resistant grease such as Valvoline X-All to the rubber switch connector grommets before tightening the caps.

Electric Box Removal/Installation (1977-1980 Models)

See **Figure 16**. On these models, the electric box halves are held together with studs. Electric box removal requires removal of the control panel and its casting in front of the bulkhead, unless the engine's top end has been removed (see *Top End Disassembly* in Chapter Four). In that case, do not remove the control panel and choke cable.

This procedure describes removal of the control panel and casting, leaving the engine fully assembled.

1. Remove the battery as described in this chapter.

2. Remove the exhaust pipe and expansion chamber as one piece; see *Exhaust Removal* in Chapter Six.

3. Detach the choke cable from the carburetor; loosen the cable set screw, remove the top adjuster locknut and pull the cable down through the carburetor bracket.

4. Remove the cable tie securing the wires to the choke cable.

5. Disconnect the choke cable bracket from the electric box (A, **Figure 17**). Open the bracket and slide it off the end of the choke cable.

6. Remove the 2 bolts with lockwashers and flat washers securing the magneto wiring connector cap to the electric box (B, **Figure 17**). Remove the cap and detach the connector from the electric box.

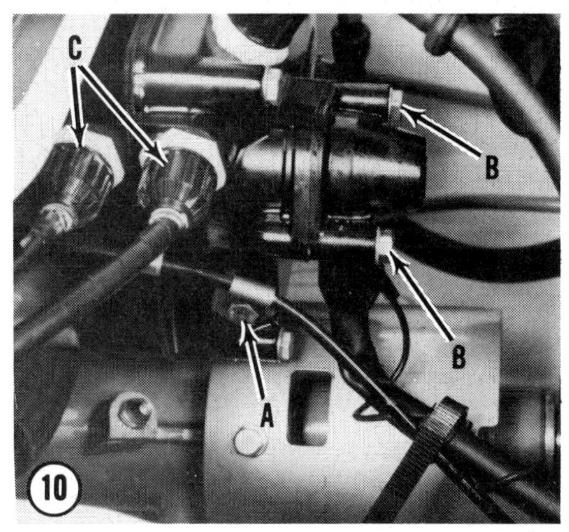
C
B
B
A
10

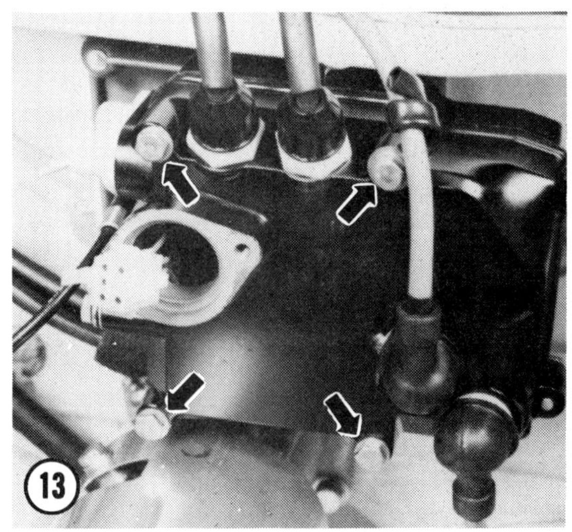
13

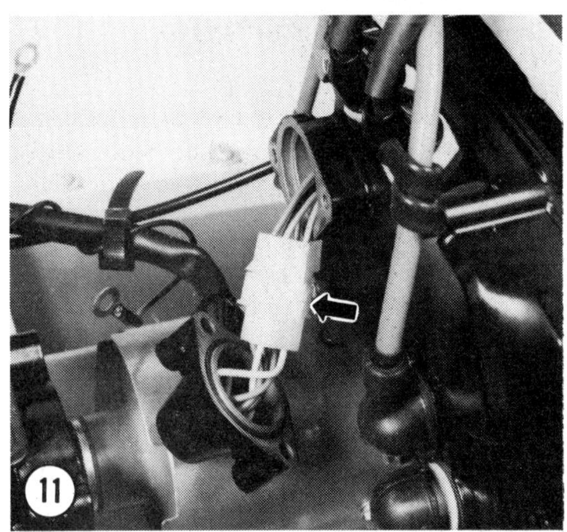
11

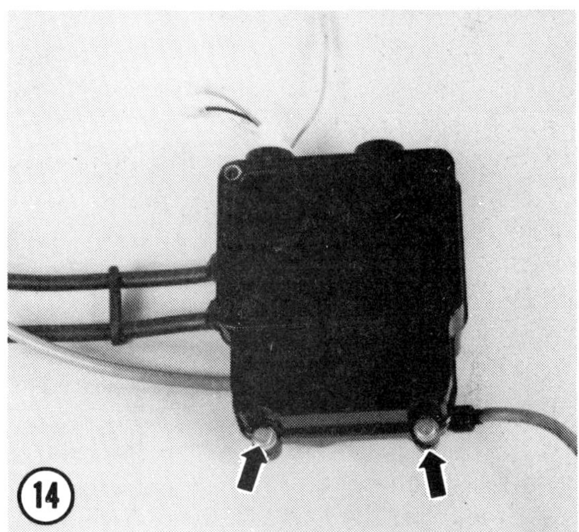
14

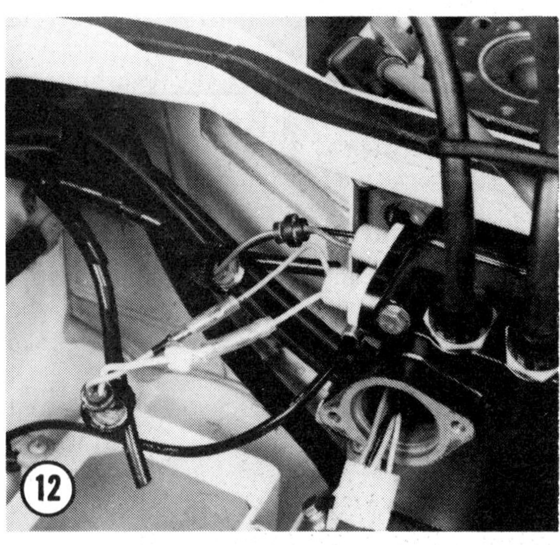
12

15

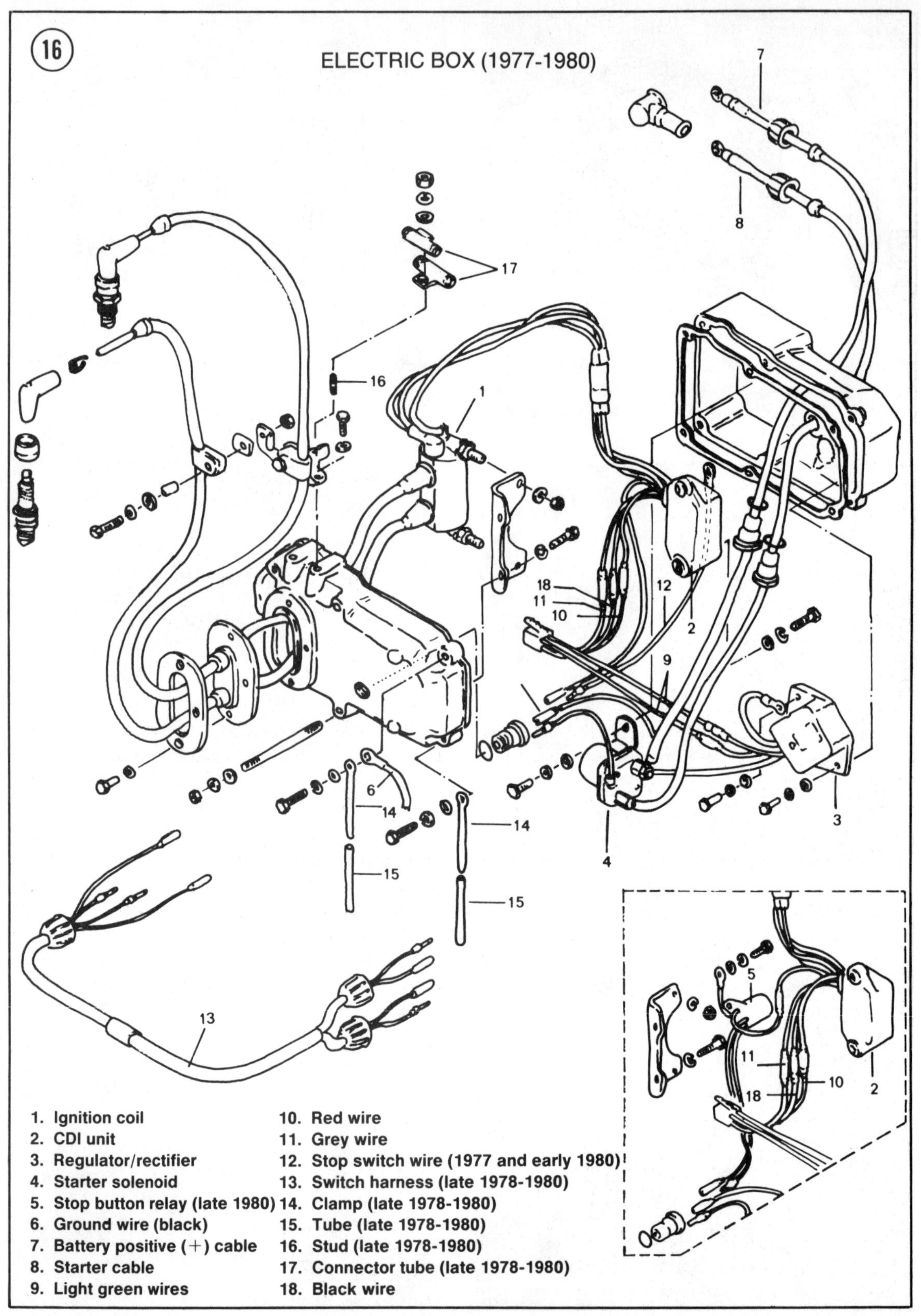

1. Ignition coil
2. CDI unit
3. Regulator/rectifier
4. Starter solenoid
5. Stop button relay (late 1980)
6. Ground wire (black)
7. Battery positive (+) cable
8. Starter cable
9. Light green wires
10. Red wire
11. Grey wire
12. Stop switch wire (1977 and early 1980)
13. Switch harness (late 1978-1980)
14. Clamp (late 1978-1980)
15. Tube (late 1978-1980)
16. Stud (late 1978-1980)
17. Connector tube (late 1978-1980)
18. Black wire

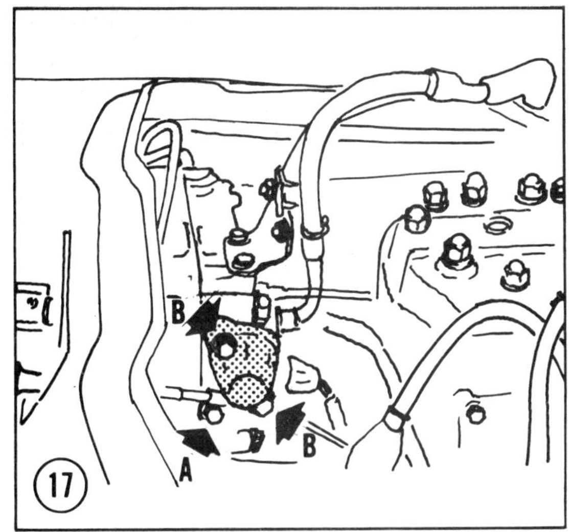

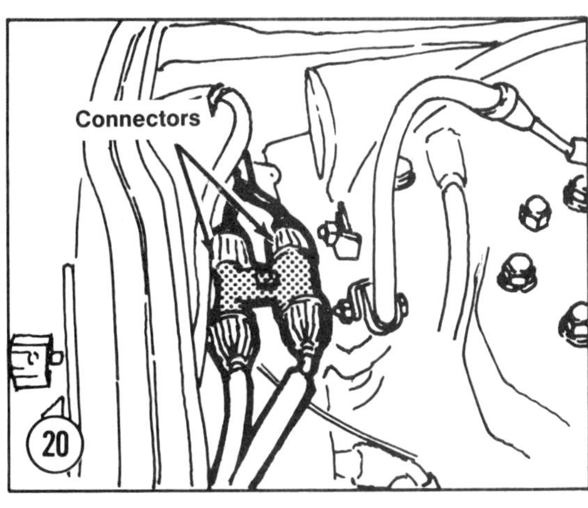

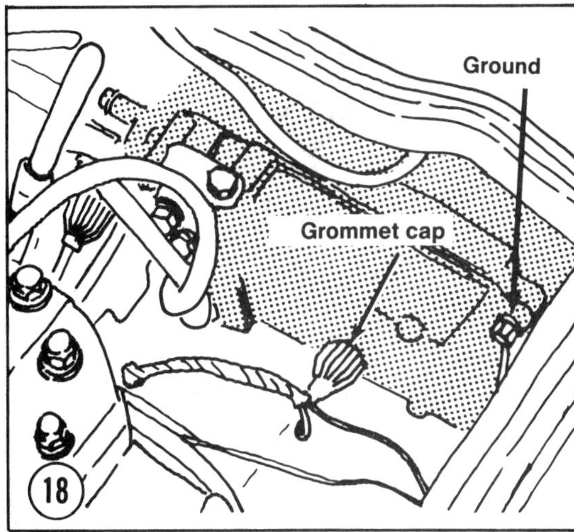

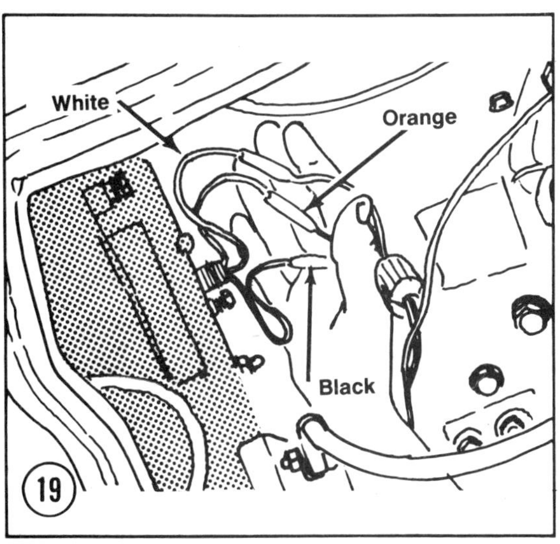

7. Pull off the spark plug leads and disconnect the starter cable at the starter (**Figure 9**).

8. Disconnect the electric box ground wire at the electric box (**Figure 18**).

9. *On 1977-early 1978 models*: Spray the start and stop switch grommet cap on the front of the electric box with WD-40 to lubricate the rubber and unscrew the cap (**Figure 18**). Spray the wires in the hole with WD-40 and pull them out of the electric box one at a time until their connectors show (**Figure 19**). Disconnect the wires.

10. *On late 1978-1980 models*: Spray the start and stop switch grommet caps on top of the electric box with WD-40 to lubricate the rubber and unscrew the caps (**Figure 20**). Pull out the wires one at a time until their connectors show and disconnect the wires.

11. Loosen the set screw that mounts the fuel valve knob and pull off the knob (**Figure 21**).

12. Remove the 4 screws that hold the control panel (**Figure 21**) and pull off the panel with the choke cable attached.

CAUTION
The control panel and its mating casting are sealed to the hull with silicone sealant. They will stick to the hull strongly unless heated a little. Be careful not to damage the hull by prying against it.

13. Pull the electric box and control panel casting assembly away from the hull (**Figure 22**).

14. Hold the electric box out of the hull and remove the 4 nuts, washers and lock washers that connect the electric box to the control panel case (**Figure 23**). Pull the electric box off of the control panel case and take the electric box out of the engine compartment.

15. To separate the electric box halves, remove the 2 short bolts, washers and lockwashers.

16. To install, reverse the removal procedure. Note the following.

  a. Make sure the start and stop switch leads are sticking out of the front case opening. If they are inside the box, separate the halves and thread the leads out the openings.

  b. Connect the color-coded wires to wires of the same color, except as follows: on 1977 models up to hull No. 10700177, the *orange* wire from the stop switch connects to a double female connector and then to the *white* wire from the electric box. The *white* wire from the start switch connects to a double male connector and then to the *orange* wire from the electric box. This is a special modification by the factory to minimize accidental short circuiting and failure of the CDI unit. Jet Skis with this modification should have a special label on top of the electric box to show that the modification has been made.

  c. Coat the electric box gasket with silicone sealant on both sides. Install a new gasket if the old one is damaged. Make sure that none of the wires are pinched between the electric box halves.

  d. Apply a light coat of water-resistant grease such as Valvoline X-All to the

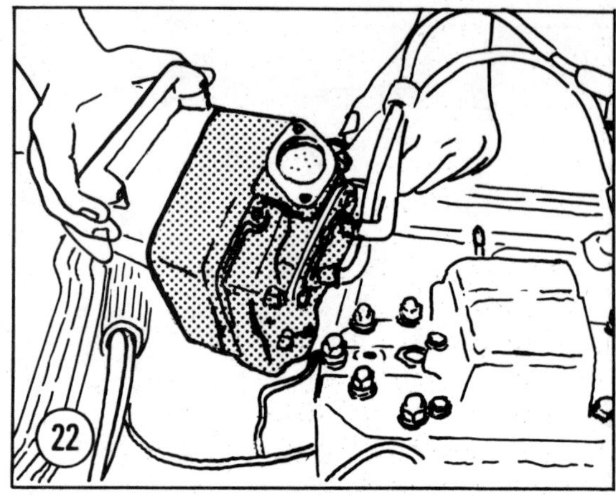

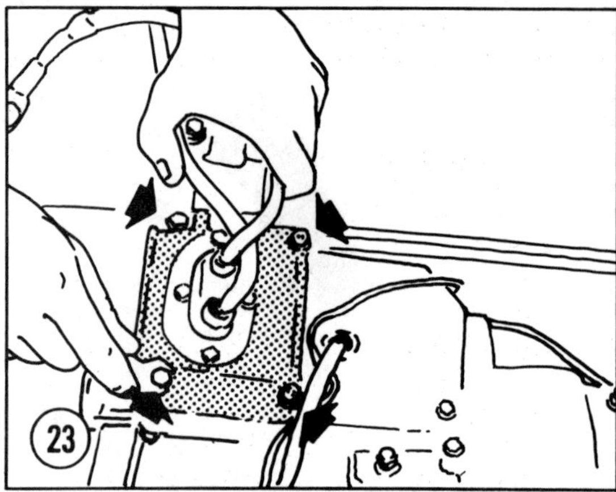

rubber switch connector grommets before tightening the caps.

  e. Use a light coat of silicone sealant on the surfaces of the control panel case and the control panel that mate with the hull.

  f. Adjust the choke cable as described under *Choke Cable* in Chapter Three.

Electric Box Removal/Installation (400 cc Models)

See **Figure 24**. On 400 cc models, you may not be able to separate the electric box halves without first removing the control panel and its casting from the front of the bulkhead, unless the engine's top end has been removed (see *Top End Disassembly* in Chapter Four). In that case, do not remove the control panel and choke cable.

This procedure describes removal of the control panel and casting, leaving the engine fully assembled.

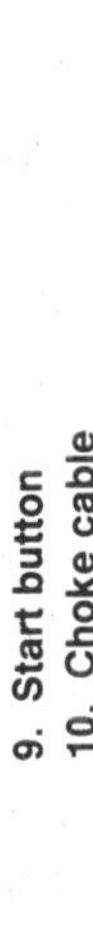

ELECTRIC BOX (400 cc)

1. Ignition coil
2. CDI unit
3. Starter solenoid
4. Regulator/rectifier
5. Starter cable
6. Battery positive (+) cable
7. Ground wire (black)
8. Stop button
9. Start button
10. Choke cable

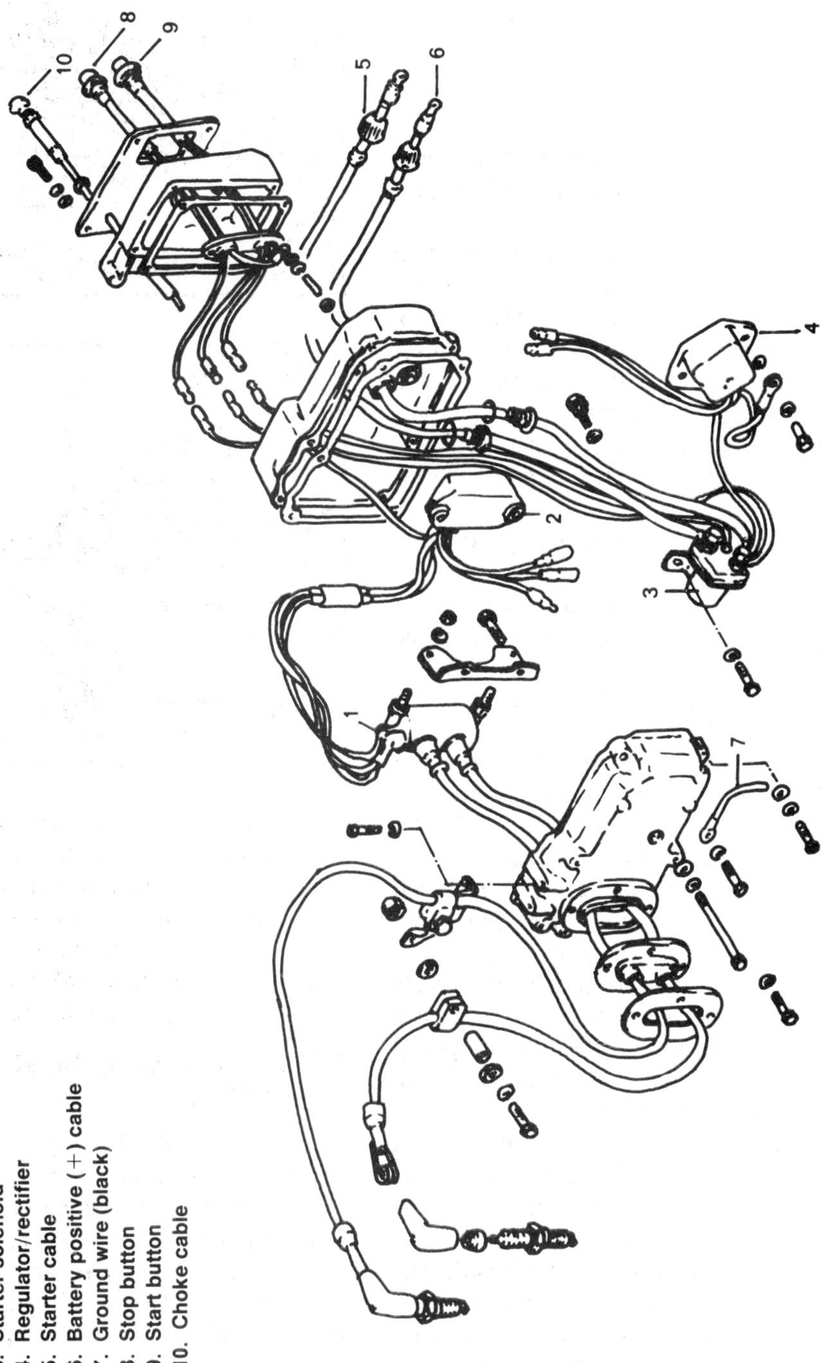

7

1. Remove the battery as described in this chapter.

2. Remove the exhaust pipe and expansion chamber as one piece; see *Exhaust Removal* in Chapter Six.

3. Remove the cable tie securing the wires to the choke cable.

4. Detach the choke cable from the carburetor; loosen the cable set screw, remove the top adjuster locknut and pull the cable down through the carburetor bracket.

5. Disconnect the choke cable bracket from the electric box. Open the bracket and slide it off the end of the choke cable.

6. Remove the plastic nut securing the choke cable to the inside of the hull. Pull the choke cable out of the hull.

7. Disconnect the spark plug leads, the electric box ground wire and the starter cable at the starter.

8. Remove the 4 screws that mount the control panel and pull the panel off of the hull bulkhead.

> *CAUTION*
> *The control panel and its mating casting are sealed to the hull with silicone sealant. They will stick to the hull strongly unless heated a little. Be careful not to damage the hull by prying against it.*

9. Pull the electric box and control panel casting assembly away from the hull.

10. Spray the magneto wiring grommet caps on the back of the electric box with WD-40 to lubricate the rubber and unscrew the caps. Spray the wires in the holes with WD-40 and pull them out of the electric box one at a time until their connectors show, then disconnect the wires.

11. Take the electric box out of the engine compartment.

12. To separate the electric box halves, remove the 6 bolts, washers and lockwashers and pull the halves apart.

13. To install, reverse the removal procedure. Note the following:

   a. Make sure the magneto wiring leads are sticking out of the rear case openings. If they are inside the box, separate the halves and thread the leads out the openings.

   b. Coat the electric box gasket with silicone sealant on both sides. Install a new gasket if the old one is damaged. Make sure that none of the wires are pinched between the electric box halves.

   c. Apply a light coat of water-resistant grease such as Valvoline X-All to the rubber connector grommets before tightening the caps.

   d. Use a light coat of silicone sealant on the surfaces of the control panel case and the control panel that mate with the hull.

   e. Adjust the choke cable as described under *Choke Cable* in Chapter Three.

CDI IGNITION SYSTEM

See **Figures 25-27** for schematic diagrams of the capacitive discharge ignition (CDI) system. The 1980 and later models have a stop switch relay that keeps the ignition OFF when the stop button is released. The solid state CDI has no wearing parts and, once assembled properly, should not require adjustment unless you want to alter the engine's performance characteristics.

A flywheel magneto mounted at the front of the crankshaft provides all the power for the CDI system. As the rotor (flywheel) turns, a magnet in the rotor passes an exciter coil on the stator assembly. This generates an AC current pulse that flows to the CDI unit where it is rectified (converted) into a DC pulse that charges the capacitor in the CDI unit. A split second later, the rotor magnet passes another coil on the stator, the trigger coil. The trigger coil sends an AC current pulse to an electronic switch (thyristor or SCR) in the CDI unit. The electronic switch allows the charged capacitor to discharge through the ignition coil primary winding. This current surge through the primary winding induces a very high voltage current in the secondary winding, firing the spark plug.

The CDI system has a built-in electronic ignition advance. As the rotor turns faster, the trigger signal builds faster in degrees of crankshaft rotation, turning the electronic switch on earlier. This advances ignition timing as rpm increases.

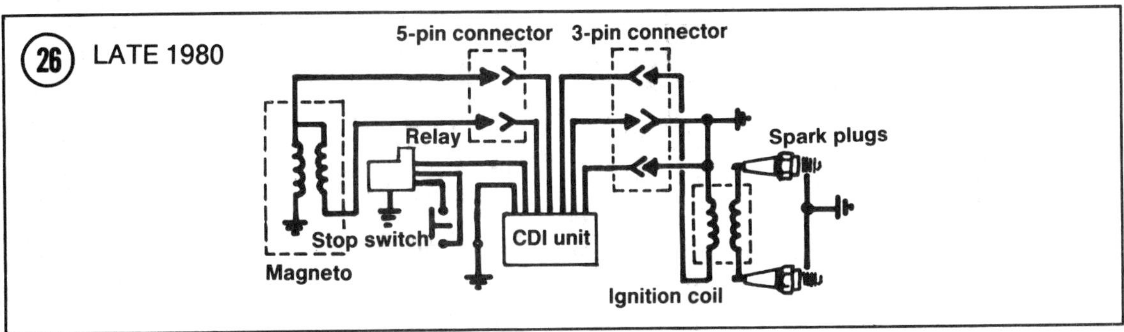

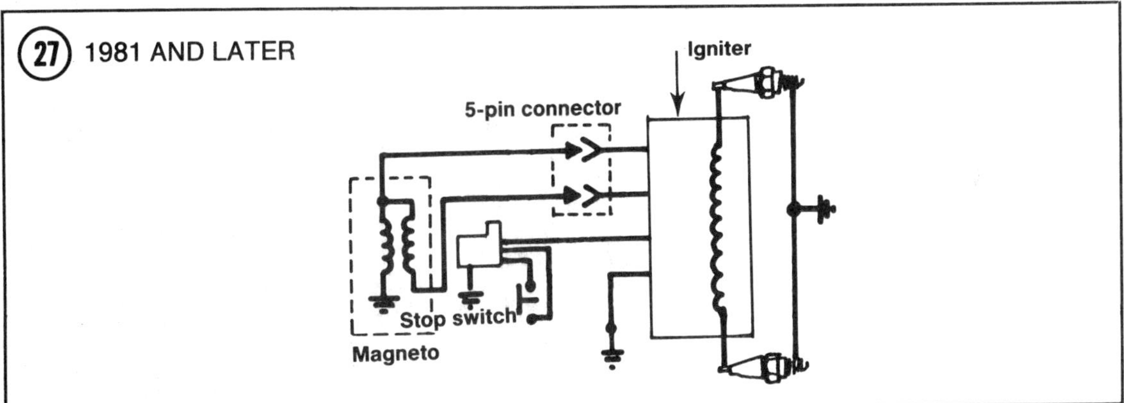

27 1981 AND LATER

IGNITION TIMING

The solid state CDI has no wearing parts and, once assembled properly with the stator base plate marks aligned (**Figure 28**), should not require adjustment unless you want to alter the engine's performance characteristics.

The dynamic timing inspection procedure given here checks CDI timing at full advance, when proper timing is critical for maximum power.

If you want to check ignition timing at exactly the specified rpm, you will need a tachometer suited for use on electronic ignition systems. Sun Instruments makes an Inductive Tach-Dwell Meter with a sensor lead that clips onto a spark plug lead. The meter is available at well-stocked auto parts stores.

1. Remove the fuel tank from the boat; see *Fuel Tank Removal* in Chapter Six. Lay it next to the boat and connect the fuel hoses to the carburetor.

2. Remove the magneto cover as described in *Rotor Removal* in this chapter.

3. Reinstall the 2 front starter mounting bolts to hold the starter in place. On 1976-early 1980 models the battery ground lead must be connected at the upper starter mounting bolt.

4. Remove the front spark plug and position the piston at top dead center (TDC). Verify that the piston is exactly at TDC by installing a dial indicator in the spark plug hole (**Figure 29**). Turn the rotor until the indicator needle reaches its maximum reading.

5. Attach a rigid pointer to one of the magneto cover bolts and line it up with the "T" mark on the flywheel while the front piston is at TDC (**Figure 29**).

> *NOTE*
> *A pointer made of sheet metal will provide a more rigid reference mark than one made of wire.*

6. Remove the dial indicator, install the spark plug and connect the spark plug lead.

7. Hook up a stroboscopic timing light according to the instrument manufacturer's instructions.

8. Connect an electronic tachometer according to the instrument manufacturer's instructions.

9. Start the engine and point the light at the pointer and timing marks. Run the engine at 6,000 rpm. The light will flash as the "F" mark aligns with the pointer if ignition timing is correct (**Figure 30**). Stop the engine immediately following this test.

> *WARNING*
> *The exhaust gases are poisonous. Do not run the engine in a closed area. Make sure there is plenty of ventilation.*

> *CAUTION*
> *Do not run the engine for more than 15 seconds without a supply of cooling*

water or the rubber parts of the exhaust system will be damaged. Prolonged running without coolant will cause serious engine damage. Do not operate the engine at maximum speed out of the water.

NOTE
If no tachometer is available, gradually increase engine speed until the "F" mark stops moving closer to the pointer.

10. If the timing is not correct, loosen the stator plate set screws through the holes in the flywheel (**Figure 31**) and turn the stator plate as required to set the timing. Turning the stator to the left (counterclockwise) advances timing. Tighten the stator screws and recheck the timing.

11. When the timing is correct, remove the timing light and the pointer.

12. Remove the 2 front starter mounting bolts.

13. Install the magneto cover as described in *Rotor Installation* in this chapter.

14. Install the fuel tank; see *Fuel Tank Installation* in Chapter Six.

ROTOR

The rotor (flywheel) must be removed to service the stator coils. Rotor replacement is usually necessary only if the rotor magnets have been damaged by mechanical shock or heat.

Rotor Removal

NOTE
This procedure is shown with the engine removed from the hull for clarity. Engine removal is not required for rotor removal.

See **Figure 32**.

1. Remove the fuel tank from the boat; see *Fuel Tank Removal* in Chapter Six.

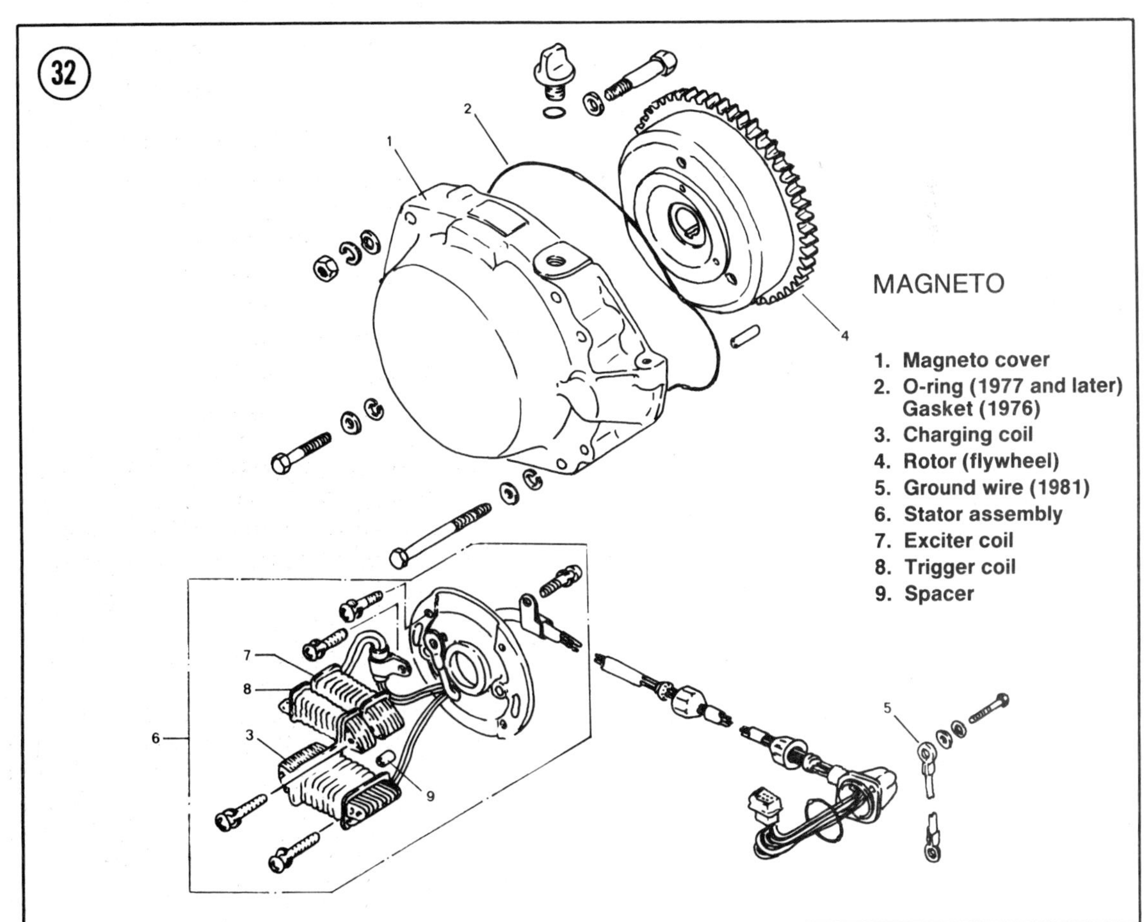

2. Remove the 2 bolts at the front of the starter (**Figure 33**).

3. Remove the 4 magneto cover bolts and the cover (**Figure 34**).

4. Fold down the tabs on the rotor lockwasher (**Figure 35**).

5. Hold the rotor steady with a rotor holding tool and remove the rotor nut (**Figure 36**).

6. Loosen the rotor with a 4-bolt Kawasaki rotor puller (**Figure 37**), part No. T57001-259. Back out the puller center bolt, screw the 3 outer bolts into the rotor, then screw in the center bolt to pull the rotor off. You may have to alternate tapping on the center puller bolt sharply with a hammer and tightening the bolt some more (**Figure 38**), but don't hit the rotor.

> *CAUTION*
> *Rotor removal requires a puller such as the one illustrated. Don't pry or hammer on the rotor itself. Damage is sure to result and you may also destroy the rotor's magnetism. You may be able to substitute an automotive steering wheel puller for the special Kawasaki puller.*

7. Remove the rotor and pull the Woodruff key out of the end of the crankshaft (**Figure 39**).

Rotor Installation

See **Figure 32**.

1. Inspect the inside of the rotor carefully for any bits of metal or small parts that may have been picked up by the rotor magnets. Remove them to prevent damage when the engine starts.

2. Wipe the rotor hole clean, apply WD-40 to the crankshaft taper and then slide the rotor onto the crankshaft, aligning the Woodruff key with the slot in the rotor.

3. Install a new tabwasher with its tongue in the rotor hole (**Figure 40**).

4. Install the rotor nut. Hold the rotor steady with a rotor holding tool (**Figure 36**) and torque the nut as specified.

   a. 440 cc engines: 115 ft.-lb. (16.0 mkg)

   b. 400 cc engines: 85 ft.-lb. (12.0 mkg)

5. Bend the tabs on the washer up against the nut (**Figure 41**).

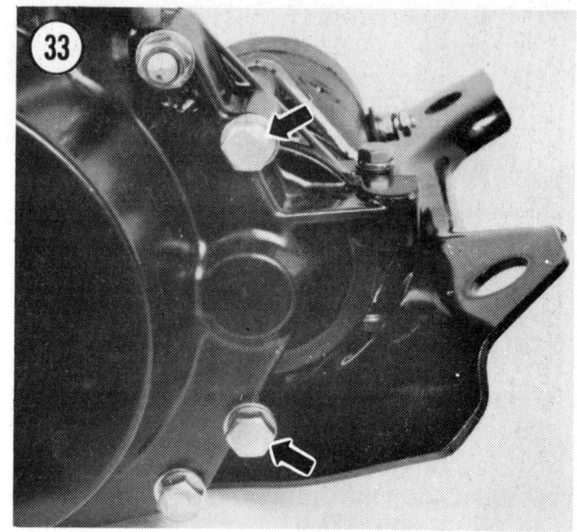

6. *On 1977 and later models*: Check that the magneto cover O-ring is in good condition. Apply a light coat of waterproof grease such as Valvoline X-All.

7. *On 1976 models*: Apply silicone sealant to both sides of the magneto cover gasket.

8. Install the magneto cover. Use a flat washer and lockwasher under each bolt head or nut.

9. Reinstall the 2 front starter mounting bolts. On 1976-early 1980 models the battery ground lead must be connected at the upper starter mounting bolt.

10. Install the fuel tank; see *Fuel Tank Installation* in Chapter Six.

STATOR

The stator contains the exciter and trigger coils for the ignition system and the charging coil for the charging system.

Stator alignment during installation establishes ignition timing. The magneto stator and coil assembly must be removed to separate the engine cases. Stator removal is not necessary for coil testing.

Stator Coil Inspection

On 440 cc engines, disconnect the 5-pin connector from the magneto (**Figure 11**) and measure the resistance between the pairs of leads listed in **Table 1**. The resistance readings are *approximate*. If the resistance is zero (short circuit) or infinite (open circuit), check the wiring to the coils and replace the coil(s) if the wiring is okay.

On 400 cc engines, coil inspection will be easiest if the rotor is removed; do not try to puncture the stator wire insulation to take test readings or you will promote corrosion of the wires.

Stator Coil
Removal/Installation

1. To remove the coils from the stator, remove the coil mounting screws (A, **Figure 42**), disconnect or cut the wires close to the coils and remove the coils.

2. When installing the trigger and exciter coils, position them as shown in **Figure 43**, with the red leads toward the right side of the Jet Ski and the grey lead toward the left side of the Jet Ski.

A. Coil mounting screws   B. Stator screws

3. Solder the new wire connections, matching color-coded wires, and insulate the connections with electrical tape. Use resin core solder, not acid core solder.

Stator Removal

See **Figure 32**.

> *NOTE*
> *The 400 cc engine's stator cable is permanently wired into the electric box and engine. Replacement requires electric box removal.*

1. Remove the magneto rotor; see *Rotor Removal* in this chapter.

2. Remove the 2 stator screws and loosen the stator (B, **Figure 42**).

3. Spray a little WD-40 on the connectors and wires at both ends of the stator cable. Loosen the connector caps.

4. Use a small pair of long-nose pliers to compress the spring retainer in each pin in the 5-pin connector (**Figure 44**) and pull each wire and pin out of the connector, one at a time.

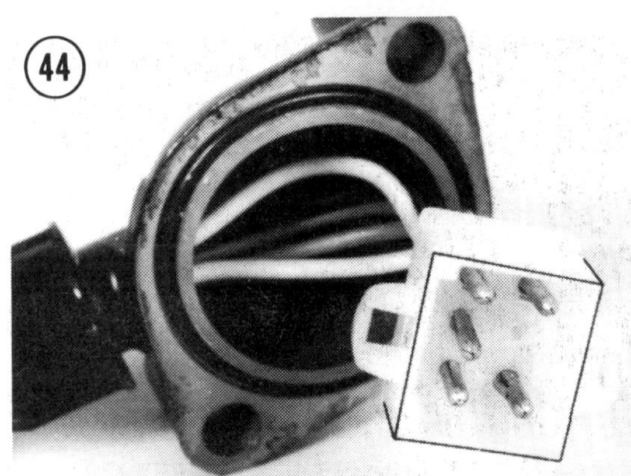

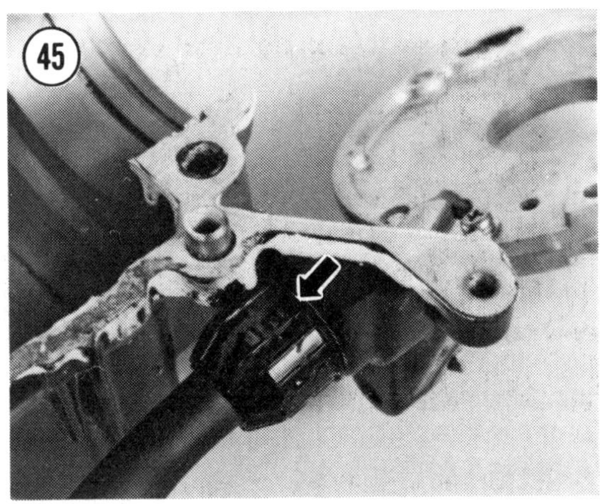

replacement requires removal of the individual stator wires.

3. Pull the wires through the outer tube and insert them through the grommet plug, after treating it with a light coat of WD-40. On 1979 and later models, the tube covering the wires between the grommets must cover the ends of the grommets by 3/8 in. (10 mm).

4. Align the 5-pin connector halves and insert the pins into the connector so that each lead will match the electric box connector lead of the same color. Make sure each pin's locking tang is seated inside the connector.

5. Position the magneto stator so that the mark on the stator plate lines up with the parting line of the crankcases (**Figure 28**). Put a small amount of silicone sealant on the threads of the 2 stator screws (B, **Figure 42**), slip on their lockwashers and flat washers and tighten them securely.

6. Solder the new wire connections, matching color-coded wires, and insulate the connections with electrical tape. Use resin core solder, not acid core solder.

7. Inspect the ignition timing as described in this chapter. Adjust it if necessary.

IGNITER
(1981-ON MODELS)

On 1981 and later models, the ignition coil and CDI unit are manufactured in one piece, called the "igniter." The igniter is inside the electric box (**Figure 46**).

5. Spray a little WD-40 on the grommet and wires and gently pull the grommet off of the wires.

6. Remove the outer tube from the wire cable.

7. Pull the wires out of the lower crankcase and remove the stator assembly.

Stator Installation

1. Push the wires through the hole in the lower crankcase half, one at a time.

2. Spray a little WD-40 on the grommet plug and insert the wires through the plug and cap. Then, apply a light coat of a water-resistant grease such as Valvoline X-All to the grommet and install the cap securely.

CAUTION
*The stator grommet cap (**Figure 45**) is made of brittle plastic. Be very careful to avoid cracking or damaging this cap, as*

Igniter Inspection

The ignition coil secondary circuit can be inspected without opening the electric box. With an ohmmeter set at R x 100, measure the resistance between the 2 high-tension leads at the spark plug connectors. The resistance should be 4,500-6,500 ohms. If the meter indicates an open circuit (no continuity), the igniter is faulty and must be replaced. The high-tension leads are not replaceable individually.

NOTE
The primary side of the coil in the igniter cannot be inspected.

Inspection of the CDI part of the igniter requires opening the electric box as described in this chapter. To avoid damaging the igniter, use a small portable multimeter such as one that is used for radio repair. Set the meter to R x 1000 range and connect the meter leads to each pair of igniter leads in turn. The readings should be as indicated in **Figure 47**.

Test the first horizontal row. If the expected readings are obtained, finish the test using this meter polarity. If the expected readings are not obtained for the first row, reverse the polarity (+ to -) of the leads at the meter and test the same row again. If the expected readings are now obtained for the first row, complete the test using this new meter lead polarity.

If the stator coils and wires are good, the igniter itself could be the source of a problem. Substitution of a known good igniter is the only way to verify a suspected CDI problem under actual running conditions.

IGNITION COIL TEST
(1976-1980 MODELS)

The ignition coil is inside the electric box. The ignition coil is a step-up transformer which increases the low voltage produced by the magneto to a high voltage required to jump the spark plug gap.

If the functional condition of the coil is in doubt, there are several checks which should be made.

1. Separate the electric box halves as described in this chapter and disconnect the 3-pin connector from the ignition coil.

2. With an ohmmeter set at R x 1, measure the resistance between each primary wire *purple* and ground *black*. The resistance should be 0.40-0.47 ohms.

3. With an ohmmeter set at R x 100, measure the resistance between the 2 high-tension leads at the spark plug connectors. The resistance should be 9,500-11,500 ohms.

4. If the meter indicates an open circuit (no continuity) in Step 3, unplug both high-tension leads from the coil and test the coil again with the meter leads connected directly to the contact pins in the coil caps.

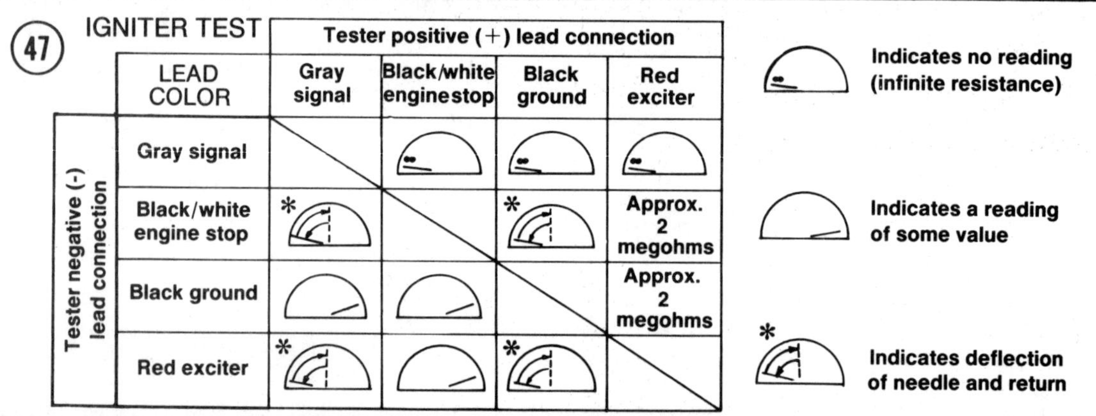

Before checking connections indicated with an asterisk, short the two CDI unit leads together to discharge any residual voltage in the capacitor. The amount of needle deflection may be slight or large. If the expected deflection is not observed, reverse the meter leads (+ to -), test the circuit, return the leads to normal polarity and check the circuit again. If the circuit is good, you will observe the deflection.

NOTE
The high-tension leads are secured with epoxy and are not available from Kawasaki as replacement parts. However, you can substitute common high-tension leads available at auto parts stores.

If there is continuity now at the coil terminals, the trouble is in the high-tension leads. It may be a bad connection at the spark plug or an internal break in the wire. Make sure the connections are good and check the leads themselves for continuity. If an open circuit is still indicated, replace the high-tension leads. If high tension leads have continuity, the coil itself is faulty and must be replaced.

Normal resistance in both the primary and secondary windings in the coil is not a guarantee that the unit is in top working order; only an operational test can tell if a coil is producing an adequate spark from the input voltage. Your Jet Ski dealer or auto electrical repair shop may have the equipment to test the coil's output. If not, substitute a known good coil to see if the problem goes away.

CDI UNIT TEST
(1976-1980 MODELS)

The CDI unit is inside the electric box. Disconnect the 3-pin connector from the ignition coil and the 3 single wire connectors from the CDI unit.

To avoid damaging the CDI unit, use a small portable multimeter such as one that is used for radio repair. Set the meter to R x 1000 and connect the meter leads to each pair of CDI unit leads in turn. The readings should be as indicated in **Figure 48** (use **Figure 49** if your CDI unit is marked "71" or higher on its case).

Test the first horizontal row. If the expected readings are obtained, finish the test using this meter polarity. If the expected readings are not obtained for the first row, reverse the polarity

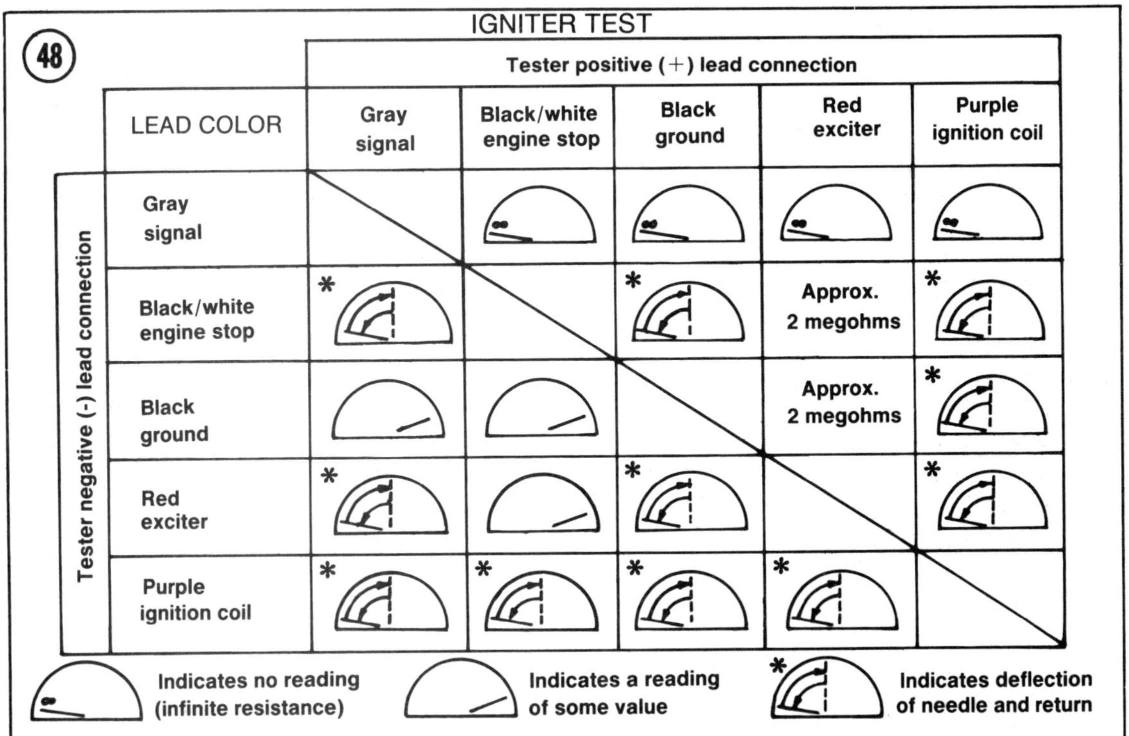

IGNITER TEST

LEAD COLOR	Tester positive (+) lead connection				
	Gray signal	Black/white engine stop	Black ground	Red exciter	Purple ignition coil
Gray signal		No reading	No reading	No reading	No reading
Black/white engine stop	* Deflection		* Deflection	Approx. 2 megohms	* Deflection
Black ground	Reading	Reading		Approx. 2 megohms	* Deflection
Red exciter	* Deflection	Reading	* Deflection		* Deflection
Purple ignition coil	* Deflection	* Deflection	* Deflection	* Deflection	

(Row labels at left are the Tester negative (−) lead connection.)

Indicates no reading (infinite resistance). Indicates a reading of some value. * Indicates deflection of needle and return.

Before checking connections indicated with an asterisk, short the two CDI unit leads together to discharge any residual voltage in the capacitor. The amount of needle deflection may be slight, or large. If the expected deflection is not observed, reverse the meter leads (+ to -), test the circuit, return the leads to normal polarity and check the circuit again. If the circuit is good, you will observe the deflection.

IGNITER TEST (CDI UNITS MARKED "71" OR HIGHER)

⑭9

LEAD COLOR	Tester positive (+) lead connection				
	Gray signal	Black/white engine stop	Black ground	Red exciter	Purple ignition coil
Gray signal		no reading	no reading	no reading	no reading
Black/white engine stop	no reading		no reading	no reading	no reading
Black ground	reading	reading		Approx. 2 megohms	* deflection
Red exciter	* deflection	reading	* deflection		* deflection
Purple ignition coil	* deflection	* deflection	* deflection	* deflection	

(Row labels at left are under "Tester negative (−) lead connection".)

	Indicates no reading (infinite resistance)		Indicates a reading of some value	*	Indicates deflection of needle and return

Before checking connections indicated with an asterisk, short the two CDI unit leads together to discharge any residual voltage in the capacitor. The amount of needle deflection may be slight, or large. If the expected deflection is not observed, reverse the meter leads (+ to −), test the circuit, return the leads to normal polarity and check the circuit again. If the circuit is good, you will observe the deflection.

(+ to −) of the leads at the meter and test the same row again. If the expected readings are now obtained for the first row, complete the test using this new meter lead polarity.

If all other ignition parts are good, the CDI unit itself could be the source of a problem. Substitution of a known good CDI unit is the only way to verify a suspected CDI problem under actual running conditions.

CHARGING SYSTEM

The function of the charging system is to keep the battery at its full potential for reliable starting. The system is composed of a charging coil and a voltage regulator, connected in circuit with the battery. See **Figure 50**.

When the magneto flywheel magnets move past the charging coil, it generates an alternating current (AC) which is fed to the regulator. The rectifier within the regulator converts the AC to direct current (DC), which flows to the battery. The regulator maintains a

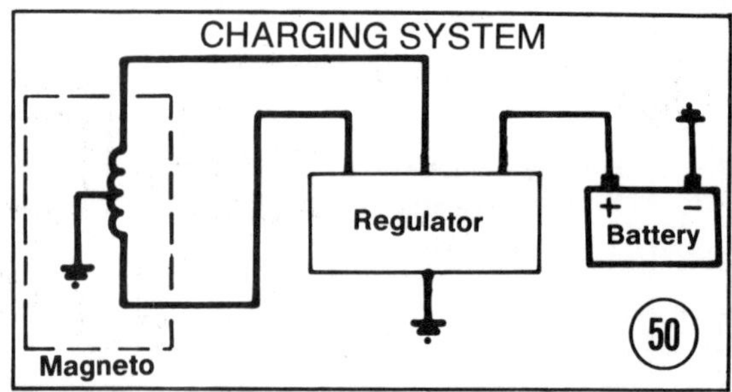

constant voltage to the battery, regardless of variations in engine speed.

Charging System Test

Inspect the charging coil resistance as described in *Stator Coil Inspection* in this chapter. If the charging coil is functioning properly, but the battery continually discharges or overcharges, the problem may be a faulty regulator. See **Figure 8**, **Figure 16** or **Figure 24** for the regulator location in your Jet Ski.

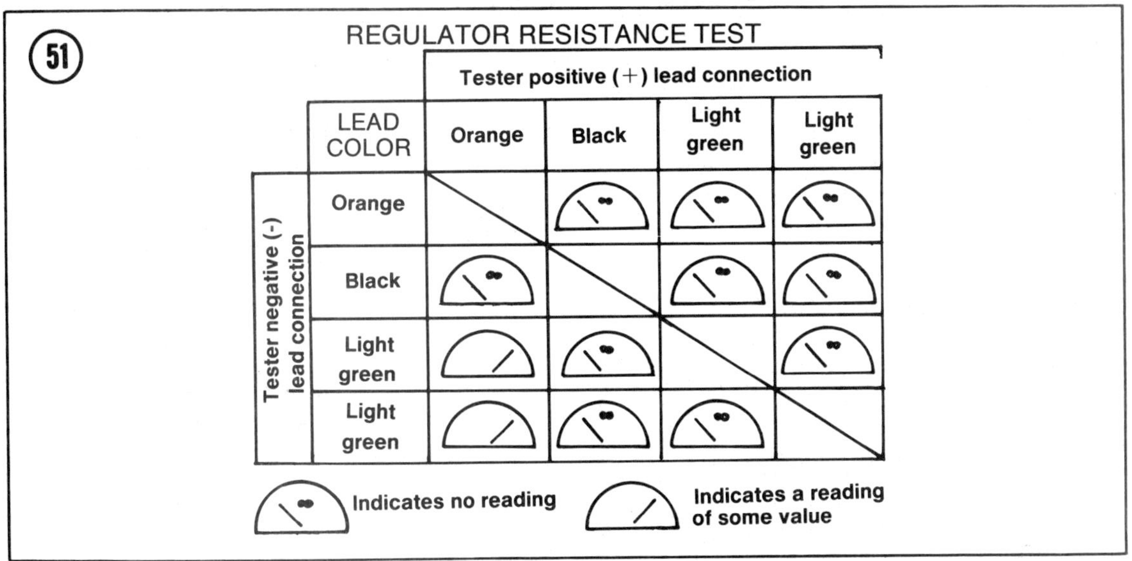

LEAD COLOR	Orange	Black	Light green	Light green
Orange		no reading	no reading	no reading
Black	no reading		no reading	no reading
Light green	reading	no reading		no reading
Light green	reading	no reading	no reading	

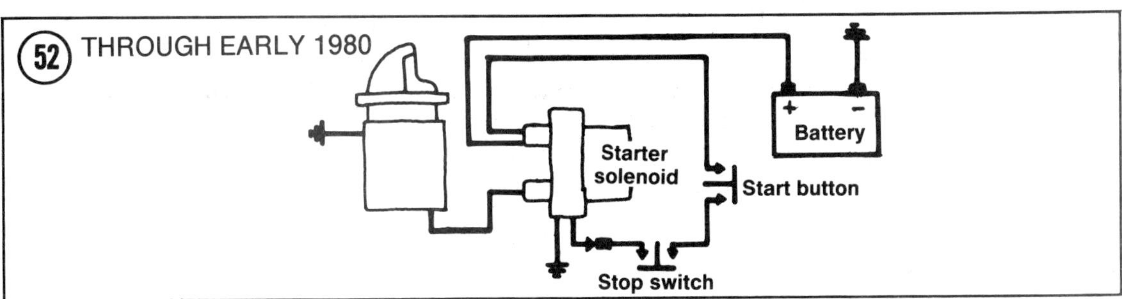

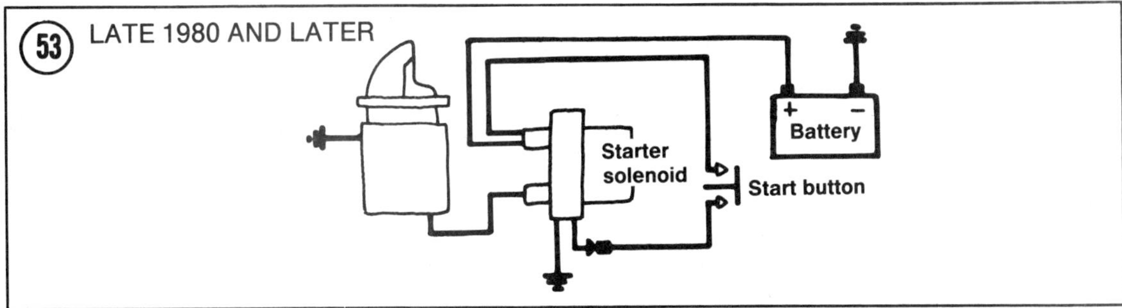

To inspect the regulator, set an ohmmeter at R x 100 and connect the meter leads to each pair of regulator leads in turn. The readings should be as indicated in **Figure 51**.

If the expected readings are not obtained, reverse the polarity (+ to -) of the leads at the meter and test the regulator again. If the expected readings are now obtained, the regulator is okay. If any readings are not as indicated with the proper meter polarity, the regulator should be replaced.

STARTING SYSTEM

The starting system consists of the stop switch (on 1976-early 1980 models only), start switch, starter solenoid, battery and starter motor. **Figure 52** and **Figure 53** are schematic diagrams of the starting systems.

When the starter button is pressed, it engages the solenoid switch which then closes the circuit. Electricity flows from the battery to the starter motor. On 1976-early 1980 models, the starter will not operate if the engine stop switch is OFF. On 1981 and later models, the starter cables can be replaced without opening the electric box (**Figure 54**). Earlier models require removal of the electric box for starter cable replacement.

Starter Removal/Installation

1. *On 1979 and later models*: Disconnect the ground lead at the engine.
2. *On 1976-1978 models*: Disconnect the ground lead at the battery.
3. Remove the exhaust pipe and expansion chamber in one piece; see *Exhaust Removal* in Chapter Six.
4. Pull back the rubber cap at the starter and disconnect the battery lead (**Figure 55**).
5. Disconnect the cooling water inlet hose from the exhaust manifold.
6. Remove the 2 bolts at the rear of the starter (**Figure 56**). Note any shims between the starter and the crankcase so the same shims can be installed later.
7. Remove the 2 bolts at the front of the starter (**Figure 57**) and remove the starter.
8. To install, reverse the removal procedure. Note the following:
   a. Apply a light coat of grease to the starter drive gear mechanism.
   b. Check the condition of the starter's O-ring, then grease it lightly and install it in the starter groove (**Figure 58**).
   c. Loosely install the starter, using 2 bolts, lockwashers and flat washers at the front and 2 at the rear bracket. Torque the 2 front bolts to 12 ft.-lb. (1.6 mkg).

   NOTE
   On 1976-early 1980 models, the battery ground cable must be attached to the upper front starter mount bolt before tightening.

   d. Measure the space between the crankcase and the rear bracket of the starter (**Figure 59**). Install shims or washers to take up any clearance, then torque the 2 rear bolts to 50 in.-lb. (0.6 mkg).

Starter Inspection

1. Remove the 4 starter end cover screws and remove the cover (**Figure 60**). The slotted

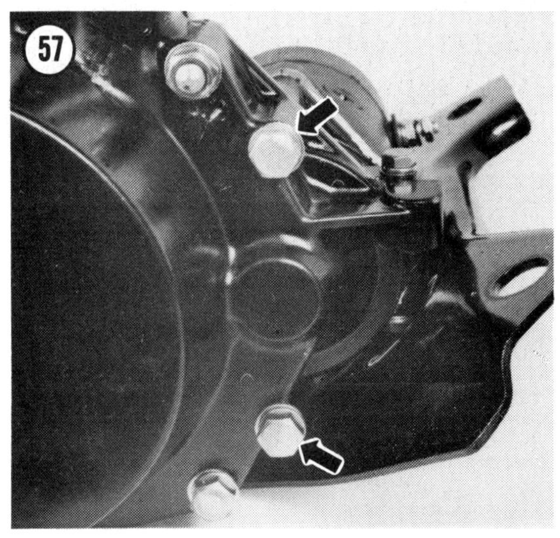

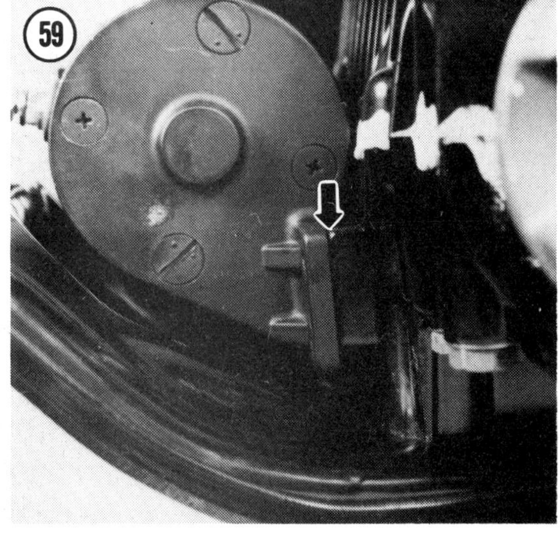

screws are very tight. An impact driver will be required to remove them.

2. Clean all grease, dirt and carbon dust from the brush holder and end cover (**Figure 61**).

3. Remove the brushes and measure the length of the brushes (**Figure 62**). If a brush is worn

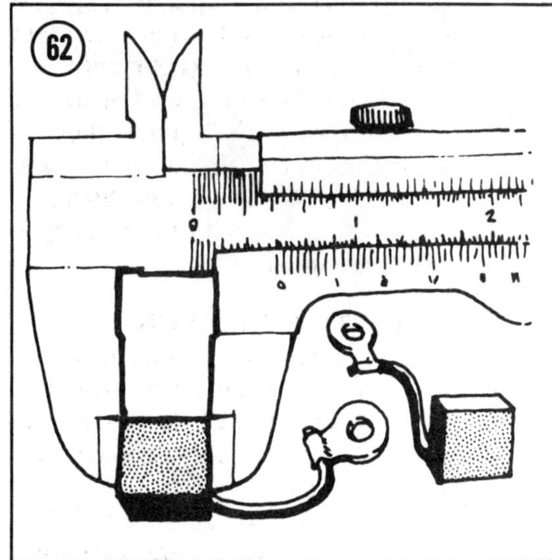

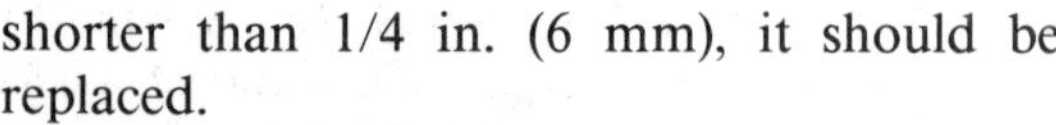

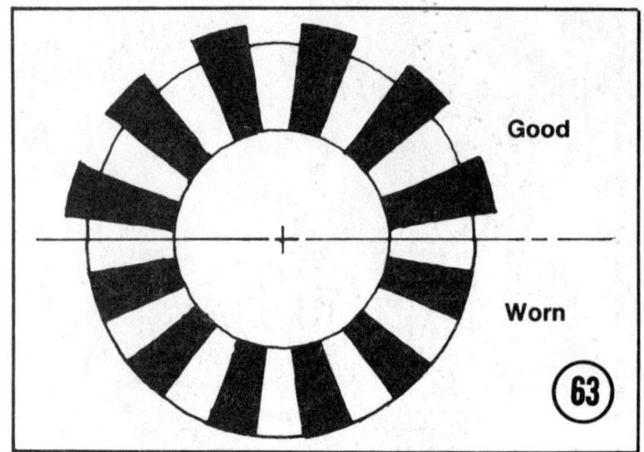

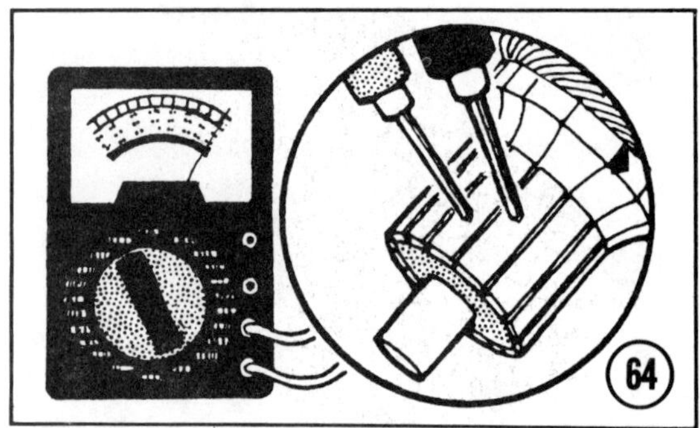

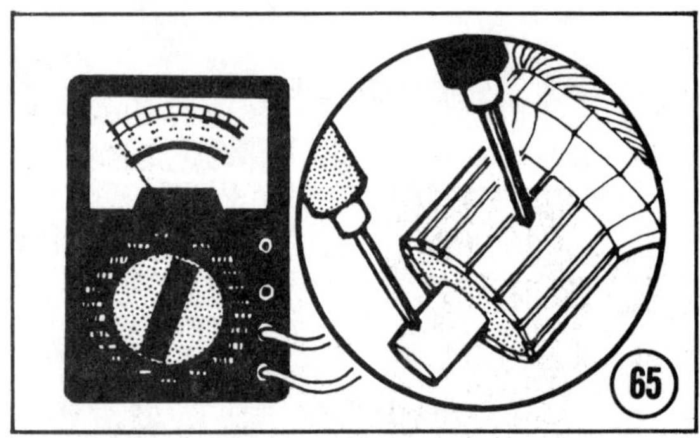

shorter than 1/4 in. (6 mm), it should be replaced.

4. Inspect the condition of the commutator (**Figure 63**). The mica in the normal commutator is cut below the copper. A worn commutator is also shown where the copper is worn to the level of the mica. A worn commutator can be undercut, but it requires a specialist. Take the job to your Jet Ski dealer or auto electrical repair shop.

5. Inspect the commutator bars for discoloration. If a pair of bars are discolored, that indicates grounded armature coils.

6. Check the electrical continuity between pairs of armature bars (**Figure 64**) and between the commutator bars and the shaft (**Figure 65**). There should be continuity between pairs of bars but no continuity between the bars and the shaft. If the results are not as described, replace the armature.

7. Inspect the field coil by checking continuity from the cable terminal to the brush wire. If there is a short or open, the case should be replaced.

8. Inspect the front and rear end cover bearings for damage. Replace the starter if they are worn or damaged.

9. Assemble by reversing the removal steps. Note the following:
   a. Reinstall any shims (**Figure 66**).
   b. Align the notch on the front end cover with the tab in the housing (**Figure 67**).

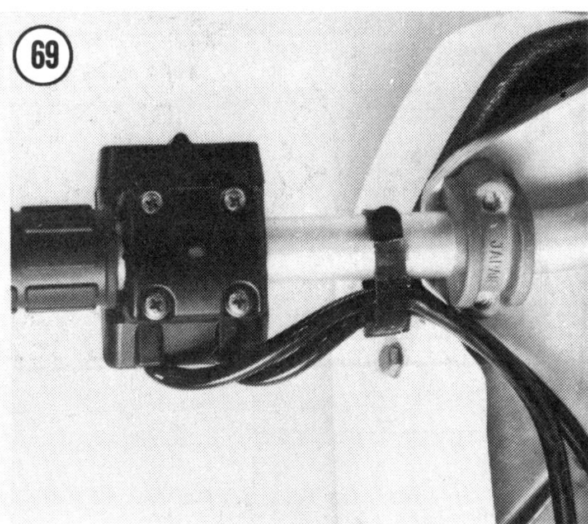

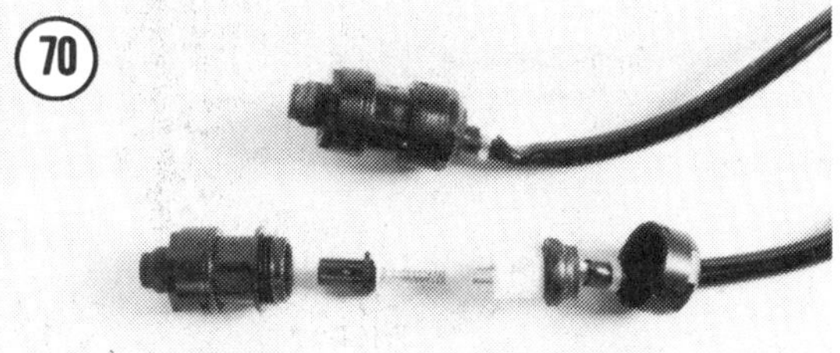

c. Align the brush plate so that the long bolts will pass through the housing and screw into the front end cover (**Figure 68**).

d. Make sure the 4 cover screw O-rings are in good condition. Replace them if necessary. Lubricate them with grease. Use WD-40 on the long screw threads.

e. Align the rear cover with the housing as shown in **Figure 60**.

STARTER SOLENOID

Before testing the starter solenoid, make sure the battery is fully charged, with adequate electrolyte, and make sure all the connections between the battery and starter are corrosion-free and tight.

The starter solenoid is inside the electric box. If the solenoid fails to operate, the starter will not get power from the battery. Before you dig into the electric box, check the solenoid's operation by connecting a voltmeter or VOM from the starter's side terminal to engine ground. On late 1980-on models, check that the safety switch is ON. On 1976-early 1980 models, make sure the red engine stop button is ON (out). Push the start button and observe the meter. If the meter reads battery voltage when the starter button is pushed, the solenoid is okay.

If the meter does not show battery voltage during the test, check the starter positive (+) cable back to the electric box for good electrical connections. To replace the solenoid, remove the electric box and open it as described in this chapter. See **Figure 8**, **Figure 16** or **Figure 24** for the solenoid location in your Jet Ski.

START AND STOP SWITCHES

The late 1980-on models have both start and stop switches in one case mounted on the handlebar. When installing the switch case, be sure to align the case peg with the hole in the handlebar and secure the switch leads with a cable tie (**Figure 69**). The 1977-early 1980 models have a separate stop switch and start switch and the 1976 models have a stop switch and start switch mounted on the control panel.

The switches are sealed to prevent corrosion and they should not be disassembled except in an emergency. **Figure 70** shows 1981 switch components.

STOP SWITCH RELAY
(LATE 1980-ON MODELS)

The late 1980 and later boats have a latching relay (**Figure 71**) connected to the stop switch so that the button need only be pressed once and released to ground the CDI unit and break the ignition circuit. Earlier boats without the relay use a latching stop switch that locks either ON or OFF.

Inspection of the stop switch relay requires opening of the electric box as described in this chapter. Use a small portable multimeter such as one that is used for radio repair. Set the meter to the R x 1 range, disconnect the relay leads and connect the meter leads to each pair of relay leads in turn. The readings should be as indicated in **Figure 72**. If the readings are not as specified, install a new relay.

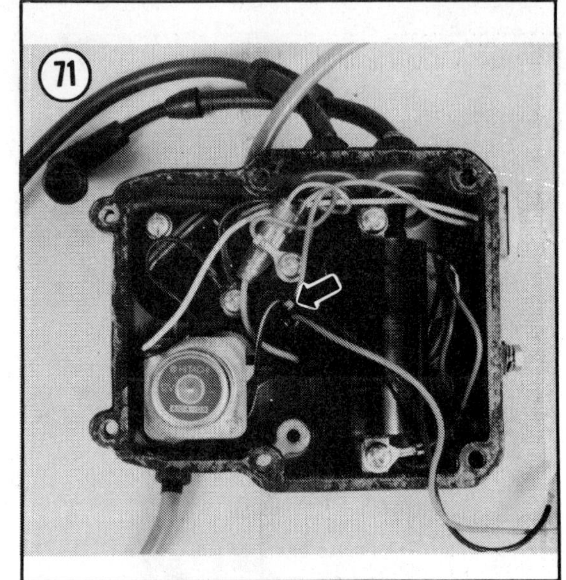

RELAY RESISTANCE TEST

LEAD COLOR	Tester positive (+) lead connection			
	Black White	Blue	Black	Brown
Black White		reading	no reading	no reading
Blue	reading		no reading	no reading
Black	no reading	no reading		reading
Brown	no reading	no reading	reading	

(Tester negative (-) lead connection — row labels)

Indicates no reading
Indicates a reading of some value

Table 1   JS400/440 ELECTRICAL SPECIFICATIONS

Alternator output	45W @ 6,000 rpm
Battery	12V, 16 AH
Charging current	
To 1980	1-2.3 amp
1981-on	1-4 amp
Ignition coil	
Primary resistance	0.43 ohm +/-10°
Secondary resistance	
1976-1980	10.5K ohm +/-10°
1981-on	5.6K ohm +/-20°
Ignition timing	25° BTDC @ 6,000 rpm, 0.139 in. (3.53 mm)
Regulator setting	
1976-1980	15.0 +/-0.5V
1981-on	14.0 +/-0.5V
Spark plugs	
U.S.	NGK B7ES; Champion N4G
Canada	NGK BR7ES
Starter motor	
Current draw	50 amp
Field coil resistance	0.006 ohm
Stator coil resistance	
Charging coil	
To 1980	3.0 ohm +/-10°
1981-on	2.7 ohm +/-20°
Exciter coil	
To 1980	270 ohm +/-10°
1981-on	250 ohm +/-20°
Trigger coil	
To 1980	65 ohm +/-10°
1981-on	25 ohm +/-20°

Table 2   BATTERY FREEZING TEMPERATURES

Specific Gravity	Freezing Temperature Degrees F.	Specific Gravity	Freezing Temperature Degrees F.
1.100	18	1.200	—17
1.120	13	1.220	—31
1.140	8	1.240	—50
1.160	1	1.260	—75
1.180	—6	1.280	—92

CHAPTER EIGHT

HULL

This chapter covers handle pole disassembly, hull repair and bilge system operation.

BILGE SYSTEM

Despite the fact that the Jet Ski is designed to prevent water from entering the engine compartment, some will always manage to get in. The purpose of the bilge system is to remove this unwanted water.

See **Figure 1**. The bilge system has no moving parts. It consists of a rubber hose connected to the jet pump outlet, a metal tube through the hull, a rubber hose to a plastic breather fitting and another rubber hose running to the bilge pickup filter in the engine compartment, below the bearing box.

On 1979 and later models the breather fitting is above and behind the battery on the bulkhead (**Figure 2**). On the 1976-1978 models the breather fitting is on the right side of the engine compartment (**Figure 3**).

When the jet pump is operating, water is forced out of the pump outlet at high speed, creating a low pressure area at the pump outlet. Mounted just in front of the steering nozzle is the bilge suction fitting, which draws water out of the engine compartment through the bilge filter, through the breather fitting and out the jet pump.

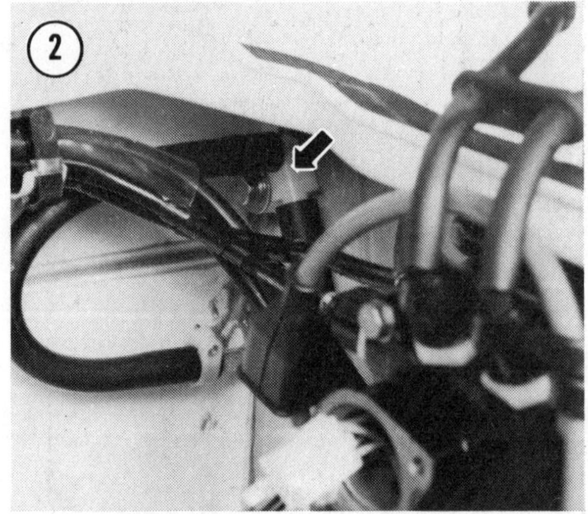

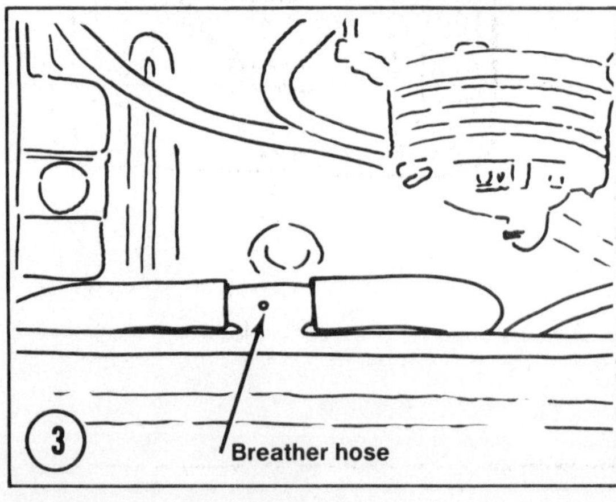

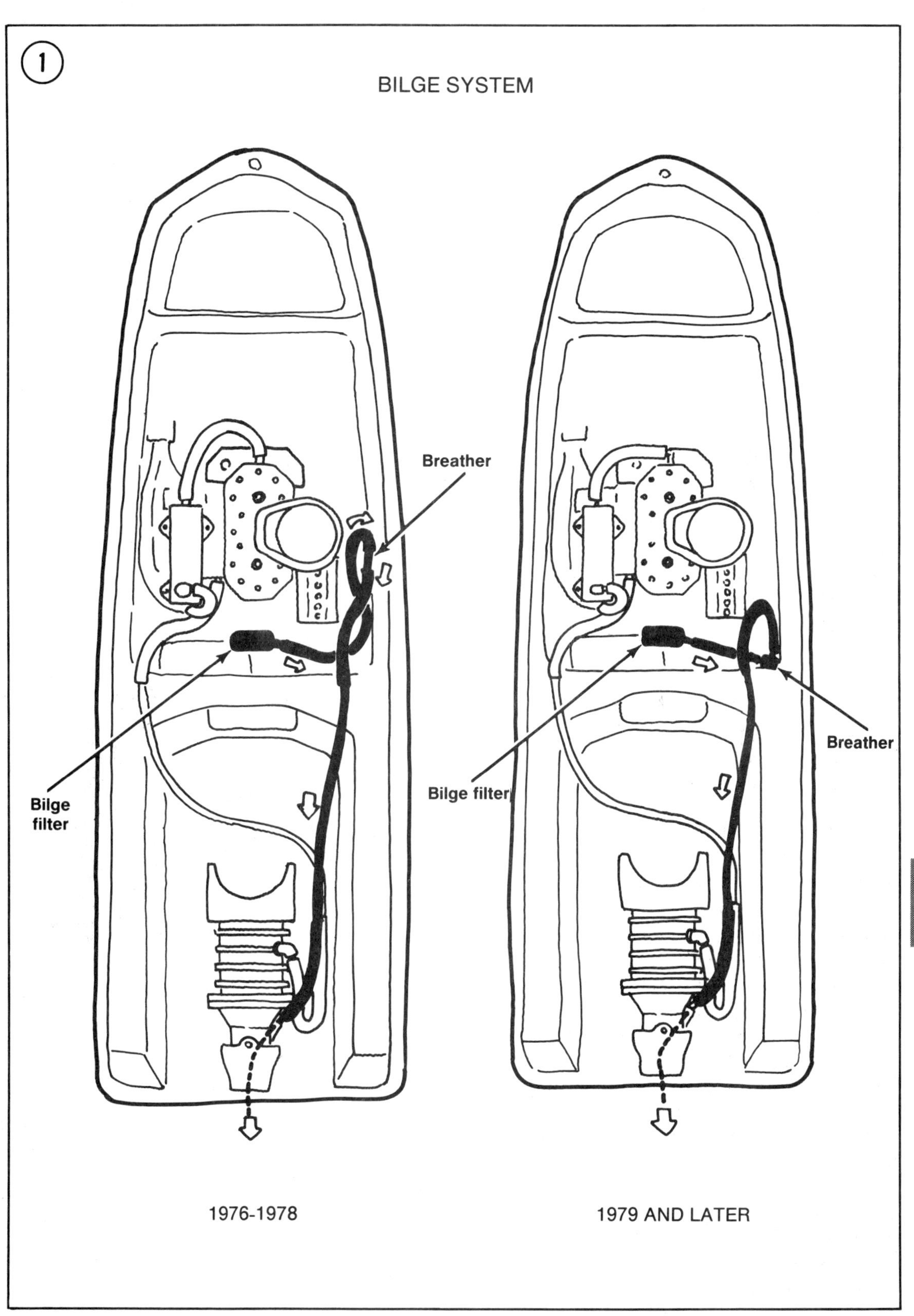

BILGE SYSTEM
Breather
Breather
Bilge filter
Bilge filter
1976-1978
1979 AND LATER
8

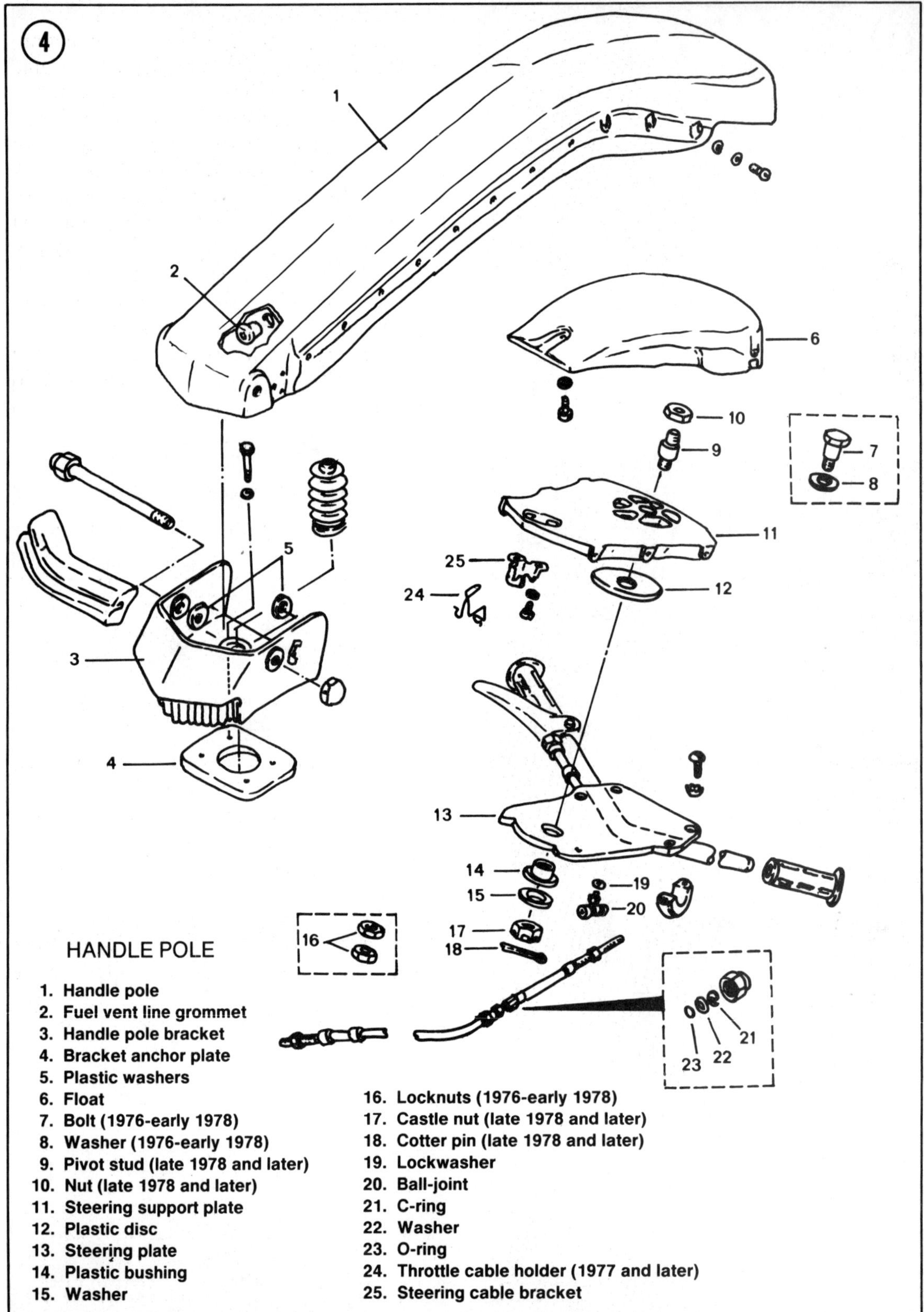

HANDLE POLE

1. **Handle pole**
2. **Fuel vent line grommet**
3. **Handle pole bracket**
4. **Bracket anchor plate**
5. **Plastic washers**
6. **Float**
7. **Bolt (1976-early 1978)**
8. **Washer (1976-early 1978)**
9. **Pivot stud (late 1978 and later)**
10. **Nut (late 1978 and later)**
11. **Steering support plate**
12. **Plastic disc**
13. **Steering plate**
14. **Plastic bushing**
15. **Washer**
16. **Locknuts (1976-early 1978)**
17. **Castle nut (late 1978 and later)**
18. **Cotter pin (late 1978 and later)**
19. **Lockwasher**
20. **Ball-joint**
21. **C-ring**
22. **Washer**
23. **O-ring**
24. **Throttle cable holder (1977 and later)**
25. **Steering cable bracket**

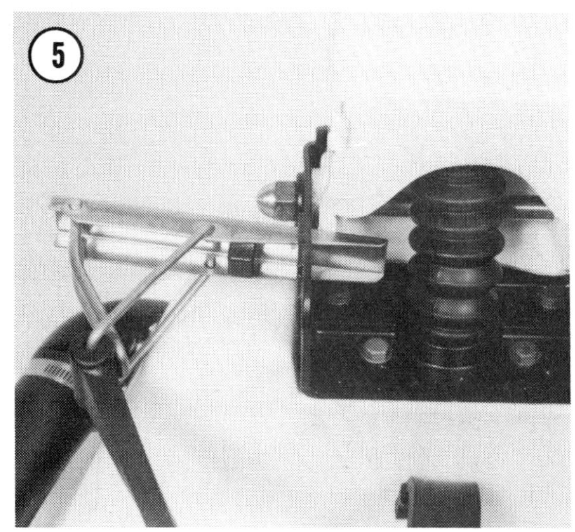

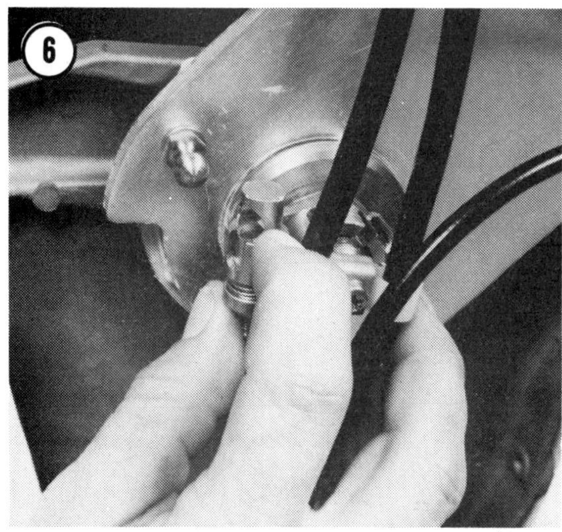

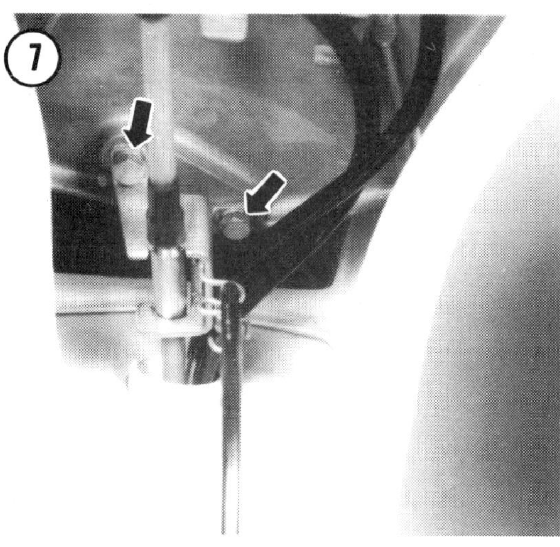

Since the bilge system depends on a fast flow of water through the jet pump to cause suction, the bilge system does not work when the engine is only idling. Water is emptied from the engine compartment when the boat is being ridden normally. The purpose of the plastic breather fitting is to prevent water from siphoning back into the boat when the engine is not running. In the top of the fitting is a tiny pin-hole that allows air to enter the bilge lines to break any possible siphoning effect. The hole is small enough to keep from interfering with normal bilge system operation. The pin-hole must be kept clear, but it must not be enlarged or the bilge system will not draw enough water to empty the engine compartment.

HANDLE POLE

Handle Pole Removal

This procedure describes handle pole removal for 1977 and later models with stop and start switches on the handlebar. If you have a 400 cc model with switches on the bulkhead control panel, disregard all steps relating to electrical wiring. See **Figure 4**.

1. To avoid short circuits while disconnecting wires, disconnect the battery ground wire. See *Battery Removal* in Chapter Seven.

2. Removal and installation of the steering, throttle and electrical cables will be easier if you first remove the water muffler. See *Exhaust Removal* in Chapter Six.

3. Lock the handle pole in the upright position (**Figure 5**).

4. Pull the fuel tank vent hose up through the cable boot or pull it down out of the handle pole and out of the rubber boot. The grommet in the handle pole is secured with sealant and it will probably come out with the hose.

5. Slide the steering cable connector's spring-loaded sleeve down and pull the connector free of the ball (**Figure 6**).

6. Remove the 2 bolts holding the steering cable bracket and remove the bracket and throttle cable holder (**Figure 7**).

7. Pull the steering cable down out of the handle pole and through the rubber boot.

8. Disconnect the throttle cable at the carburetor, or at the throttle lever, and pull it out of the handle pole.

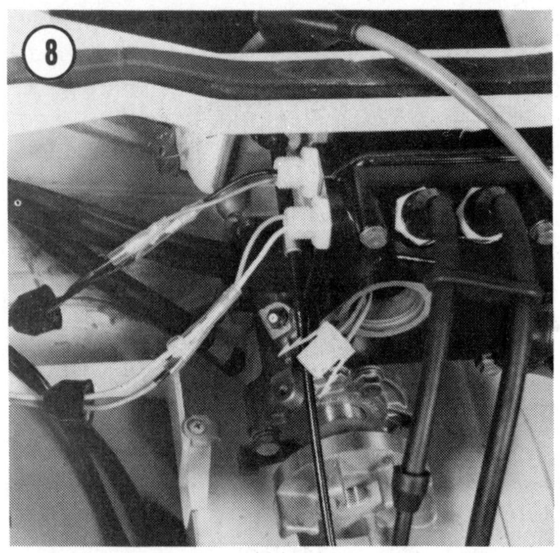

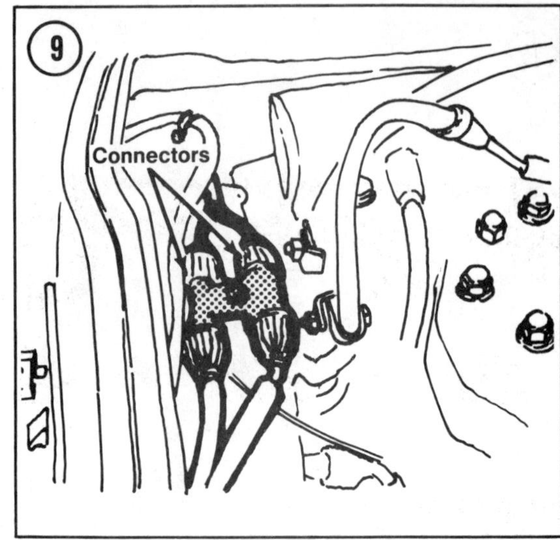

9. *On 1981 and later models*: Spray the start and stop switch grommet caps at the electric box with WD-40 to lubricate the rubber and unscrew the caps. Pull the switch leads out of the electric box carefully, one at a time until their connectors show (**Figure 8**) and disconnect them.

> *NOTE*
> *If the connectors pull apart inside the box, the box halves must be opened to reconnect the wires during installation. See **Electric Box Removal** in Chapter Seven.*

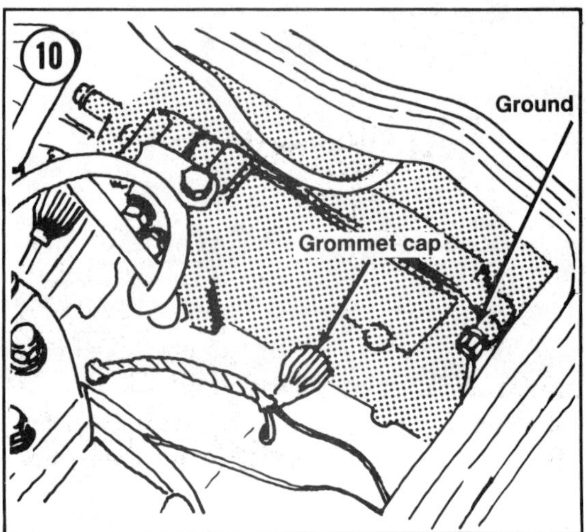

10. *On late 1978-1980 models*: Spray the start and stop switch grommet caps on top of the electric box with WD-40 to lubricate the rubber and unscrew the caps (**Figure 9**). Pull out the leads and disconnect the wires.

11. *On 1977-early 1978 models*: Spray the start and stop switch grommet cap on the front of the electric box with WD-40 to lubricate the rubber and unscrew the cap (**Figure 10**). Spray the wires in the hole with WD-40 and pull them out of the electric box one at a time until their connectors show (**Figure 11**). Disconnect the wires.

> *NOTE*
> *Pull the **black/white** connector out of the box first, followed by the **orange**, then the **white** connector. If the connectors pull apart inside the box, the box halves must*

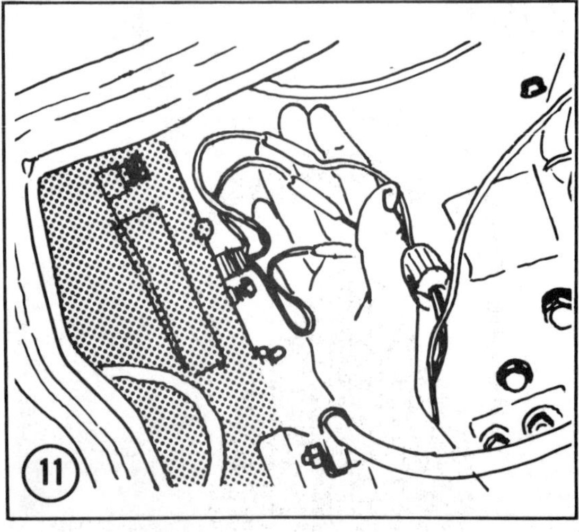

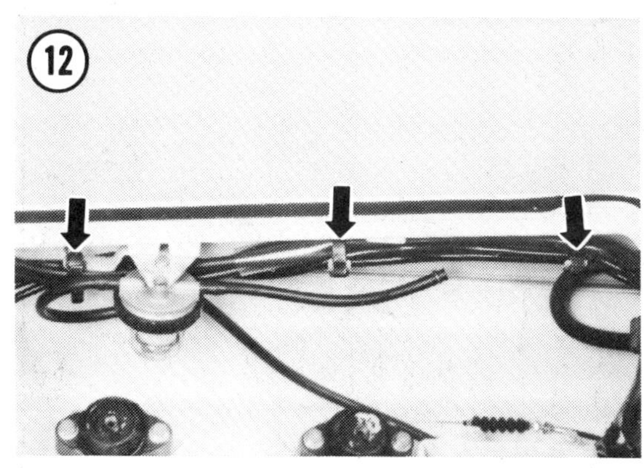

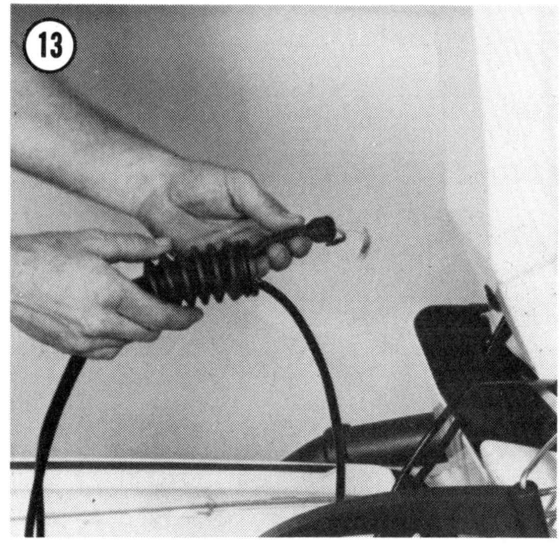

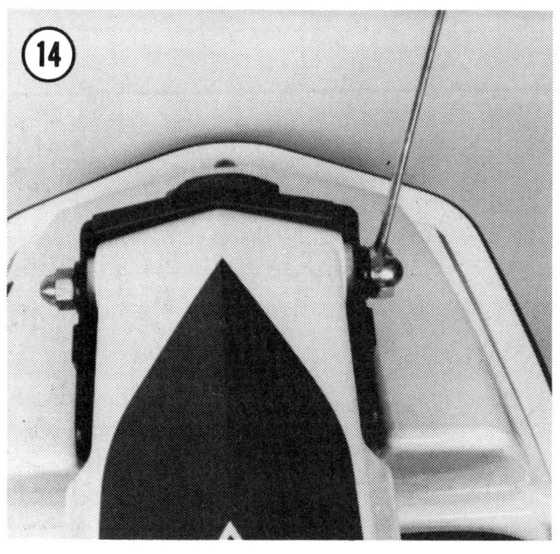

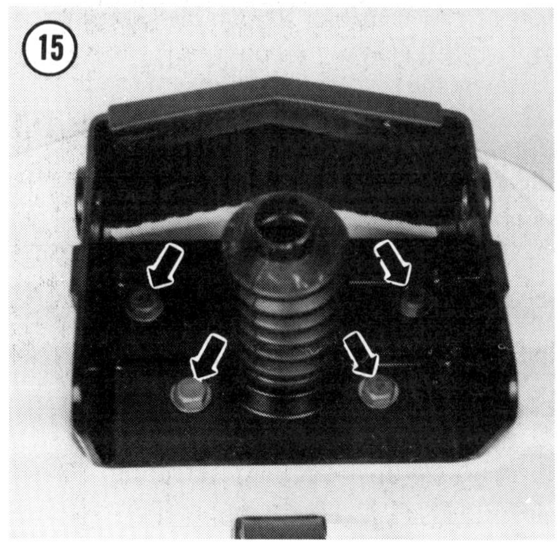

*opened to reconnect the wires during
installation. See **Electric Box Removal**
in Chapter Seven.*

12. Remove the cable ties securing the wiring
loom to the boat (**Figure 12**).

13. Detach the rubber boot at the handle pole
and carefully pull the start and stop switch
wiring up out of the boot (**Figure 13**).

14. Unscrew the acorn nut from the right side
of the handle pole pivot bolt (**Figure 14**) and
remove the bolt and washers.

15. Pull the handle pole up and back out of its
bracket.

16. To remove the handle pole bracket,
remove the 4 bolts (**Figure 15**).

Handle Pole Installation

This procedure describes handle pole
installation for 1977 and later models with stop
and start switches on the handlebar. If you
have a 400 cc model with switches on the
bulkhead control panel, disregard all steps
relating to electrical wiring. See **Figure 4**.

1. If you removed the handle pole bracket,
apply Loctite Stud N' Bearing Mount to the 4
bolts (**Figure 15**) and torque them to 16 ft.-lb.
(2.2 mkg).

2. Slip the handle pole into position in the
bracket. Grease the handle pole pivot bolt and
2 nylon washers and place one nylon washer

between each side of the handle pole and its bracket (**Figure 16**).

3. Insert the pivot from the left side and screw it into the bracket. Torque the pivot bolt to 10 ft.-lb. (1.4 mkg). There should be no side play at the pivot, but it must not be so tight that it binds.

4. Install the acorn nut on the pivot bolt. Hold the pivot bolt tight and torque the nut to 25 ft.-lb. (3.5 mkg). Make sure that the handle pole still moves up and down smoothly. If it does not, loosen the acorn nut and readjust the pivot bolt.

5. If you removed the electrical cables, spray them with WD-40 for easy installation. Thread them down through the handle pole and the rubber boot (**Figure 13**).

6. Put the rubber boot in place and thread the throttle cable and steering cables up through the boot and handle pole (**Figure 17**).

7. Push the vent line through the boot and insert it into the grommet in the bottom of the handle pole. The grommet should be secured to the pole with silicone sealant. Be sure the vent line reaches at least 4 in. (100 mm) into the handle pole.

8. Assemble the steering cable bracket onto the cable and mount the bracket on the handle pole (**Figure 18**). Tighten the 2 bolts securely.

9. Attach the steering cable to the ball-joint on the handlebar steering plate.

10. Check that the steering cable is routed through its rubber guides (**Figure 19**).

11. Attach the throttle cable holder to the steering cable bracket and install the throttle cable in it (**Figure 18**).

12. Route the stop and start switch leads along the right side of the boat and secure the straps (**Figure 12**).

13. Reconnect the stop and start switch wires at the electric box.

> *NOTE*
> *If the connectors pulled apart inside the box, the box must be opened to reconnect the wires. See **Electric Box Removal** in Chapter Seven.*

> *NOTE*
> *On 1977 models up to hull No. 10700177, the **orange** wire from the stop switch connects to a double female*

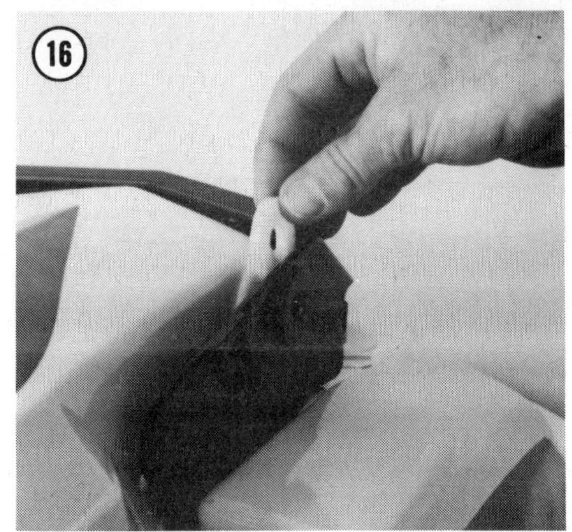

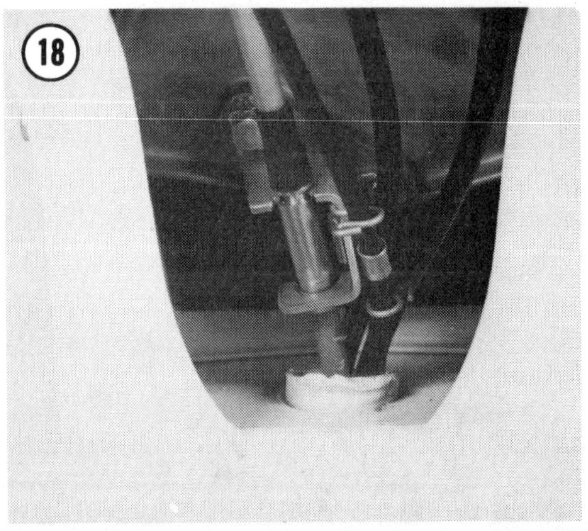

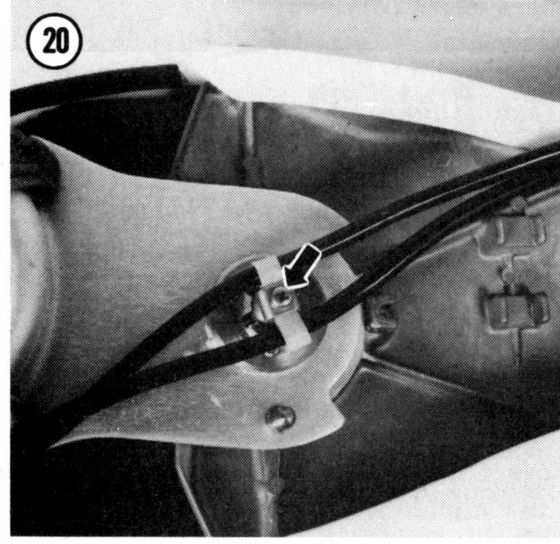

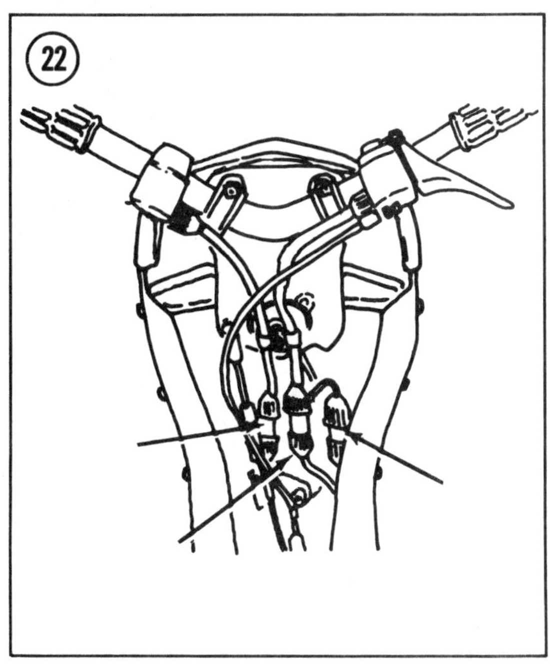

*connector and then to the **white** wire from the electric box. The **white** wire from the start switch connects to a double male connector and then to the **orange** wire from the electric box. This is a special modification by the factory to minimize accidental short circuiting and failure of the CDI unit.*

14. Apply a light coat of a water-resistant grease such as Valvoline X-All to the connector cap threads and grommets and screw the caps on.

15. Adjust the steering; see *Steering* in Chapter Three.

16. Adjust the throttle cable play; see *Throttle Cable* in Chapter Three.

Steering Disassembly

See **Figure 4**.

1. *On 1979 and later models*: Remove the wiring clamp screw and clamps from the pivot (**Figure 20**).

2. *On 1980 and later models*: Remove the cable tie and remove the start/stop switch assembly (**Figure 21**).

3. *On 1977-1979 models*: Spray the wiring connector caps with WD-40 (**Figure 22** or

Figure 23). Remove the caps and disconnect the wires.

4. Remove the 6 bolts that secure the steering support bracket to the handle pole (**Figure 24**). Remove the steering assembly.

5. If the handle pole float must be removed, take out the 3 screws and the float (**Figure 25**).

6. *On 1979 and later models*: Remove the cotter pin from the pivot nut and remove the nut, washer and bushing (**Figure 26**).

7. *On 1976-1978 models*: Unscrew the 2 locknuts from the steering plate pivot (**Figure 27**) and remove the washer and bushing.

8. Remove the steering plate from the support and take out the nylon bushing disc (**Figure 28**).

9. To remove the handlebar from the steering plate, remove the 4 screws with an impact driver.

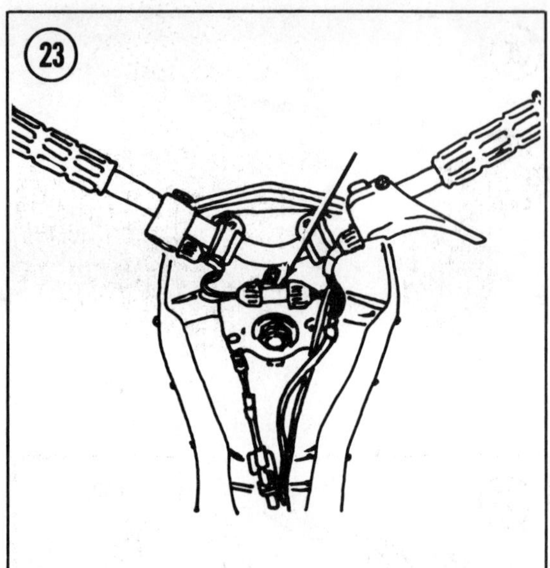

> *NOTE*
> *Do not try to remove the handlebar unless it is damaged. The mounting screws are secured with a permanent locking agent.*

10. *On 1977-1979 models*: To remove the start and stop switches from the handlebar, it may be necessary to cut and remove the handle grips. Remove all traces of tape from the handlebar with acetone or naptha.

> *WARNING*
> *Acetone is very flammable and poisonous. Avoid prolonged contact with skin and keep away from open flame. Use only in a well-ventilated area.*

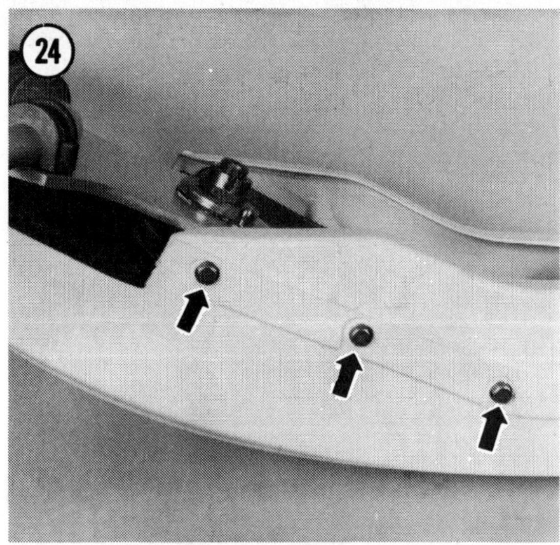

Steering Assembly

See **Figure 4**.

1. Install the handlebar on the steering plate with its 4 screws. Tighten the screws with an impact driver.

2. *On 1976-1979 models*: Install the start and stop switches, but don't tighten the clamp screws. Position the start switch about 2 3/8 in. (60 mm) from the left grip and the stop switch about 1 3/4 in. (45 mm) from the right grip.

3. *On 1980 and later models*: Install the throttle lever assembly. Position the throttle lever about 1 3/4 in. (45 mm) from the right grip.

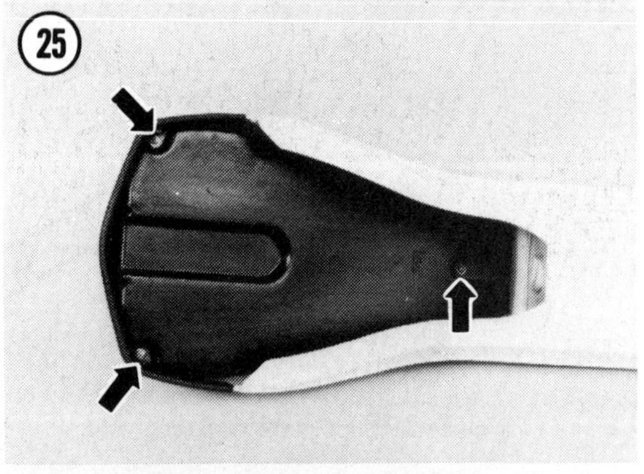

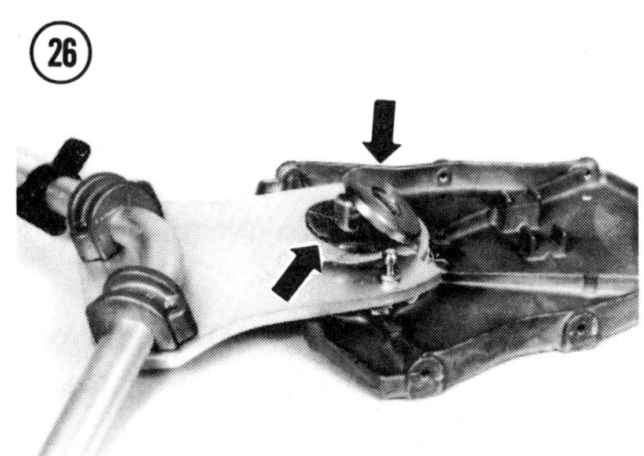

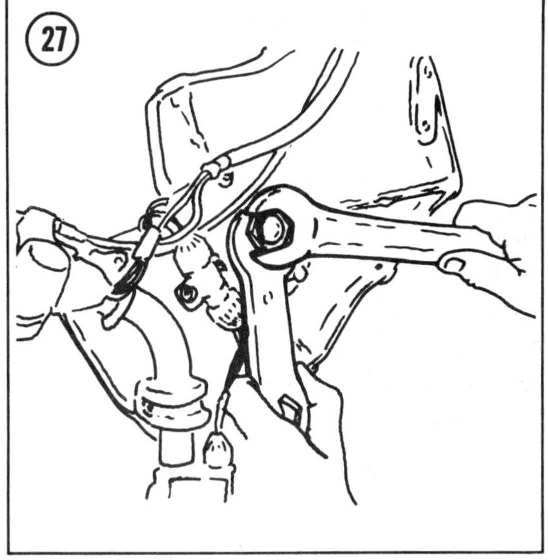

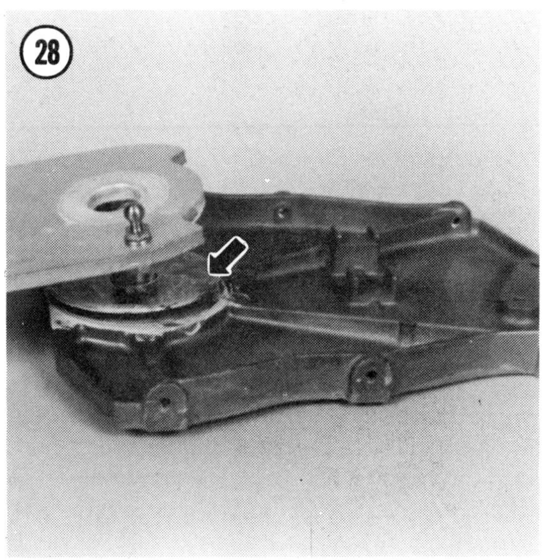

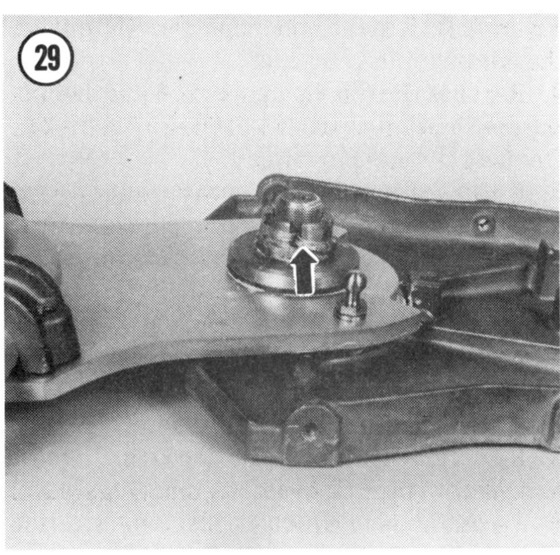

4. To install new hand grips, use a piece of sandpaper to rough up the ends of the handlebar and then clean them with solvent. Wrap the handlebar ends with double-sided tape such as 3M Scotch No. 400 or No. 410. Do not overlap layers of this tape. Treat the inside of the handle grip with a small amount of acetone or gasoline and push the grip onto the handlebar.

> *WARNING*
> *Acetone is very flammable and poisonous. Avoid prolonged contact with skin and keep away from open flame. Use only in a well-ventilated area.*

5. Apply a water-resistant grease such as Valvoline X-All to lubricate the nylon pivot bushings. Assemble the steering support, plate, bushings and washer.

6. *On 1980 and later models*: Install the castellated locknut and tighten it just enough so that the handlebar rotates smoothly without too much drag and with a minimum of vertical free play. Install a new cotter pin and spread the ends (**Figure 29**).

7. *On 1976-1979 models*: Install the adjuster nut and tighten it just enough so that the handlebar rotates smoothly without too much drag and with a minimum of vertical free play. Install the second nut and tighten it while holding the adjuster nut to keep it from turning.

8. If the float in the handle pole was removed, install it with its 3 screws.

9. Install the steering support in the handle pole.

10. *On 1977-1980 models*: If the grommet caps were removed from the connector tubes, connect the wires, apply a light coat of a water-resistant grease such as Valvoline X-All to the grommets and install the caps (**Figure 22** or **Figure 23**).

11. *On 1980 and later models*: Install the stop/start switch assembly. A pin cast into the switch housing fits into a hole in the handlebar.

12. *On 1977-1979 models*: Lower the handle pole and rotate the switches until they point upward at about a 30° angle. Tighten the clamp screws securely.

HULL REPAIR

The 440 cc Jet Ski hull is made of sheet molded compound, a machine-pressed and cured, chopped fiberglass sheet. The 400 cc Jet Ski hull is made of hand-laid fiberglass. Hull repairs covered here are limited to hairline cracks up to 8 inches long and small punctures. Larger cracks and punctures require professional repair or replacement of the damaged parts. If there is *any* structural damage to the handle pole, it must be replaced.

Repair Materials

Many commonly available fiberglass repair kits will not work well on the Jet Ski. Kawasaki provides a hull SMC Repair Kit (Kawasaki part No. W61080-001) and a Paint Touch-up Repair Kit (Kawasaki part No. W61061-001) for damage to the hull. The paint supplied by Kawasaki is not the same as the original white epoxy paint; it is for cosmetic touch-up only. The original paint used on the Jet Ski is a 50/50 mixture of DuPont Imron paints No. 555U and 817U, available from marine suppliers. This is an epoxy paint and requires a catalyst to cure. A solvent such as acetone must be used to clean and prepare surfaces for bonding.

> *WARNING*
> *Acetone is very flammable and poisonous. Avoid prolonged contact with skin and keep away from open flame. Use only in a well-ventilated area.*

> *NOTE*
> *When mixing the epoxy hull repair filler, use a smooth non-porous surface. Do not use cardboard for filler mixing.*

Scratches and Gouges

Use this procedure when the hull is scratched or lightly damaged.

1. Clean the damaged area with acetone. Push on the area around and, if possible, underneath the damage to determine the extent of the damage.

2. Use an electric drill with a burr bit or a hand file to make a V-shaped groove along the whole length of the scratch or gouge (**Figure 30**). Taper the sides of the groove at a 45° angle, but be careful not to make the groove any deeper than the existing damage.

3. Use No. 80 emery cloth or sandpaper to remove the flaky edges and to sand away the paint up to 1 or 2 inches away from the damage.

4. Clean the area with a clean cloth moistened with acetone.

5. Refer to the repair kit instructions and mix enough filler to fill in the area. Use a plastic squeegee to apply and spread the filler, making sure to remove all air bubbles. The filler should extend a little above the original surface (**Figure 31**). Let the filler cure according to the kit instructions.

6. Use a sanding block to sand the area smooth. Start with No. 80 grit and finish with No. 400 grit.

7. Use the Paint Kit to repaint the area, following the kit instructions.

Structural Damage

Use this procedure when the hull is cracked anywhere except at the engine cover rail.

1. Clean the damaged area with acetone. Push on the area around and, if possible, underneath the damage to determine the extent of the damage.

2. Use an electric drill with a burr bit or a hand file to make a V-shaped groove along the whole length of the crack or gouge. Open a 1/8 in. gap along the crack (**Figure 32**). On the hull bottom and the front deck (where the handle pole attaches), open the gap to 1/4 inch (**Figure 33**). Taper the sides of the groove at a 45° angle. If

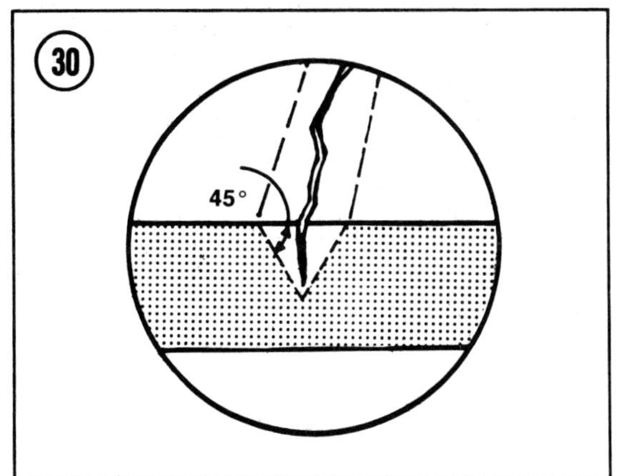

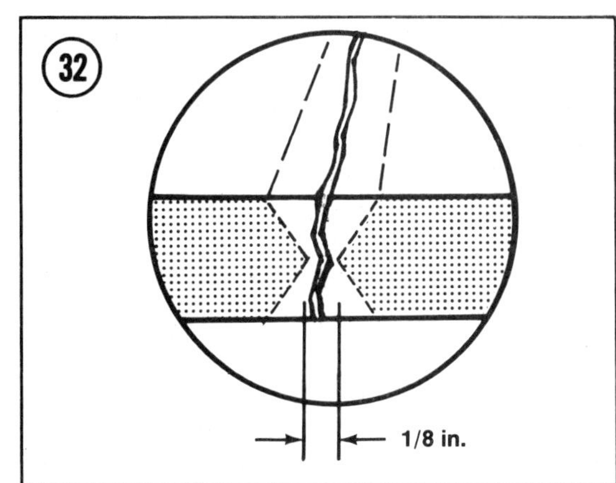

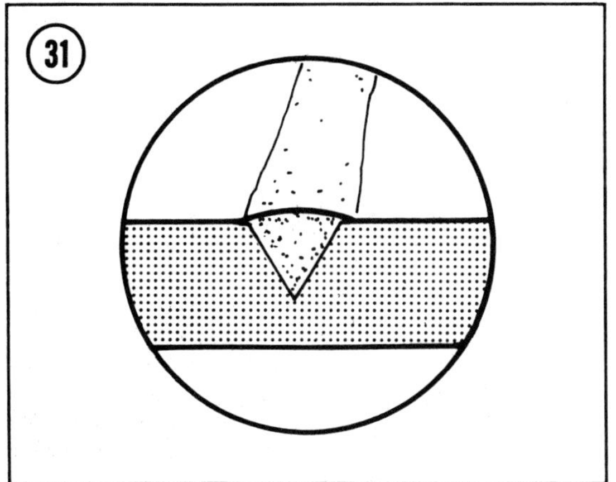

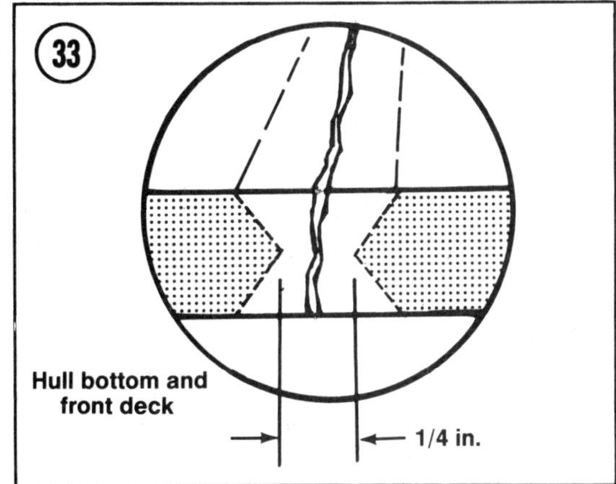

both sides of the hull are accessible, groove both sides.

3. Use No. 80 emery cloth or sandpaper to remove the flaky edges and to sand away the paint about 4 inches away from the damage.

4. Clean the area with a clean cloth moistened with acetone.

5. Refer to the repair kit instructions and mix enough filler to fill in the area. Use a plastic squeegee to apply and spread the filler, making sure to remove all air bubbles. The filler should extend a little above the original surface (**Figure 31**).

6. Before the filler sets up, lay 4 oz. fiberglass cloth over the crack, inside and outside, so that the cloth extends about 2 inches beyond the crack on each side.

7. Tap the cloth into the filler until filler comes through the cloth. Spread a light coat of filler over the cloth, inside and outside, and let the filler cure according to the kit instructions.

8. Use a sanding block to sand the area smooth. Start with No. 80 grit and finish with No. 400 grit.

9. Use the Paint Kit to repaint the area, following the kit instructions.

Crack At Engine Cover Rail

See **Figure 34**. A crack in this area must be reinforced with wood for strength.

1. Clean the damaged area with acetone. Push on the area around and, if possible, underneath the damage to determine the extent of the damage.

2. Use an electric drill with a burr bit or a hand file to make a V-shaped groove along the both sides of the whole length of the crack. Open a 1/4 in. gap along the crack. Taper the sides of the groove at a 45° angle (**Figure 33**).

3. Use No. 80 emery cloth or sandpaper to remove the flaky edge and to sand away the paint about 4 inches away from the damage.

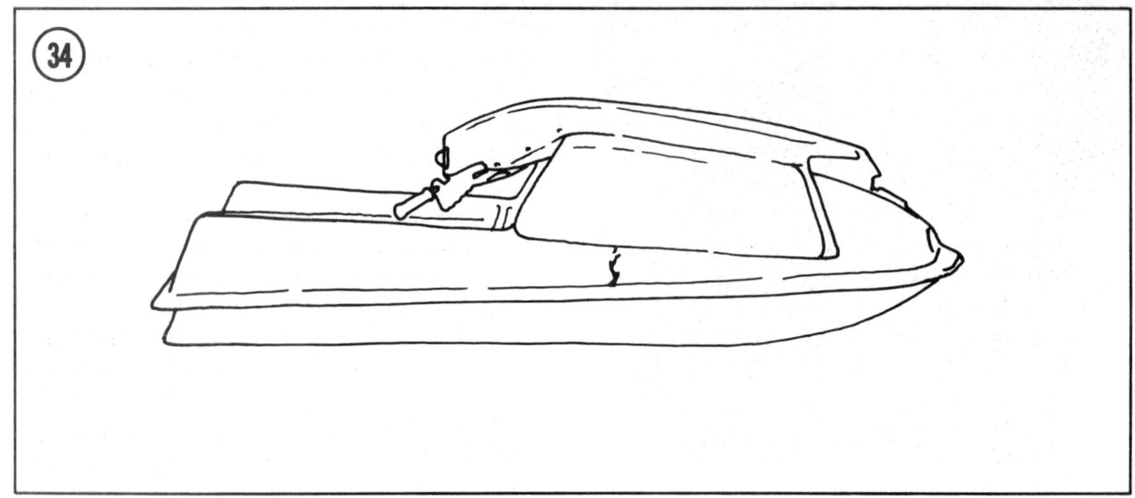

4. Clean the area with a clean cloth moistened with acetone.

5. To align the rail and add rigidity, cut a piece of marine plywood 3/8 in. thick, 3/4 inch wide by 3 inches long, center it over the crack inside the deck and clamp it at each end.

6. Refer to the repair kit instructions and mix enough filler to fill in the area. To bond the wood to the deck on both sides of the crack, apply filler to the center of the wood and the inside wall of the deck. Use a plastic squeegee to apply and spread the filler, working it into all the cracks and voids making sure to remove all air bubbles.

7. Before the filler sets up, lay 4 oz. fiberglass cloth over the crack, inside and outside, so that the cloth extends about 2 inches beyond the crack on each side. Make sure the cloth completely covers the wood on the inside.

8. Tap the cloth into the filler until filler comes through the cloth. Spread a light coat of filler over the cloth, inside and outside, and let the filler cure according to the kit instructions.

9. Use a sanding block to sand the area smooth. Start with No. 80 grit and finish with No. 400 grit.

10. Use the Paint Kit to repaint the area, following the kit instructions.

Hull Extensions

The hull extension tips (**Figure 35**) are available as replacement parts. They should be bonded to the hull with the same hull repair epoxy used for repair of cracks.

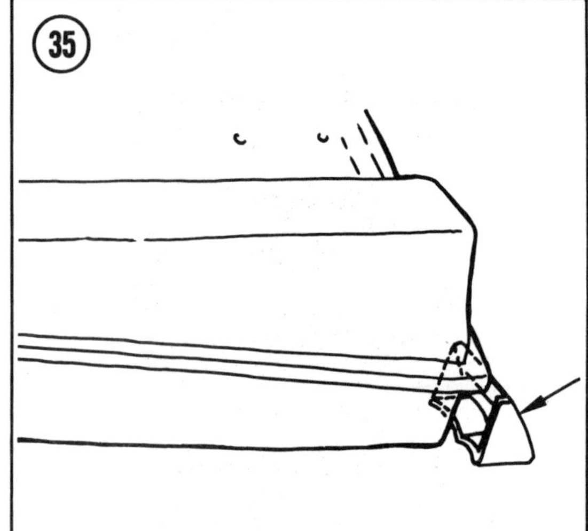

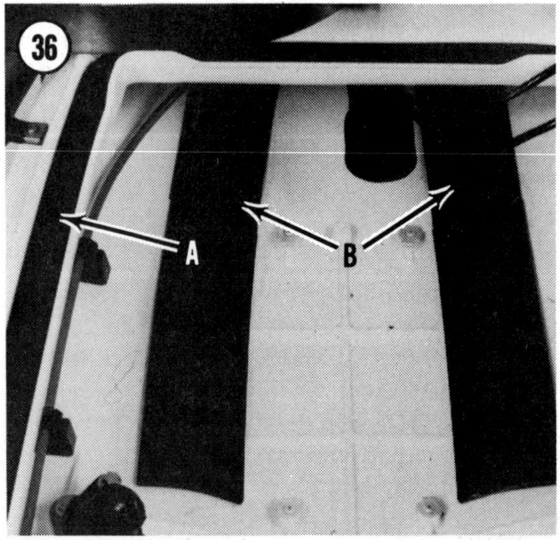

Rubber Parts

1. To replace the rider's mat, thoroughly clean the deck surface and use waterproof contact cement such as Goodyear Pliobond to glue the mat down. Refer to the adhesive container for instructions.

2. The engine cover gasket (A, **Figure 36**) and the fuel tank and water muffler dampers (B) should be attached with a waterproof contact cement such as Goodyear Pliobond.

3. The bumper strip on the front of the boat, the handle pole bracket cover (**Figure 37**) and the steering cable guides (**Figure 19**) should be secured with a cyanoacrylate cement such as Loctite Super Bonder. Refer to the adhesive container for instructions. Goodyear Plio-Grip adhesive may also be used.

PERFORMANCE IMPROVEMENT

The first thing you should consider doing when you decide to modify or race your Jet Ski is to contact the U.S. Jet Ski Boating Association (address is given in **Table 1** at the end of the chapter). The U.S. Jet Ski Boating Association offers race schedules, rules, insurance and a periodic newsletter that often contains advertisements from the many suppliers of performance equipment and services. Organized competition sanctioned by the association has grown tremendously in a short time, with races spread across the United States and up to $10,000 purses.

Although the performance of a standard Jet Ski is very good, there is still a lot of room for improvements which will not diminish the dependability of the machine. The technology used in the original design incorporated a large amount of "over design" in the engine. The powerplant and connecting water jet components can be upgraded without noticeably shortening engine life or reliability.

The components that we will be discussing here come primarily from West Coast Jet Ski, one of the leaders in Jet Ski components and current holder of numerous national records in Jet Ski competition. West Coast Jet Ski has been in business more than 5 years and is currently selling items to Jet Ski owners across

the U.S. and in such far away places as Australia, South Africa and the Middle East. Jet Ski parts are also available from other sources; **Table 1** (at the end of the chapter) lists these suppliers.

RACING IMPELLERS

These racing impellers (or props) are made from highly polished aluminum and incorporate both a better blade design and a longer shaft (**Figure 1**). Because of the design changes the impeller is 1/2 in. farther away from the pump and is capable of pushing a higher volume of water, resulting in better low

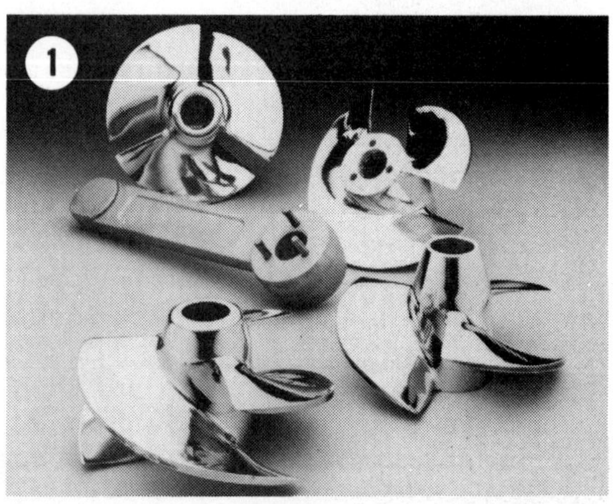

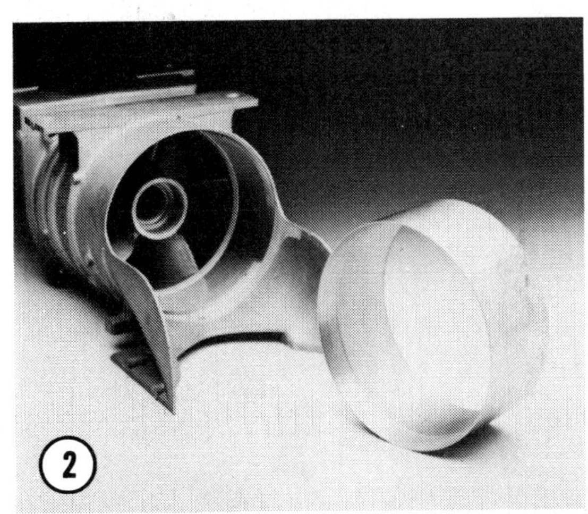

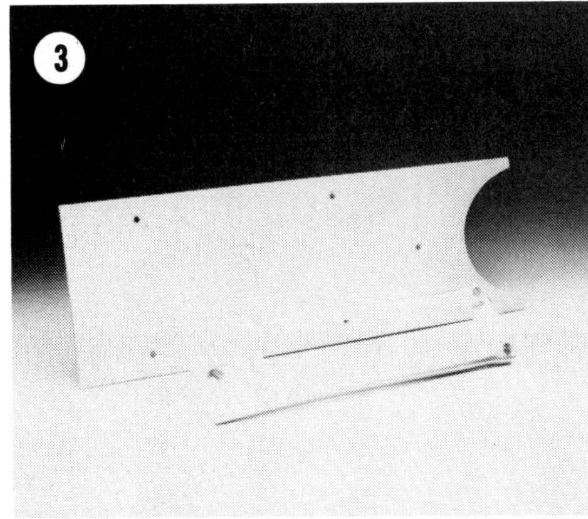

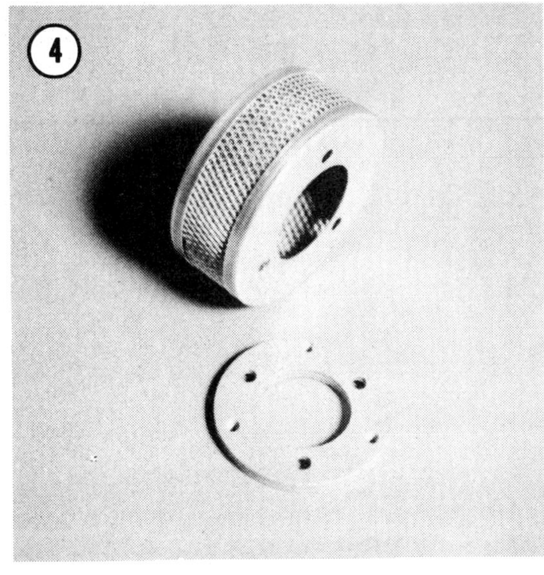

end torque and mid-range power. West Coast Jet Ski offers 4 different impellers ranging from a polished stock design impeller to an extended nose impeller. The stock polished impeller is more suitable for pleasure riding, while the power thrust unit is designed to work in conjunction with high-performance engine modifications.

REMACHINED PUMPS

Many Jet Ski owners loose a lot of potential forward thrust because their Jet Ski's pump wall is worn. The inner wall of the Ski's pump is gradually worn down by the impeller blades. West Coast Jet Ski will bore the inner diameter of the pump, then install a precision machined stainless steel insert with closer blade-to-pump clearance (**Figure 2**). This increases pump efficiency. Because of the liner, the modified pump will outlast the stock pump from 10 to 15 times before needing to be rebored.

RACING GRATES

Through the use of higher side walls, these racing grates and stabilizer speed plates will increase the water intake for the more efficient pump (**Figure 3**). The stabilizer plate not only makes the Ski more stable, but increases the overall speed from 2 to 4 miles per hour. The racing grates also improve the handling and allow the rider to turn sharper and deeper in corners. The design results in a grate that is larger and rounder, which reduces the chance of falling off the "edges" while taking tight corners.

FLAME ARRESTOR KITS

These modified flame arrestors increase air intake into the engine, allowing for better mid-range power. The arrestors come with high-quality bolts and information on how to safety-wire the bolts for vibration-free riding (**Figure 4**). All West Coast arrestors are Coast Guard approved.

RACING PIPES

By enlarging the center cone area and changing the rear dimensions of the pipe, racing pipes help improve low-end torque and mid-range power by allowing exhaust gases to

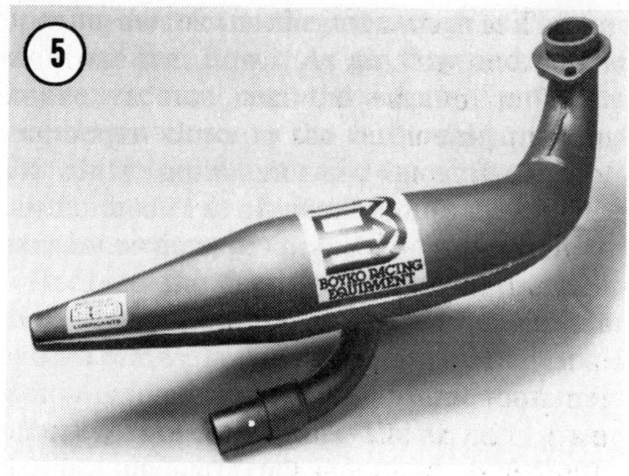

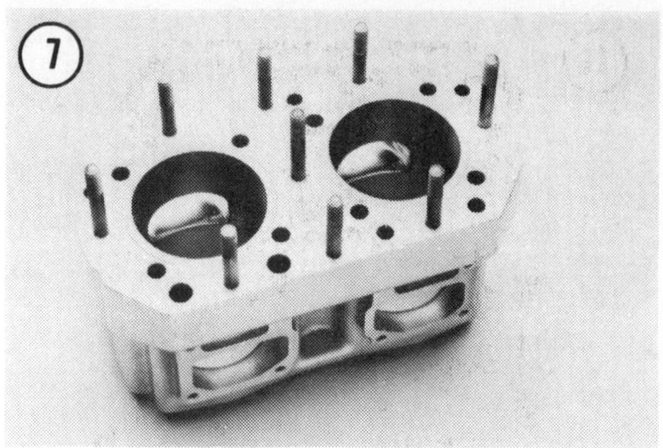

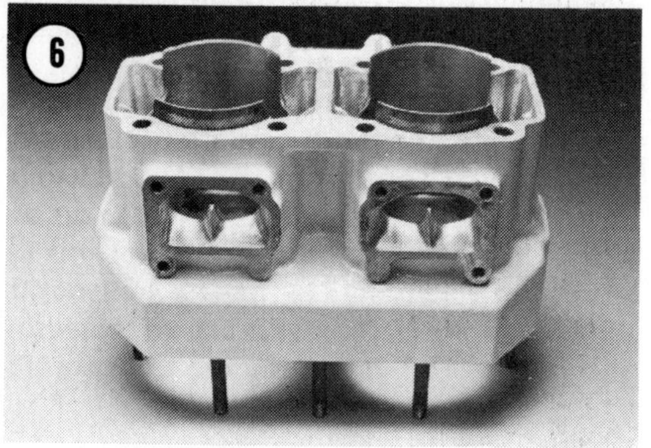

exit the engine faster than the stock pipe. These racing pipes are the biggest single improvement you can make for your Jet Ski engine (**Figure 5**). Good performance pipes are die-stamped to eliminate cracking from vibration. Flexible mounting, because of the constant engine movement, is another important factor when buying pipes. The combination of an impeller and pipe will result in a speed increase of about 6 mph for most Jet Skis.

The pipe utilizes the same space as the standard pipe and doesn't require any modifications to install. It is slightly louder than stock (an increase of approximately 15%) but is still well within the legal noise limits.

CYLINDER PORTING

The engineers left a lot of extra "buffer room" inside the Jet Ski engine, so internal engine hop-ups can go a long way without lowering the machine's reliability. Porting is one of the most popular ways to increase horsepower. This consists of enlarging the

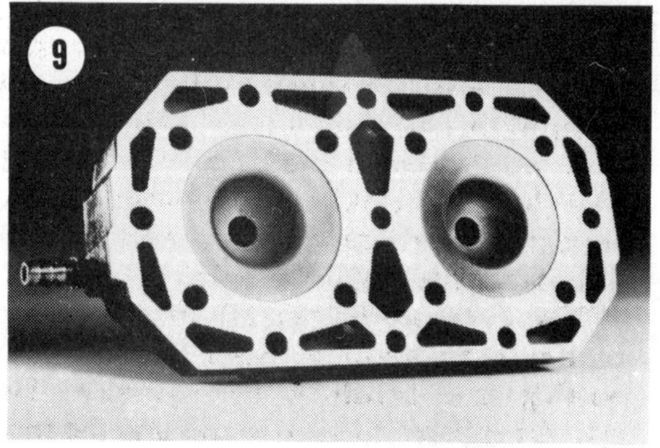

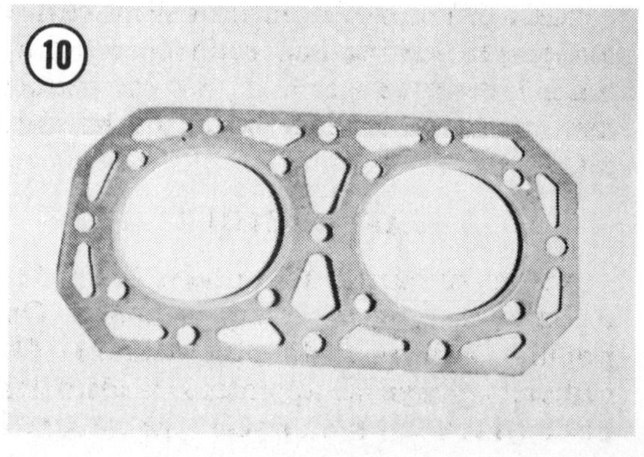

intake and exhaust ports. The inlet ports are enlarged and elongated to allow fuel to enter the cylinders sooner during the intake stroke (**Figure 6**). The exhaust port is raised to allow the spent gases to completely escape. The exhaust port is also machined to a high polish finish to reduce carbon build-up (**Figure 7**).

All transfer ports in the cylinder are matched to the transfer passages in the cases to ensure efficient fuel flow. The end result is a Ski which better utilizes the fuel it is fed. Although the rpm won't rise noticeably, the overall powerband of the Ski will be broader. The Ski becomes more responsive and has an all-around "healthy" engine feel.

West Coast Jet Ski offers 3 different engine porting configurations. Stage 1 consists of porting and polishing the cylinder. The cylinder is bored to 1st oversize and the head is milled to increase compression. Stage 2 consists of raising the engine's displacement along with porting and cylinder polishing. Stage 3, designed specifically for competition use, consists of an even larger displacement kit.

CARBURETORS

A larger carburetor allows more fuel and air to enter the engine during operation. One popular unit is a 42 mm Mikuni. The carburetor design incorporates a standard float bowl system and motorcycle-type carburetor jets. The carburetor is more resistant to vibration than the standard unit and will not "slip" out of tune. It comes complete with the matching manifold and all hardware required for installation (**Figure 8**).

There are other carburetion combinations available for the Jet Ski, ranging from a 38 mm Mikuni (slightly smaller than stock) on up to a set of dual downdraft 42 mm Mikuni units. Many riders prefer the 38 mm carburetor over the stock unit because of the tuning method used. The smaller carburetor uses standard numbered jets so that the owner can "tune by the numbers" and change jets rather than turn spring-loaded screws. This makes it easier to precisely tune the carburetion of the Ski.

MILLED HEAD

Head milling consists of shaving off some of the cylinder head surface area to reduce the available volume area in the combustion chamber (**Figure 9**). Since the intake portion of the motor is still pumping in the standard volume of air-fuel mixture, the mixture is compressed into a smaller area. The result is a higher compression engine. This increases the low-end torque of the engine and allows the Ski rider to drive out of corners harder and faster.

THIN HEAD GASKETS

West Coast suggests using thinner head gaskets with their milled or standard cylinder heads (**Figure 10**). These thinner gaskets create slightly higher engine compression. The gasket material is stronger than standard Kawasaki gaskets and the retail price is much lower than the OEM piece. Due to the possibility of water penetration, you should install new head gaskets after each 30 hours of Jet Ski use. This will help to ensure that nothing gets into the cylinders and damages the pistons or cylinder walls.

BIG BORE PISTON KITS

Although the standard engine is potent, many Jet Ski owners are looking for an increase in horsepower and performance. This can be quickly achieved (on 1977-1980 models) through big bore piston kits which raise the displacement to 474, 480 or 500cc (**Figure 11**).

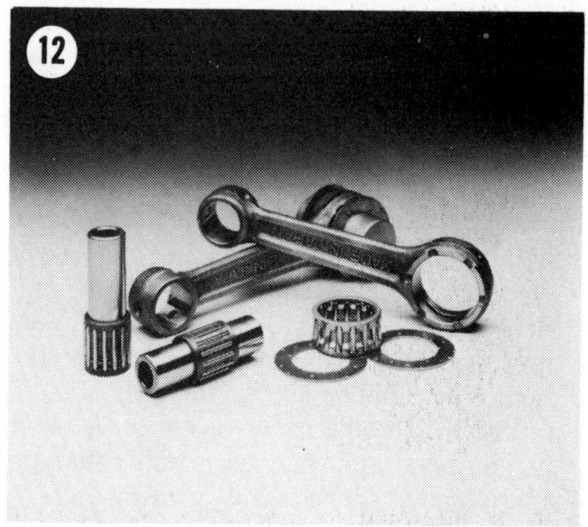

The larger pistons, rings, piston pins and all the hardware will result in a 25% increase in overall Ski power. The kit also requires that the cylinder sleeves be bored out to accommodate the larger pistons. This can be done by West Coast or a machine shop in your area. You will need the pistons and rings in order to get precise measurements for the bore work.

The 1981-on Jet Ski's solid cast iron cylinders cannot be bored larger than the factory's 0.020 in. (0.50 mm) oversize limit.

HIGH PERFORMANCE RODS AND CRANK PINS

Even if you stick to the stock displacement of your Jet Ski, you should consider replacing the stock rods and crank pins during your next off-season teardown. The standard Jet Ski rods have slightly substandard oiling capabilities. Replacement H-1 rods are taken directly from the road racing engines (**Figure 12**). The rods are lighter and provide better oiling than stock Ski rods. The crank pins are specially heat treated and precision ground.

CRANKSHAFT AND FLYWHEEL MODIFICATIONS

Trueing and welding the crankshaft (**Figure 13**) is a very important step in building a lasting and dependable performance Jet Ski engine. Many ski owners want the performance of a built engine but are concerned about losing reliability. West Coast Jet Ski will true and weld crankshafts to eliminate the possibility of crank slipping.

The flywheel is one of the weak points of the engine and also needs attention. The flywheel flange is welded to the housing to reduce rivet fatigue. Then, additional holes are bored to lighten the unit and all surfaces are machined to reduce the rotating mass. Symmetrical balance is unchanged (**Figure 14**).

ALUMINUM DRIVE SHAFTS

One of the easiest ways to increase performance of the Jet Ski engine is through the use of lighter components. An aluminum drive shaft (**Figure 15**) is 4 pounds lighter than the stock steel shaft and comes complete with stainless steel sleeves at the pump bushing and seal wear points. The aluminum shaft will let the engine work more efficiently and will result in better throttle response.

HANDLING COMPONENTS

Just as engine performance can be improved through components, the handling and response of the Jet Ski can be upgraded through various aftermarket parts. The simplest and

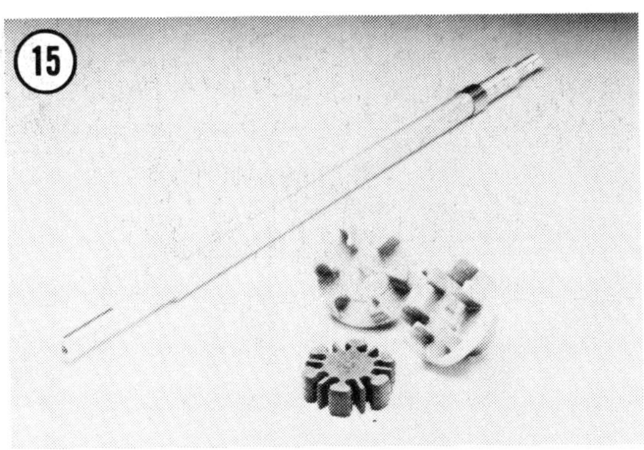

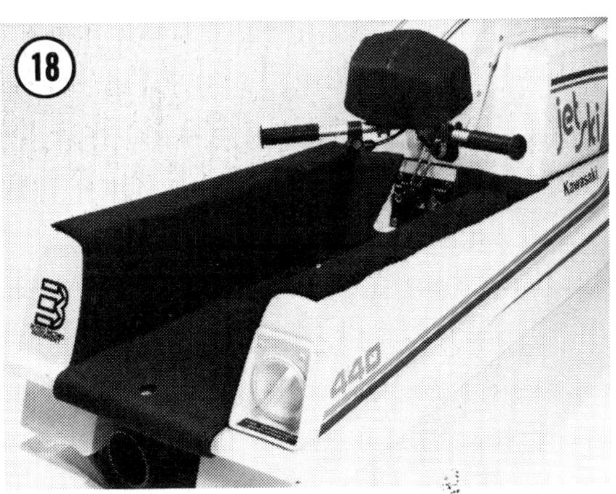

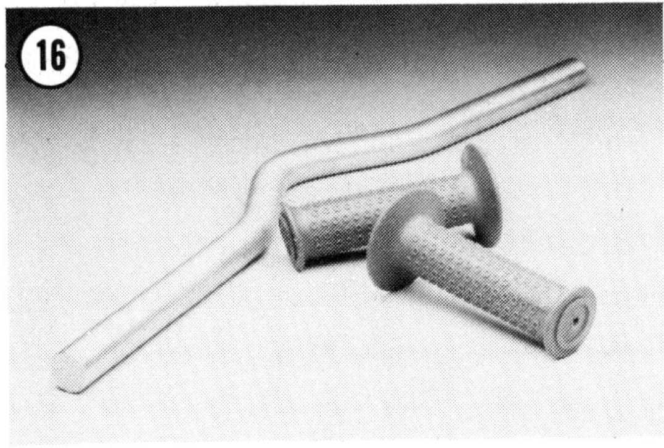

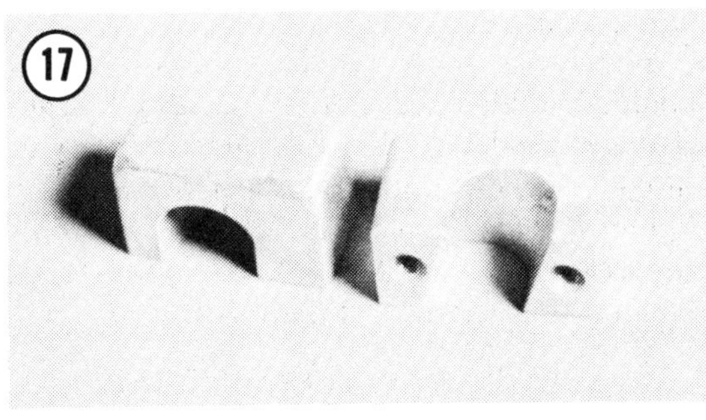

most noticeable improvement is the addition of a Quick Steering Kit. This is a complete steering linkage system which allows the Jet Ski to turn tighter in corners. The kit reduces the steering ratio of the Ski, which results in better response when you turn the handlebars. With the Quick Steering Kit installed, the Ski will turn quicker, sooner and tighter, requiring less movement of the handlebars to initiate the change of direction.

RACING HANDLEBARS

Racing bars are designed to work in conjunction with the Quick Steering Kit, but can be mounted to a standard Ski and still improve response (**Figure 16**). The bars have a more comfortable bend and are narrower, which not only increases response but also reduces the chance of getting hit by the handlebars when falling off the Ski.

HANDLEBAR CLAMPS

These aluminum machined clamps (**Figure 17**) change the angle of the handlebars and help reduce back soreness during long Jet Ski rides. The clamps allow the operator to stand or kneel in a more comfortable position slightly farther back than normal. The clamps increase the maneuverability of the Ski and reduce the demand for perfect balance while riding.

PAD KITS

Most Jet Ski owners quickly realize that it's easy to bruise elbows, shins and ribs when falling off the Ski. The West Coast Pad Kit is a complete set of special non-corrosive, non-slip neoprene rubber mats which are glued into the gunnel area and over the top of the turn handle (**Figure 18**). The pad kit greatly reduces the chance of bangs and bruises to the operator and offers a more secure standing area because of the better mat traction.

GRIPS

Many riders find that the standard grips are too slippery and too hard. This results in an insecure grip and lots of blisters. Oakley Grips are made from a soft rubber compound which offers a comfortable and secure grip (**Figure 19**). With Oakley Grips many riders find they can ride without gloves and have a better "feel" while operating the Ski.

OVERALL

The Jet Ski is one of the most exciting forms of recreational water fun. A lot of people plan a whole day around riding the Jet Ski and don't enjoy having the day cut short because of Ski problems. By following the basic maintenance procedures in this book you can make sure that each time the Ski is set in the water it is capable of running at its very best all day long. The performance improvements described in this chapter can increase your fun.

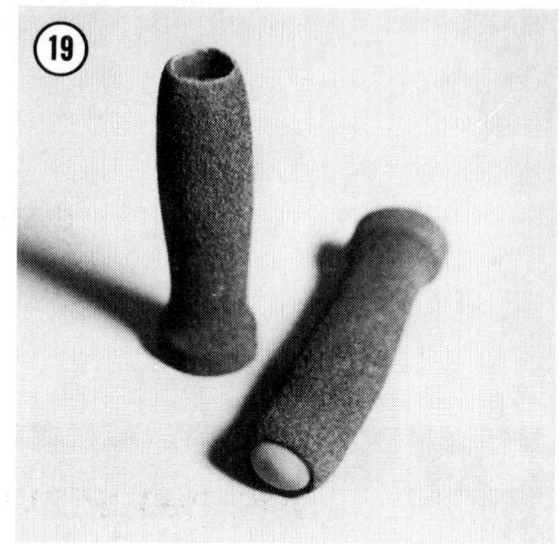

Table 1   SUPPLIERS

Supplier	Services
Arcadia Jet Ski 300N. Santa Anita Dr. Arcadia, CA 91102	Engine and pump modifications, crankshaft rebuilding, hull parts, carburetors, expansion chambers
Butch's Jet Ski Shop 727 28th St. S.E. Grand Rapids, MI 49507	Engine and pump modifications, crankshaft rebuilding, hull parts, carburetors, expansion chambers
Custom Jet Ski 889 Grossmont Ave. El Cajon, CA 92020	Engine and pump modifications, crankshaft rebuilding, hull parts, carburetors, expansion chambers, nitrous oxide injection
Dickinson Design 11542 Knott St., Unit 3 Garden Grove, CA 92641	Engine and pump modifications, crankshaft rebuilding, hull parts, carburetors, expansion chambers
R&E 2028 Woodard Road San Jose, CA 95124	Engine and pump modifications, crankshaft rebuilding, hull parts, carburetors, expansion chambers
West Coast Jet Ski 3842 E. Eagle Dr. Anaheim, CA 92807	Engine and pump modifications, crankshaft rebuilding, hull parts, carburetors, expansion chambers
U.S. Jet Ski Boating Association P.O. Box 18948 Irvine, CA 92713	Race schedules, rulebook, insurance, newsletter

SUPPLEMENT

1982-1983 SERVICE INFORMATION

The following supplement provides additional information for servicing these 1982 and later models:

a. 1982 JS440-A6.
b. 1982 JS550-A1.
c. 1983 JS440-A7.
d. 1983 JS550-A2.

Other service procedures remain the same as described in the basic book, Chapters One through Nine.

The chapter headings in this supplement correspond to those in the main portion of this book. If a chapter is not referenced in this supplement, there are no changes affecting that chapter; follow the procedures described for the comparable models in the basic book.

If your Jet Ski is covered by this supplement, carefully read the appropriate chapter in the basic book before beginning any work.

CHAPTER ONE

GENERAL INFORMATION

Model year and suffix designation for 1982 and later models are listed in **Table 1**.

SPECIFICATIONS

Refer to **Table 2** for general specifications for 1982 and later JS550 models.

Table 1   MODEL YEAR/SUFFIX DESIGNATION

Year	Model suffix	Hull number begins
1982	JS440-A6	403011081
1982	JS550-A1	434010382-B
1983	JS440-A7	463510882-A
1983	JS550-A2	472511082-B

Table 2   GENERAL SPECIFICATIONS (JS550)

General	
Engine type	2-stroke two cylinder, piston port, 180° firing, water-cooled
Lubrication system	Premixed gas/oil (40:1)
Starting system	Electric starter
Ignition system	CDI (capacitor discharge ignition)
Charging system	Alternator, rectifier/regulator
Carburetion	Mikuni BN38
Fuel tank capacity	3.5 gal. (13 liter, 2.9 Imp. gal.)
Engine	
Displacement	32.4 cu. in. (531 cc)
Max. horsepower	36 @ 5,750 rpm
Max. torque	33 ft.-lb. (4.5 mkg) @ 4,500 rpm
Compression ratio	6.0:1
Port timing	
Intake	76.2° BTDC & ATDC
Transfer	58.0° BBDC & ABDC
Exhaust	84.5° BBDC & ABDC
Drive train	
Jet pump type	Mixed flow, single stage
Jet pump diameter	N.A.*
Jet pump thrust	340 lb. (155 kg)
Steering	
Type	Pivoting outlet nozzle

(continued)

Table 2 GENERAL SPECIFICATIONS (JS550) (continued)

Braking	
Type	Water drag
Electrical	
Ignition system	CDI (capacitor discharge ignition)
Advanced timing	28° BTDC @ 6,000 rpm, 0.174 in. (4.42 mm)
Charging system	Alternator, rectifier/regulator
Alternator output	45W @ 6,000 rpm
Battery	12V, 16AH
Dimensions and performance	
Length	84 in. (2140 mm)
Width	24 in. (610 mm)
Height	25 in. (640 mm)
Draft	4 in. (100 mm)
Dry weight	247 lb. (112 kg)
Maximum speed	37 mph (60 kph)
Fuel consumption	
At full throttle	4.0 gal./hour (15 liter/hour)
Crusing range	
At full throttle	31 miles (50 km), 0.9 hours
Noise level	83 dbA @ 50 ft. @ full throttle

* N.A.=Information not available.

CHAPTER THREE

LUBRICATION, MAINTENANCE AND TUNE-UP

SERVICE INTERVALS

Refer to **Table 3** for service intervals for all 1982 and later models.

TUNE-UP

Tune-up specifications unique to 1982 and later models are listed in **Table 4**.

Table 3 MAINTENANCE SCHEDULE (1982-ON)

Initial 10 hours	• Check all nuts, bolts and fasteners • Check all hose clamps • Torque cylinder head nuts
Every 25 hours	• Check all nuts, bolts and fasteners • Check all hose clamps • Torque cylinder head nuts • Check battery electrolyte level • Clean and regap spark plugs • Grease throttle cable and choke cable fittings
	(continued)

Table 3 MAINTENANCE SCHEDULE (1982-ON) (continued)

Every 25 hours (continued)	• Lubricate throttle and choke cables • Lubricate drive shaft bearing holder • Lubricate jet pump bearing • Lubricate magneto housing • Disassemble and lubricate handlebar pivot • Clean fuel sediment filter and bowl • Adjust carburetor • Inspect fuel vent check valve • Flush bilge line and filter • Flush cooling system*

Every 100 hours	• Inspect flame arrester and clean as required
	• Remove and inspect impeller blade for damage
	• Decarbonize cylinder head, pistons and
	  exhaust manifold
	• Check ignition timing
	• Torque flywheel nut
	• Inspect coupling rubber; replace as required
	• Inspect carburetor throttle shaft spring
	  and bushing for wear; replace as required

* Flush after each use in salt water.

Table 4   TUNE-UP SPECIFICATIONS

Idle speed	
JS440	1,800 ±100 rpm
JS550	1,500 ±100 rpm
Needle adjustments	
Low-speed needle	
JS440	
1982	1 1/16 turns
1983	1 turn
JS550	1 turn
High-speed needle	
JS440	
1982	7/8 turn
1983	5/8 turn
JS550	5/8 turn
Ignition timing	
JS550	28° BTDC @ 6,000 rpm
Dial indicator	0.174 in. (4.42 mm)

CHAPTER FOUR

ENGINE

Table 5 lists engine specifications and **Table 6** lists engine tightening torques for the JS550 engine.

Table 5 ENGINE WEAR LIMITS (JS550)

Item	Wear limit in. (mm)
Cylinder diameter	
Overbore	2.959 (75.17)
Replace	2.975 (75.59)
Piston diameter	2.947 (74.78)
Piston pin hole inside diameter	0.633 (16.08)
Piston pin outside diameter	0.628 (15.96)
Connecting rod small end inside diameter	0.789 (20.05)
Piston ring thickness	0.075 (1.92)
Piston ring-to-groove clearance	0.008 (0.22)
Piston ring free gap	0.137 (3.5)
Piston ring installed gap	0.027 (0.7)
Crankshaft runout	0.003 (0.08)
Crankshaft end play	0.029 (0.75)
Connecting rod big end clearance	0.027 (0.7)
Connecting rod radial clearance	0.789 (20.05)

Table 6 ENGINE TORQUES (JS550)

	ft.-lb.	N•m
Cylinder head nuts	16	22
Cylinder head brace	52 in.-lb.	6
Engine bed bolts (to hull)	27	37
Engine bed bolts (to engine)	35	48
Engine mount damper bolts	16	22
Engine mount bolts	12	16
Rotor nut	115	160
Crankcase large bolts	16	22
Crankcase small bolts	52 in.-lb.	6
Coupling	20	27
Exhaust manifold bolts	52 in.-lb.	6
Front exhaust pipe bolts	52 in.-lb.	6
Rear exhaust pipe nut	12	16
Spark plugs	20	28
Starter bolts		
Front	12	16
Rear	52 in.-lb.	6

CHAPTER FIVE

DRIVE TRAIN

JET PUMP
(JS550)

Refer to **Figure 1**.

Jet Pump/Impeller Inspection

Normal wear of the pump case and impeller can reduce jet pump thrust and top speed, even when the engine is running perfectly, but more often the problem is caused by obstructions in the pump or damaged pump case and impeller blades.

Check for nicks and gouges in the impeller blades and the pump case blades. If they are minor, they can be smoothed out with abrasive paper or carefully filed away. It is especially important for the blade edges to be smooth. If there is major damage to the impeller or pump case blades, replace the parts.

Bearing and Seal Removal/Installation

CAUTION
The bushings and seals will be damaged by removal. Do not remove them unless you intend to install new ones. If the bushing and/or seals are hard to remove or install, don't take a chance on expensive case damage. Have the work done by a Jet Ski dealer.

1. Using an Allen wrench, remove the grease fitting cover (**Figure 2**).
2. Referring to **Figure 3**, remove the grease fitting and remove the cap bolts and the cap.
3. Position the seal protector (Kawasaki part No. 57001-3003) over the pump shaft

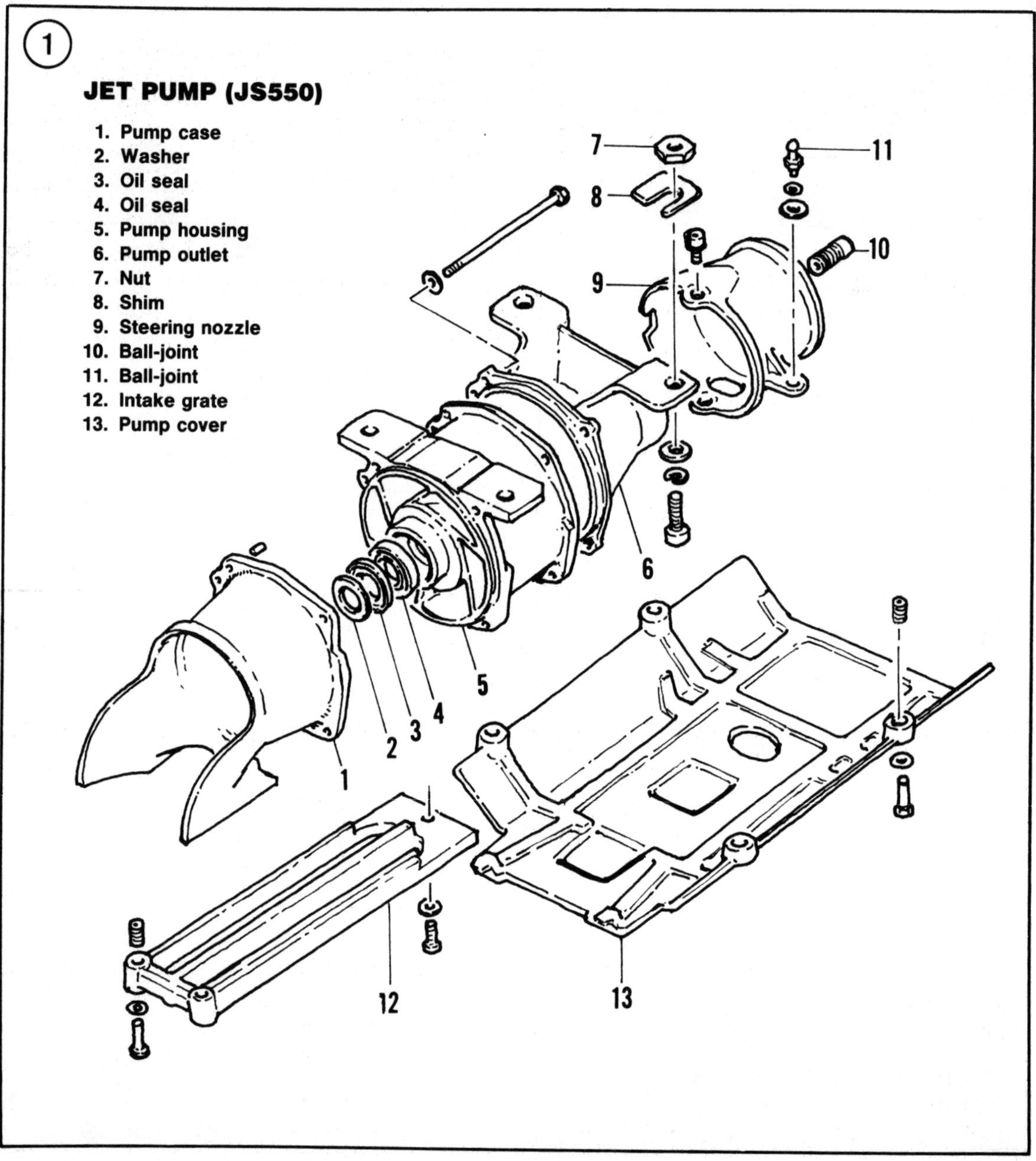

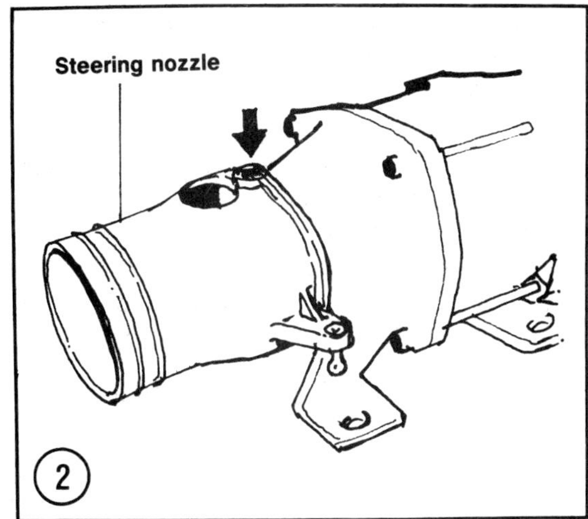

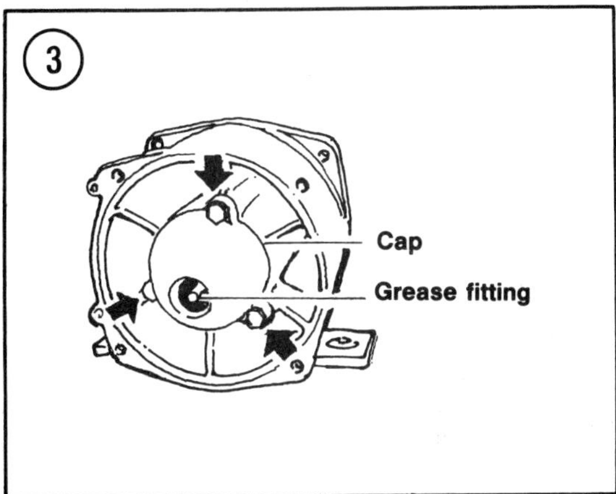

threads. Then tap the shaft out of the casting using a soft faced hammer. See **Figure 4**.

> *NOTE*
> *Have an assistant catch the shaft to prevent damage once it is removed from the housing.*

4. If the shaft end plug is to be removed, knock it out with a long punch. See **Figure 5**.

5. To replace the bearings, have a machine shop or a Kawaskai dealer press the bearings off the shaft and then install new bearings.

> *NOTE*
> *When the new bearing are pressed on, they both rest against the large diameter part of the shaft.*

6. Pull the grease seals out with a hook.

7. To install the seals, perform the following:
   a. Grease the outside of both seals.
   b. Install the plain seal first, so that the open side of the seal faces up. Then fill the inside of the seal with grease.
   c. Install the second (ridged) seal into the hole in the same direction as the plain seal. Press the seal in until the seal ridge fits into the stopper groove.
   d. Fill the inside of the second seal with grease.

8. Install the shaft plug with the flat side of the plug facing down (**Figure 6**).

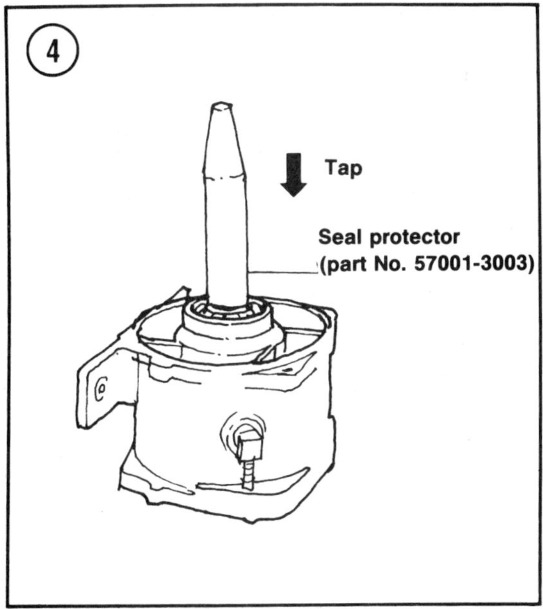

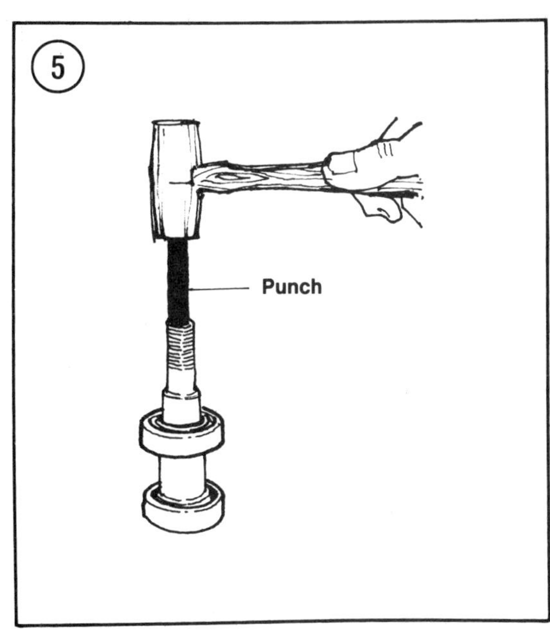

9. Position the seal protector (Kawasaki part No. 57001-3003) over the pump shaft threads. Then tap the shaft into the pump case until the bearings bottom against the inside of the case.

10. When the shaft/bearing assembly is correctly installed, measure from the outer bearing race to the edge of the casting (**Figure 7**). Then measure the length of the end cap from the mounting position to the end of the cap (**Figure 8**).

11. To determine bearing and cap clearance, subtract the cap length measurement from the bearing depth measurement. For example, if the bearing depth is 12 mm and the cap length is 11.5, the calculated clearance is 0.5 mm. Now compare the calculated clearance with shim thickness requirements in **Table 7** and install the correct shim.

> *NOTE*
> *Shims are available from your Kawasaki dealer.*

12. Before installing the cap, make sure the plug is installed (flat side first) and that the cap O-ring is installed and greased.

13. Install the shims (if required) and install the cap and bolts. Tighten the bolts to 52 in.-lb. (6 N•m).

14. Install the grease fitting (**Figure 3**). Then use a grease gun and fill the housing with Shell Alvania EP1 or Shell MP grease. Continue to apply grease until it comes out of the seal lips on the opposite end of the housing.

Impeller/Jet Pump Installation

Procedures used to install the jet pump on JS550 models are the same as for JS440 models, except that some specifications and tightening torques have changed. Refer to **Table 8** and **Table 9** during installation.

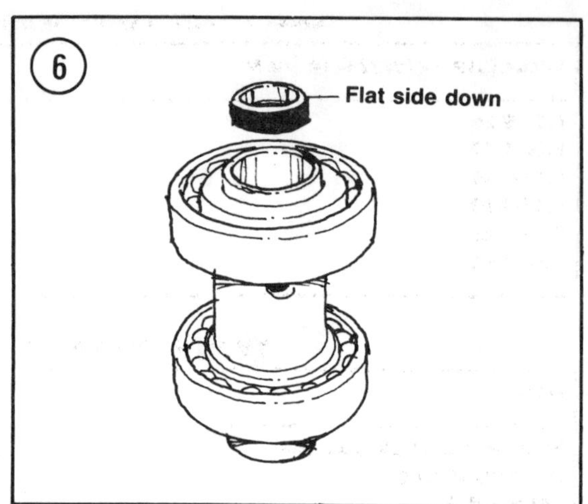

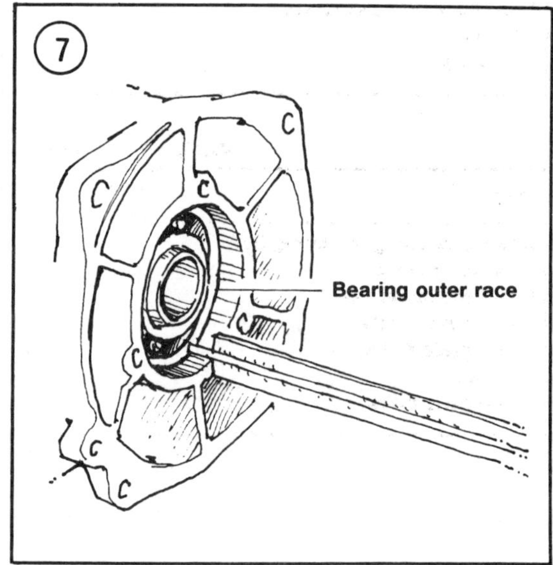

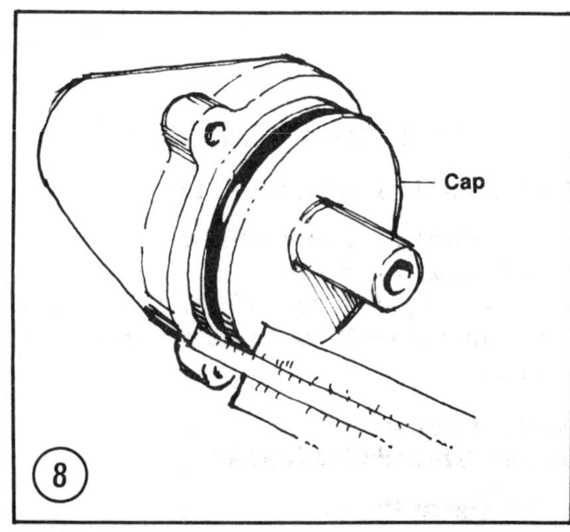

Table 7   JET PUMP BEARING SHIM SELECTION (JS550)

Calculated clearance (mm)	Shim thickness (mm)
0.10-0.25	None
0.26-0.40	0.15
0.41-0.55	0.30
0.56-0.70	0.15 + 0.30
0.71-0.85	0.30 + 0.30
0.86-0.94	0.15 + 0.30 + 0.30

Table 8   DRIVE TRAIN WEAR LIMITS (JS550)

Item	in. (mm)
Impeller maximum clearance	0.023 (0.6)
Drive shaft runout	
At point A	0.004 (0.1)
At point B	0.020 (0.5)
Shaft-to-tunnel clearance	
At top	3.0 (77)
At sides	Equal to both sides

Table 9   DRIVE TRAIN TORQUES (JS550)

Item	ft.-lb.	N•m
Bearing housing mounting bolt	12	16
Coupling torque	20	27
Pump mounting bolts	16	22
Pump cover bolts	7	10
Pump grate bolts	7	10
Impeller	14	20
Pump case bolts	48 in.-lb.	5.5

CHAPTER SIX

FUEL AND EXHAUST SYSTEMS

CARBURETOR SERVICE

Carburetor Removal/Installation

Procedures used during carburetor removal and installation remain the same as for 1981 models, except that the carburetor mounting braces for the JS440 model have changed. See **Figure 9**.

Flame Arrestor Removal/Installation (JS550)

See **Figure 10**.

1. Remove the bolts from the top of the flame arrester cover.
2. Lift the flame arrester up and off the carburetor as a unit.
3. Installation is the reverse of these steps, noting the following:
   a. Make sure the gasket is in place under the flame arrester.
   b. Before installing the flame arrester housing bolts, apply a small amount of Loctite Lock N' Seal to each bolt. Then tighten to 52 in.-lb. (6 N•m).

EXHAUST
(JS550)

Exhaust Removal/Installation

The exhaust system used on all 1982 and later JS550 models is shown in **Figure 11**. Procedures used to remove and install the exhaust system are the same as described in Chapter Six of the main book, noting the following:

a. When installing the expansion chamber, position it so that it is 1/8-1/4 in. (3-6 mm) from the rear exhaust pipe. Then turn the expansion chamber so that its weld is aligned with the arrow on the exhaust pipe. See **Figure 12**.

b. After installing the expansion chamber, check that there is at least 1/2 in. (10 mm) clearance between the expansion chamber and the engine bed. Reposition the expansion chamber as required.

RPM LIMITER SYSTEM
(JS550)

The limiter system used on all 1982 and later JS550 models is shown in **Figure 13**.

Limiter Valve
Removal/Installation

1. Unscrew the limiter valve cap at the electric box.
2. Loosen the clamps and disconnct the 3 fuel lines at the limiter valve.
3. Remove the screws securing the limiter valve to the fuel filter bracket and remove the limiter valve assembly.
4. Installation is the reverse of these steps, noting the following:

a. Apply a small amount of waterproof grease to the limiter valve cap threads and grommet before installation.

b. Apply a small amount of Loctite Lock N' Seal to the limiter valve bolt threads and tighten the bolts to 52 in.-lb. (6 N•m).

Limiter Relay
Removal/Installation

1. Remove and open the electric box as described in Chapter Seven of the main book.

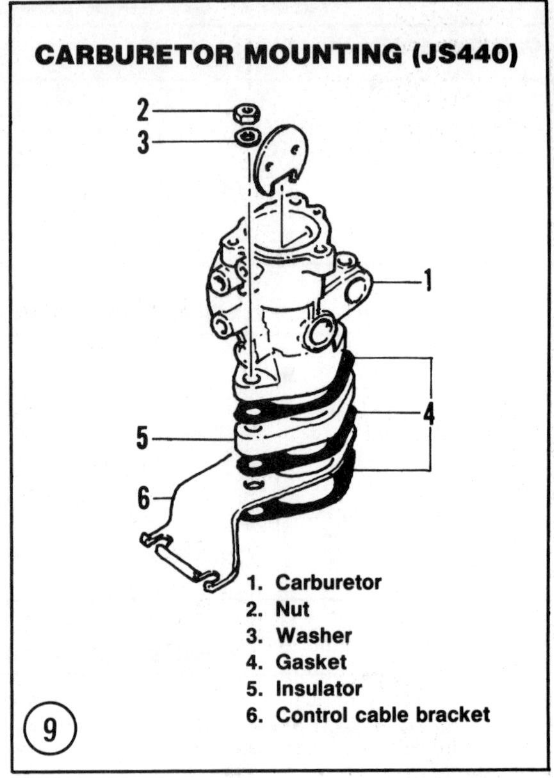

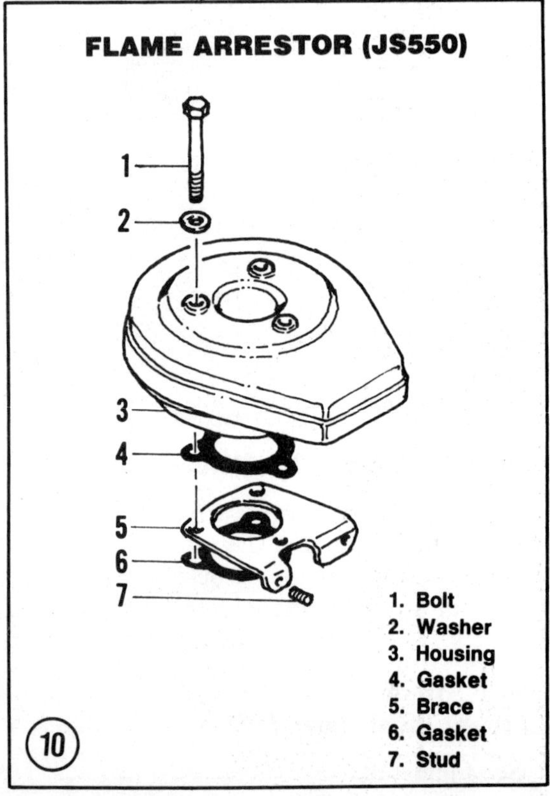

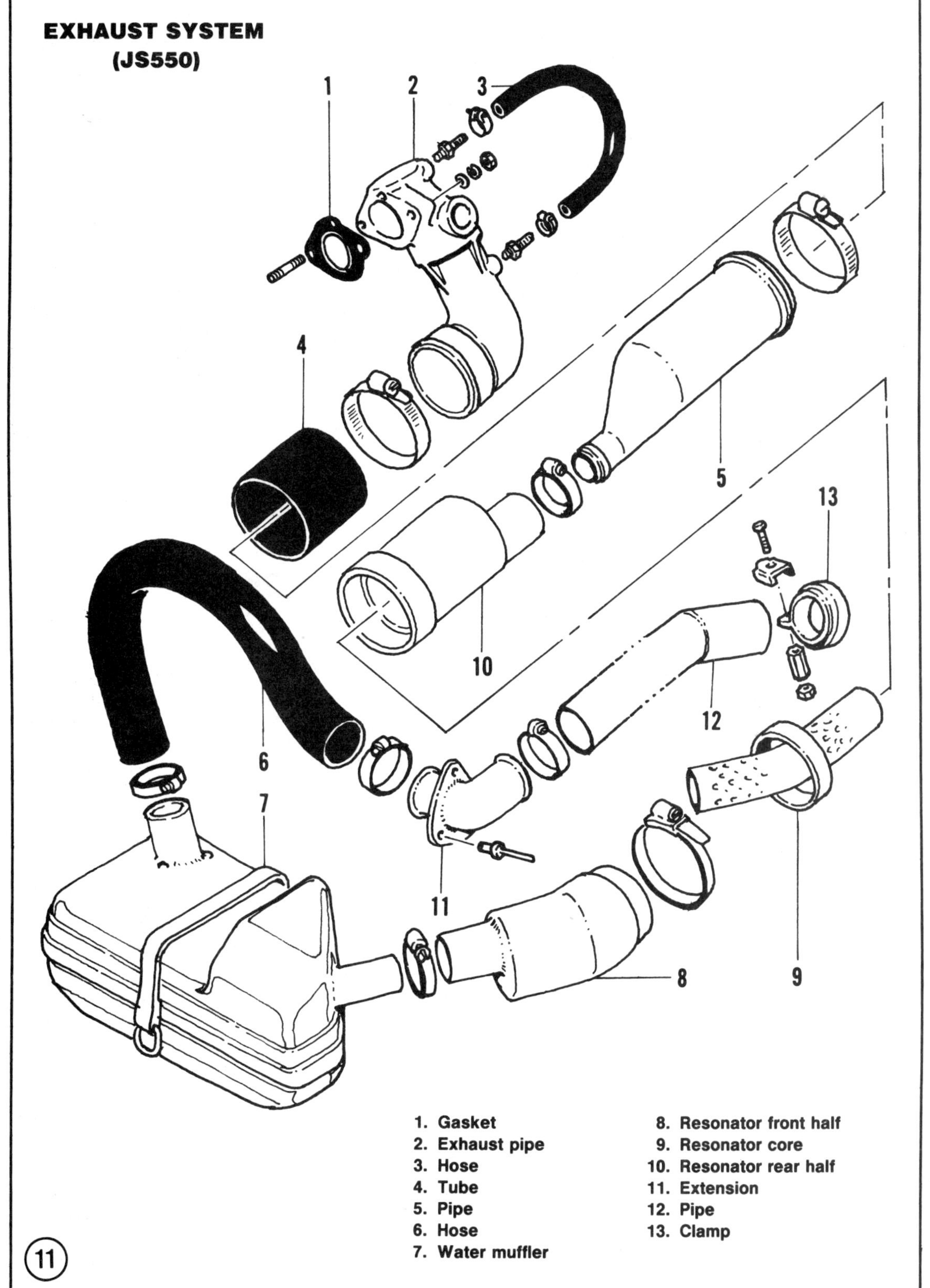

1. Gasket
2. Exhaust pipe
3. Hose
4. Tube
5. Pipe
6. Hose
7. Water muffler
8. Resonator front half
9. Resonator core
10. Resonator rear half
11. Extension
12. Pipe
13. Clamp

(12)

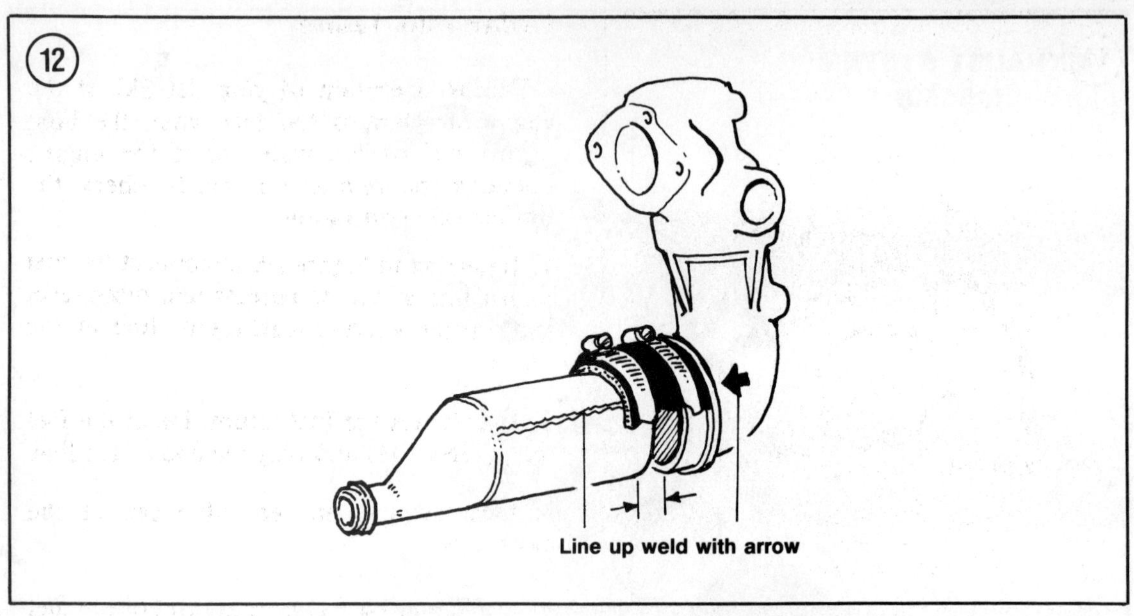

RPM LIMITER SYSTEM

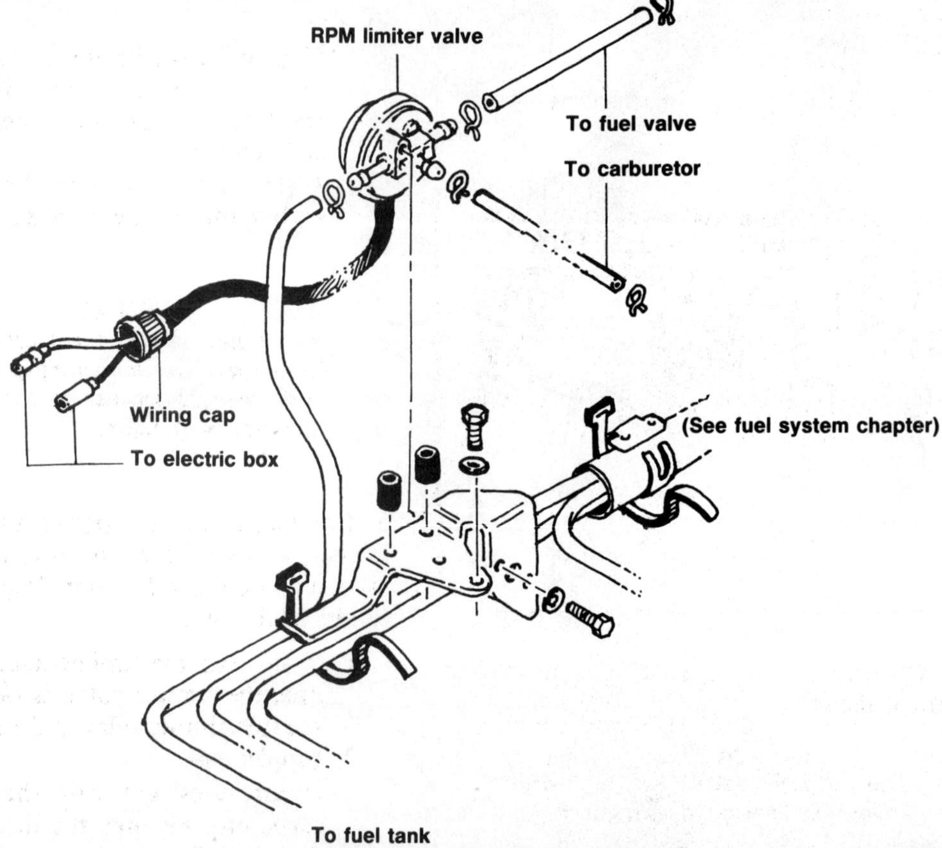

(13)

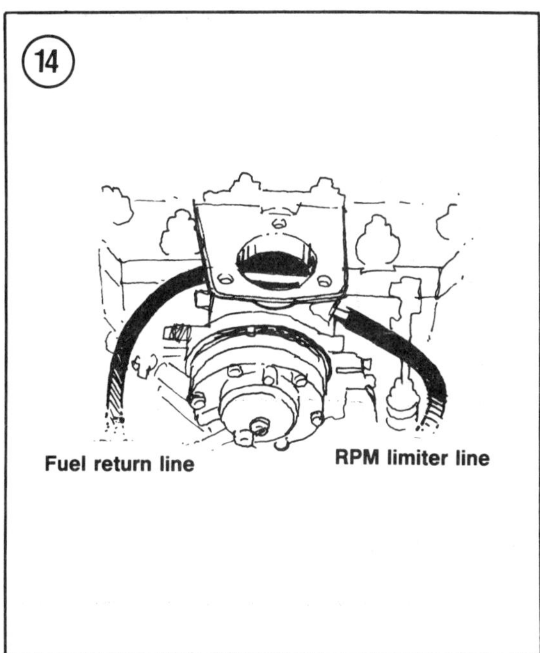

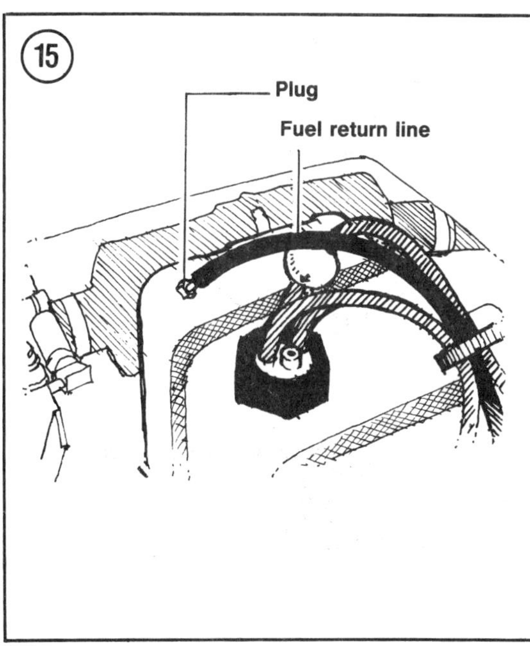

2. Remove the limiter relay screws and remove the relay.

> *NOTE*
> *The limiter relay has 3 wires: brown/red, brown and light green.*

3. Close and install the electric box as described in Chapter Seven of the main book.

Limiter Valve Testing

During operation of your Jet Ski, if the engine accelerates too fast when the boat jumps out of the water or if the engine operates too rich at all speeds, check the limiter valve operation.

1. Referring to **Figure 14**, disconnect the fuel return line at the carburetor and disconnect the limiter valve-to-carburetor line at the valve.

2. Disconnect the fuel return line at the fuel tank (**Figure 15**) and plug the end of the line.

3. Unscrew the limiter valve cap at the electric box.

4. See **Figure 16**. Connect the end of the fuel return line to a hand operated pump (such as Kawasaki part No. T96000-001). Blow air into the fuel return line; interpret results as follows:

   a. If air exits the limiter-to-carburetor air line, the limiter valve is damaged. Replace it as described in this supplement.
   b. If air does not exit the limiter-to-carburetor air line, proceed to Step 5.

> *CAUTION*
> *In the next step, do not attach the limiter valve to the battery power for more than 15 seconds or the limiter valve will be damaged.*

5. Connect a 12 volt power source to the limiter valve wire connectors (**Figure 13**). Blow air into the valve as in Step 4. Interpret results as follows:

   a. If air exits the limiter-to-carburetor air line, the limiter valve is okay. Replace the rpm limiter relay as described in this supplement.
   b. If air does not exit the limiter-to-carburetor air line, the limiter valve is damaged. Replace it as described in this supplement.

10

CHAPTER SEVEN

ELECTRICAL SYSTEMS

STATOR

Stator Coil Inspection

Disconnect the 6-pin connector from the magneto and measure the resistance between the pairs of leads listed in **Table 10**. If the resistance is zero (short circuit) or infinite (open circuit), check the wiring to the coils. Replace the coil(s) if the wiring is okay.

Stator Coil Removal/Installation

Procedures used to replace the stator coil(s) are the same as described in Chapter Seven of the main book, except when reinstalling the electrical wire pins to the 6-pin connector. During installation, note that the holes in the 6-pin connector are numbered as follows:

a. Pins 1 and 3 are light green.
b. Pin 4 is red.
c. Pin 5 is black.
d. Pin 6 is grey.

Make sure to install the correct colored wire in the proper pin hole.

IGNITER

As with 1981 models, the ignition coil and CDI unit are manufactured in one piece, called the "igniter." The igniter is positioned inside the electric box (**Figure 17**). However, while the ignition coil secondary circuit can be tested as described in Chapter Seven of the main book, testing the CDI part of the igniter now requires the use of a special Kawasaki ignition tester. Therefore it is recommended to refer all CDI electrical testing to your local Kawasaki dealer.

CHARGING SYSTEM

Charging System Test

New regulator testing specifications are indicated in **Figure 18**. Procedures used to test the regulator are the same as described in Chapter Seven of the main book.

STARTING SYSTEM

Starter Removal/Installation (JS550)

Procedures to remove the starter on JS550 models are the same as those described in Chapter Seven of the main book, except that it is not necessary to remove the exhaust pipe and expansion chamber.

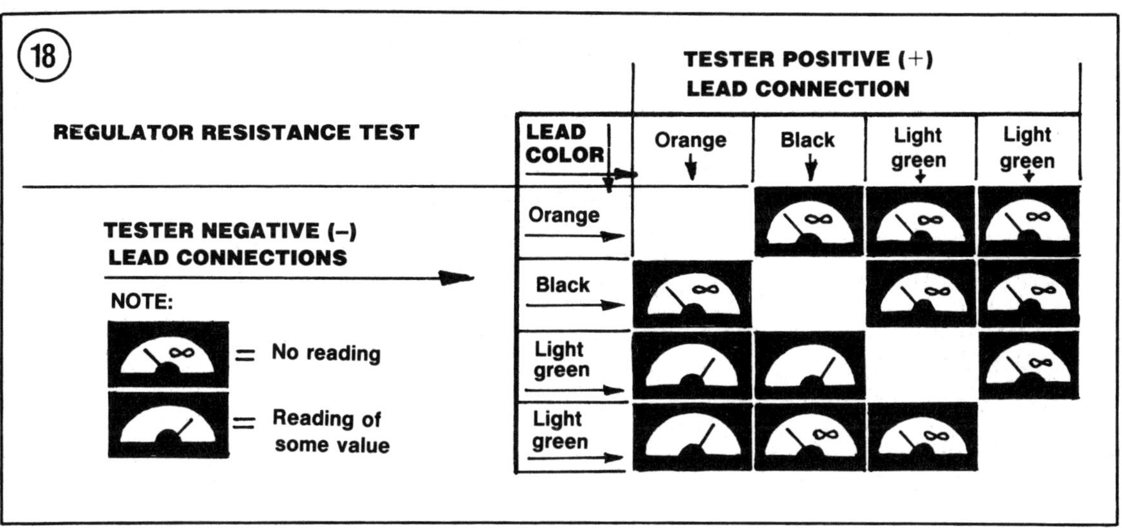

Table 10   ELECTRICAL SPECIFICATIONS

Exciter coil resistance (red to black)	270 ±20% ohms
Pulser coil resistance (red to black)	25 ±20% ohms
Charging coil resistance	
Light green to black	1.5 ±20% ohms
Light green to light green	3.0 ±20 ohms
Charging coil output test (light green to black)	12-15 volts
Ignition timing (JS550)	28° BTDC @ 6,000 rpm
Dial indicator	0.174 in. (4.42 mm)

INDEX

JS400 A3

ENGINE
MAGNETO
STARTER MOTOR
SPARK PLUGS
IGNITION COIL
BATTERY
STARTER SOLENOID
REGULATOR
CDI UNIT
ELECTRIC BOX
ENGINE STOP SWITCH
START BUTTON
DIAGRAM KEY
CONNECTORS
GROUND
FRAME GROUND
CONNECTION
NO CONNECTION

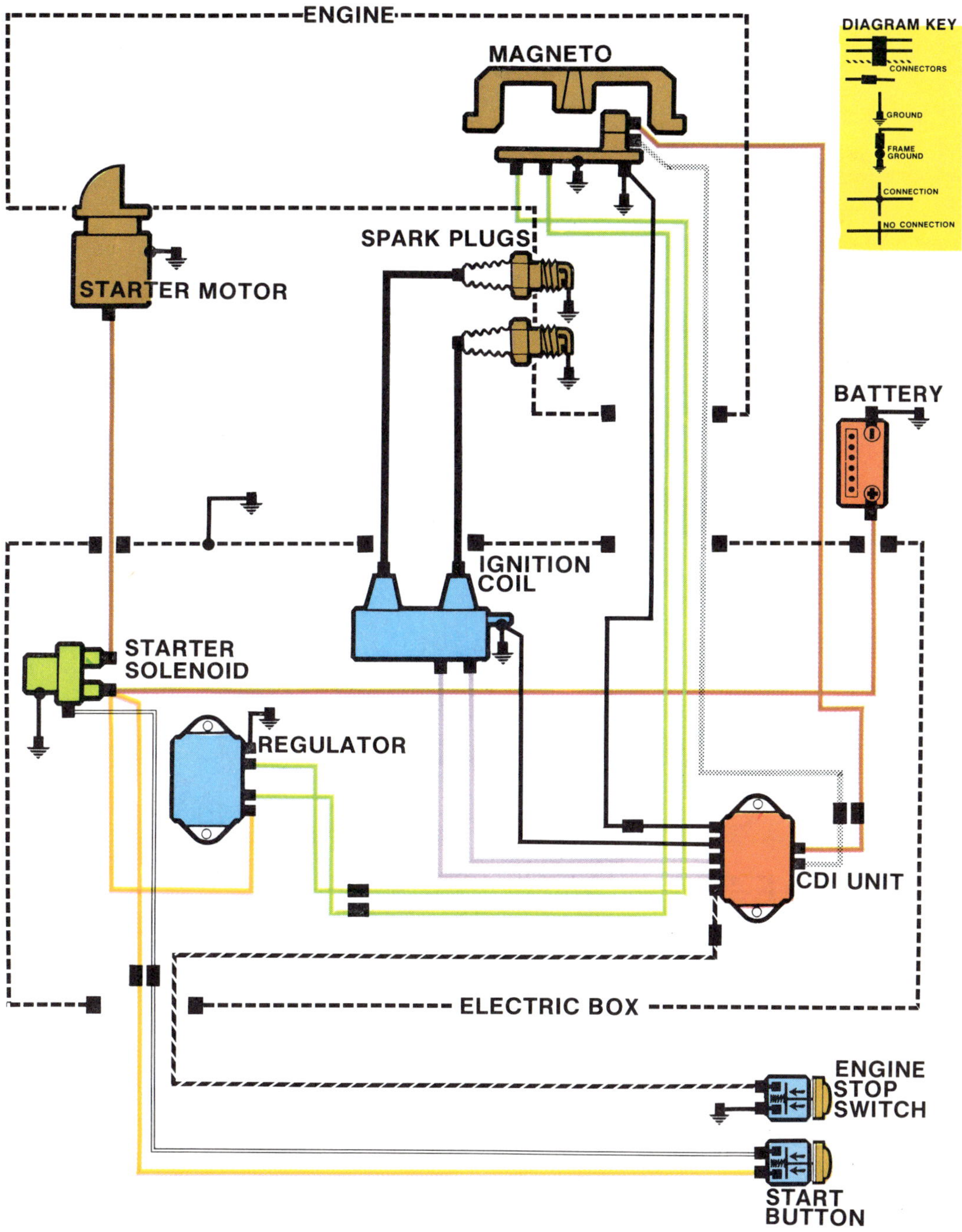

JS440 A1, A1A, A2, A3, A4

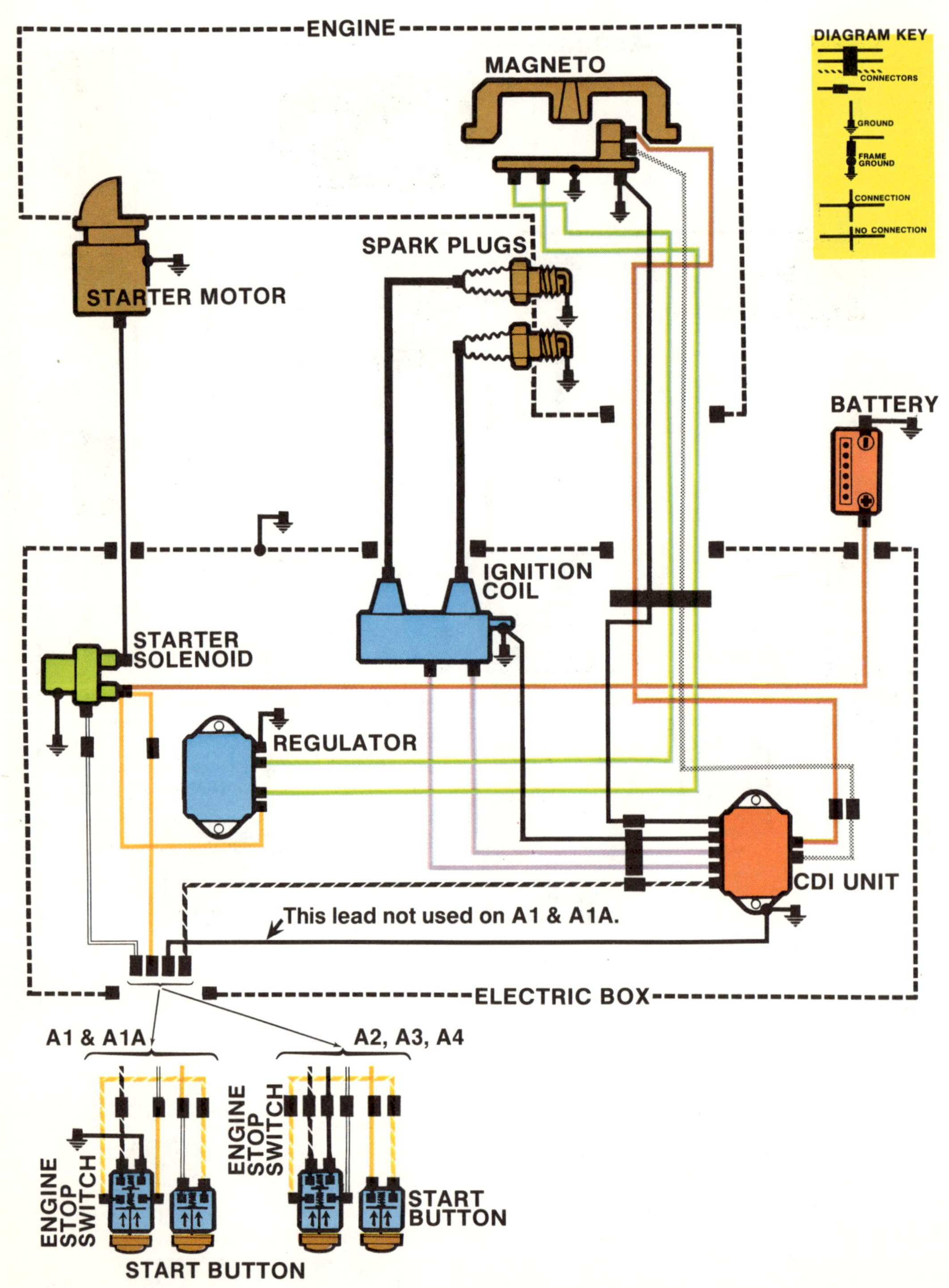